(Old) Rappahannock County, Virginia Deed Book Abstracts 1688-1692

Ruth and Sam Sparacio

The Antient Press Collection
from

Colonial Roots
Millsboro, Delaware
2016

ISBN 978-1-68034-225-3

Originally printed 1990 by The Antient Press
Printed in the United States of America

CONTENTS

[this page intentionally blank]

(OLD) RAPPAHANNOCK COUNTY, VIRGINIA
Deed Book No. 8
1688 -1692

p. 1 The marke of a black and white heifer given to JOHN HOWELL by his Mother is a staple on the left Eare and a crop and a slit in the right; the mark of a Brindle Heifer given to ELIZA. HOWELL by her Mother being four years old is three Slitts and a crop in the left Eare and a Slitt and a crop and underkeel in the right. The marke of a Cow of nine years old given to SARAH HOWELL by her Mother is three slitts and a crop in the left Eare and a crop and two slitts in the right; the colour of the sd being black and white

Recordr. Teste WM. COLSTON Cl. Cur.

January Court 1682

Two crops and upper Keele in the Right Eare to JOS: LEWIS

Recordr. Teste WM. COLSTON Cl. Cur.

KNOW ALL MEN by these presents that I WILLIAM GRIFFIN of the County of Rappa:, Plantr., have for and in consideration of the sum of Eight hundred pounds of Tobb: and Caske to me already in hand paid, bargained sold enfeoffed and confirmed and by these presents do bargain sell aline and confirm unto JAMES JACKSON his heires or assigns forever a certain parcel of land containing about Twenty acres more or less lying in the Westward side of ORCHARDS SWAMP bounded by the Run there of being part of a Tract of land contayning Seventy five acres which the aforesaid JACKSON sold unto my Father, WM. GRIFFIN deced, as by a Deed granted may more fully appear; To have and to hold the sd parcell of land with all pertinances and herditaments there unto belonging by him the sd JACKSON his heirs and assigns forever without the lett molestation Interruption Eviction or ejection of me the said GRIFFIN my heirs or Admrs. or any other person or persons whatsoever claiming my right or title thereunto and I the sd GRIFFIN do further oblige my self my heires to warrant the sale of the sd land unto the said JACKSON his heires or assigns or any other person or persons whatsoever claimining in by from or under me my heirs and Admrs.; I doe alsoe oblige myself my heirs & Admrs. to acknowledge this Deed in the County Court of Rappa: within six months after the date of these Presents that it may be enroled according to Law and that I will cause my Wife to do the same. In Witness whereof I have hereunto set my hand and Seale this first day of January 1688/9

Signed Sealed and Delivered in presence of

JAMES HARISON, WM. GRIFFIN

ALEXR. DONIPHAN

Recognitr in Cur Compt Rappa 2nd die Janry Ano 1688 Test WM. COLSTON Cl Cur.

p. 2 KNOW ALL MEN by these presents that I WILLIAM GRIFFIN of County of Rappa: Planter, for and in consideration of the sum of four thousand two hundred pounds of Tobb: in Cask to me in hand paid by these presents do sell and confirm unto JAMES HARISSON of County aforesd. Gent. his heirs a certain tract of land containing Seventy and four acres which my Father, WILLIAM GRIFFIN deced, purchased from JAMES JACKSON situate lying and being in County of Rappa: on North side of the River about half a mile back of JAMES ORCHARDs Plantation begining at a Maple in a Great Swamp and runing thence East to a Stake by two small red Oakes neere an old field, thence W. cuting over a main branch to a Stake by a Hickory and a small Walnut, thence W: S: to another Stake upon a Hill side by a Hickory, thence S: East to the first mentioned Maple; To have and to hold occupie and enjoy the aforesd. Tract of land by him said JAMES HARISSON his heirs with all houses, orchards fences and all other appurtenances and hereditaments thereunto belonging or anywise appertaining without the lett interruption eviction of me my heirs or Admrs. or any other person whatsoever only the aforesd. HARISON must lay no claim to a small Peice of land on the Westward side of ORCHARDS SWAMP about 15 or 20 acres more or less which is included within the aforementioned bounds but lately sold by me to JAMES JACKSON whereon he now lives and the Run in the swamp make the Division and I the said GRIFFIN do hereby for myself my heirs warrant the sale of the premises to the said HARISSON his heirs from the claime or title of any person or persons whatsoever and further I do oblige myself my heirs to acknowledge the Deed in the County Court of Rappa: within six months after date of these presents that it may be there recorded according to Law. In Witness whereof I have in confermation of the premises hereunto set my hand and Seale this first day of January 1688/9

Signed Sealed and Delivered in the presence of

ALEXR: DONIPHAN, WILLIAM GRIFFIN
JAMES JACKSON

Recognitr. in Cur: Cort. 2nd die January Ano 1688

pp. 2-3 KNOW ALL MEN by these presents that I WILLIAM COOPER of County of Rappa: and Dominion of Virginia with the free and voluntary consent of my Wife, ELIZABETH COOPER for a valuable consideration in hand received do bargain grant and sell unto JOSEPH LEWIS of BRISTOLL to him his heirs from me the sd WILLIAM COOPER my heirs one part or parcel of land containing One hundred and fifty acres of land lying and being in County of Rappa: on the North side of the River bounding Begining at a Red Oak in Mr. PATTONs line corner tree to LANE and runing thence by an old Crooked Line South West to a red Oak, thence N: E: to a small Hickory saplin marked with a Knife, thence N: E: to a Stake by two red Oakes, thence along the sd line South West to the first mentioned Tree; To have and to hold the sd land forever with all its rights and hereditaments whatsoever as Fishing, Fowling, Hawking, Hunting with all woods underwoods and water courses in as large maner as is expressed in his Maties order for ye holding of Lands in this Dominion and to be safly possed with the same free from the Molestation and interruption of any person claiming Interest from or under the sd WM: COOPER my heirs them or any of them and likewise from any person whatsoever. Furthermore I the sd WM: COOPER with my Wife, ELIZABETH, do engage to acknowledge the same in Court whensoever the sd JOSEPH LEWIS shall require the same. In Confermation thereof we the said WILLIAM and ELIZABETH COOPER do sett our hands and Seals the 1st day of January 1688/9

Teste: XPHER ASCOUGH, WM. COOPER
RALPH RYMER ELIZA: COOPER

Acknowledged in Rappahannock County Court by WM. COOPER and ELIZABETH his Wife the 2nd day of January 1688/9 and recorded the 12th day of said month and yeare
Teste WM. COLSTON Cl Cur

pp. 3-4 THIS INDENTURE made the 13th day of April in the year of our Lord 1688 and in the 4th yeare of the Reign of our Sovereign Lord James the Second by the grace of God of England, Scotland, France and Ireland, King Defendr. of the Faith &c. Between ANGELL JACOBUS and ELIZABETH his Wife and FRAN: GOWRE of the one parte and HENRY LEWIS of the other part all of Rappa: County and Parish of North Farnham Witnesseth that said ANGELL JACOBUS and ELIZABETH his Wife and FRAN: GOWRE for two thousand pounds Tobb: and Caske in hand paid the Receipt whereof said

ANGELL JACOBUS, ELIZABETH his Wife and sd FRAN: GOWRE do hereby acknowledge to have reced full satisfaction have bargained sold and confirmed unto sd HENRY LEWIS his heirs all that Tract or parcell of land situate lying and being in the lower side of RAPPA: CREEKE formerly sold by GEO: BRUCE to Mr. HENRY CLARKE, Father in Law to us the said ANGELL JACOBUS and FRANS. GOWRE, and bounding upon the Plantation of JNO. ESSEX, Colnll. WALKER, Majr. PRICE and Collnll. WM. LOYDE being ninty and six acres of land next and adjoining to the foure fore rented tracts of land as may appeare by a Survey and Plat of the sd Ninty and six acres of land Surveyed pr. Mr. WM. MOSELEY the then Surveyor of the said County of Rappa: Togeather with all ways waters and all other the appurtinances unto sd HENRY LEWIS his heirs yeilding and paying the Rents and Services therefore first and of right accustomed Further the said ANGELL JACOBUS, ELIZABETH his Wife and FRAN: GOWRE hath covenanteth and promiseth to and with sd HENRY LEWIS his heirs and every of them shall and may lawfully and peaceably have possess and enjoy the aforesd. premises with their and every of their appertinances without any lawfull vexation suit incumbrance disturbance impediment or let of them the said ANGELL JACOBUS, ELIZABETH his Wife and FRAN: GOWRE or either of them their heirs or any other person whatsoever shall and will from time to time and at all times warrant save defend forever the sd HENRY LEWIS his heirs In Witness whereof we have hereunto set our hands and Seals the day and year above written

Sealed and Delivered in presence of us

GEO: EALE	ANGELL JACOBUS
THO: WARD	ELIZABETH JACOBUS
	FRAN: GAWRE

Acknowledged in Rappa: Court by ANGELL JACOBUS and FRAN: GAURE the Third day of Janry. 1688 and recorded the 15th said month. WM. COLSTON Cl. Cur.

KNOW ALL MEN by these presents that I ELIZA. JACOBUS, the Wife of ANGELL JACOBUS, Cooper, of Rappa: County in Parish of North Farnham do freely and voluntarily constitute and order my well beloved Friend DAVID BARWICK, Carpenter, of the aforesd. County and Parish, to be my lawfull Attorney and in my name and in my stead to acknowledge parcell of land HEN: LEWIS of the aforesd. County and Parish, Plantr., which he the said HENRY LEWIS bought of my Brother, JOHN CLARK deced., the which land lying and joyning to GEORGE BRUCE and LUKE THORNTON by Estimation Ninty six acres as being one of the heires now by Law and he the said HENRY LEWIS paying me for my acknowledgement do relinquish all my right title and interest unto HENRY LEWIS and his heirs forever As Witness my hand and Seale this 6th day of March 1688

ELIZABETH JACOBUS

Recognitr in Cur Court Rappa 6th Martie Ano 1688

pp. 4-5 THIS INDENTURE made the 3d day of Decembr. in year of our Lord God 1688 according to the Compaticon of the Church of England in the 4th yeare of the Reigne of our Sovereigne Lord King James the second by the Grace of God of England Scotland &c., King Defendr. of the faith &c., Between JOHN MARTIN of County of Rappa: of one part and JAMES ORCHARD of sd County of other part Witnesseth that the sd JOHN for divers good and weighty causes thereunto moving and for a valuable consideration in hand already received by these presents do give bargain sell and confirm unto said ORCHARD his heirs from me the sd MARTIN my heirs all my title and Interest of what land I the sd MARTIN do lay claime to on the North side of the RAPPA: RIVER in the Parish of SITTENBURNE and lying between the line of Majr. JOHN WEIRE deced and CHARLES his Beaver Dam being three hundred and eighty acres more or less. Now Know yee that I the sd MARTIN for the divers good and valuable consideration reced aforementioned do bargaine and sell the Three hundred and Eighty acres of and

within mentioned from my Exrs. Admrs unto the aforesaid JAMES ORCHARD his heirs he or they peaceably enjoy the sd tract of land aforesaid without the lett hindrance trouble or evasion whatsoever of me my heirs and in consideration of my assent and consent of the premises aforesaid and to all true intents and purposes I have in consideration hereof sett my hand and Seale the day and yeare first above mentioned
Signed Sealed and Delivered in the presence of us

GEO: LUKE, JOHN ◯ MARTIN
CHARLES SOPES

Recognitr in Court Rappa: 6 die Marty Ano 1688

KNOW ALL MEN by these presents that I MARGARETT MARTIN, Wife of JOHN MARTIN, do constitute and appoint unto my loving RICHD. MATHEWS to acknowledge my part of a parcel of land by my Husband, JOHN MARTIN, unto JAMES ORCHARD his heirs &c. as by a Deed bearing date the 3rd day of 10ber 1668 doth appear and do ratifie my assent and consent to the same and what my said Attorney shall do to be as legal and authentick as if I were there my self As Witness my hand and Seale this 5th day of March 1688
Signed Sealed and Delivered in the presence of us

JOHN W WILLIAMS, MARGARETT O MARTIN
JOHN STRANGE

pp. 5-6 Videe Folio 148. These presents Witnesseth that wee PHILLIP HUNNINGS and ELIZABETH HUNNINGS, Wife of the sd PHILLIP HUNNINGS of North Farnham Parish in Rappa. County do assigne and make over from us or either of us our Right title and Interest of the Plantation and land with all the Priviledges thereunto belonging which is here written expressed unto JOHN GRIFFIN his heirs or assignes forever in consideration of Forty pounds Sterling already reced, and farther we the sd PHILIP and ELIZABETH HUNNINGS do warrant the same unto the abovesd GRIFFIN his heirs or assigns In Witness whereof we have hereunto sett our hands and Seals the first day of August 1688.
Sealed Signed and Delivered in the presence of us

RALPH WHITING, PHILLIP HUNNING
JOHN CARY ELIZA. HUNNING

Recognitr in Cur: Court Rappa: 6 die Marty Ano 1688 et Record 12 die

KNOW ALL MEN by these presents that I ELIZABETH HUNNING, Wife of PHILIP HUNNING, of Rappa: County do make constitute and appoint Mr. JOHN BAVEMAR of the aforesd County my lawfull Attorney to acknowledge for me and in my name all my right of all that parcell of land my Husband now lives on joyning upon TOTESKEY CREEKE unto JOHN GRIFFIN, Ship Carpenter, of the aforesd. County and his heirs forever. In confermation I have hereunto sett my hand and Seale this Fifth day of March 1688/9

Teste RALPH WHITING, ELIZABETH HUNNINGS
JOHN SIMPSON

pp. 6-7 THIS INDENTURE made the 26th day of February in yeare of our Lord 1688/9 and in the 4th year of the Reign of our Sovereign Lord King James the second over England, Scotland, France and Ireland, Defr. of the Faith &c. Between JAMES ORCHARD of County of Rappa: of the one partie and FRANCIS TAYLER of the other partie Witnesseth that sd ORCHARD for a valuable consideration of One thousand pounds toba: and Caske pd. by the sd TAYLER to the sd ORCHARD as by a Bill bearing date with these presents Wrightings and in the hands of the said TAYLER and THO: SNEAD will appeare doth give grant bargain and sell unto sd TAYLER and THO: SNEAD heirs forever a parcell of land containing Eighty acres being a parcell of land reserved by

JOHN MASON out of a Tract of land of 441 1/2 acres being the half part of a PATENT of 883 acres of land granted to CHARLES SNEAD deced, bearing date the 26th Apr: 1659 and by the said SNEAD to PHILLIP SHERWOOD as by a Deed bearing date the 2nd Jany. 1659 doth appeare and by the sd SHERWOOD sold to JOHN MASON as by a Deed bearing date the 31st day of January 1660 doth appeare and sold by the said MARTIN to ROGER CLOTHWORTHY and JOHN BRADWAY only this Eighty acres excepted as by Deed doth appeare. Now Know yee that I JAMES ORCHARD doth for myself my heirs &c. for the consideration aforesd. doth bargain sell and estrange the land aforesd. being Eighty acres unto FRANCIS TAYLER and THOMAS SNEAD their heirs forever. Further I the sd ORCHARD do warrant the same of and from all persons that shall at any time lay any clame to the sd Eighty acres and will at all times defend the same from all claimes whatsoever As Witness my hand and Seale the 26th day of February 1688/9
Signed Sealed and Delivered in the presents of us

HAWKINS SNEAD, JAMES ORCHARD
WM. MOSELEY

Recognitr in Cur: Comt. Rappa: 6 die Martii Ano 1688

MARY ORCHARD the Wife of JAMES ORCHARD doth give her consent & assent to the sale of the land within mentioned as Witness my name Subscribed the 6th day of March 1688/9

Teste LAW: MANLEY, MARY her mark M ORCHARD
JOHN I DEREY

pp. 7-8 KNOW ALL MEN by these presents that I JAMES ORCHARD and MARY his Wife both of County of Rappa: for and in consideration of a valuable sum of Three thousand Six hundred pounds of good lawfull Tobaco in Caske according to Act by us in hand reced. as also a Gold Ring of Ten Shillings price the Receipt whereof we the sd. JAMES ORCHARD and MARY ORCHARD do hereby acknowledge ourselves thereby to be fully satisfied therewith and by these presents have granted sold and confirmed fully clearly and absolutely unto JOHN BURKETT of the County aforesd. his heirs a certain parsell or tract of land conteyning One hundred Eighty five acres lying in the sd County on the North side of the River and on the South East side of the CLEFT CREEK being part of a Patent of Three hundred acres granted to Capt. JOHN WARE bearing date the last day of March 1655. Beginning at a Maple standing by the Cleare Branch of CLIFT CREEK, Corner tree to a parcel of land sold by me the said ORCHARD to JAMES JACKSON and extending thence E. N. to a Stake by Mr. HARISONs Cornfield Fence, thence S. by E. to a Stake by a Spanish Oake, thence W. by S: to the Wester Course of the sd CLIFTS CREEK, thence up the sd Creeke S. to the first mentioned Maple. We the said JAMES ORCHARD and MARY ORCHARD do hereby grant sell convey and make over from us our heirs unto JOHN BURKETT his heirs To have and to hold the same with all its rights and Priviledges of all woods waters and whatsoever else peaceably and quietly without any let hindrance suit denyal or disturbance of us the sd JAMES ORCHARD and MARY ORCHARD our heirs or any other person whatsoever claiming or pretending any claim lawfull to any part of the demised premises also wee the sd JAMES ORCHARD and MARY ORCHARD do oblige ourselves our heirs to make what further assurance he the said JOHN BUCKETT or Councell learned in the Law shall require in that case and do further engage ourselves to acknowledge this our Deed of Sale before the Court of Rappa: there to be enrolled when thereunto lawfully called by the said JOHN BURKETT or his heirs, he or they yeilding and paying all dues or impositions which are or shall be charged and for further confermation hereof we the sd JAMES and MARY have hereunto set our hands and Seals this 6th of March 1688

Signed Sealed and Delivered in the presence of us
WM. MOSELEY, JAMES ORCHARD
JOAN (blank) MARY Sig. M ORCHARD
Recognitr in Cur Court Rappa. 6 die Martii 1688

pp. KNOW ALL MEN by these presents that I ANDW. BOYER being very sick and weak
8- but blessed be God of Sound and perfect memory. Imprs. I the said ANDREW
9 BOYER doth acquit and discharge my INDIAN WOMAN comonly known by the
name of MARY CAPER from all manner of Services from me and my Wife after the decease of me the sd ANDREW BOYER and SARAH my Wife and I the sd BOYER doth freely and voluntarily give unto the sd MARY CAPER & her Son during their said natural lives so much ground as the said INDIAN WOMAN and THOMAS her Son can tend with Indian Corne and Tobb: and also Housing for the sd INDIAN WOMAN and her Son for the housing of the sd Indians crop of Corn and Tobb: and for to dwell in dureing both their naturall lives, all which I give as aforesaid after me and my Wife decease out of the tract or divident of land where now I the sd BOYER now liveth and also I give and bequeath unto the said Parties above mentioned one Cow, one Saw, one Bed and an Iron Pott all which I do freely give after my decease aforesd. of me ANDW. BOYER and SARAH my Wife. As Witness our hands and Seales this 6th day of August 1687
Teste XPHER ASCOUGH, ANDW. marke BOYER
WM. MARKERS SARAH a BOYER
March 6th 1688. Upon the everment of Colo. JOHN STONE that ANDREW BOWYER beefore his decease requested to have the above Deed of Gift recorded, the Court have ordered it to be of Recd.

KNOW ALL MEN by these presents that wee ANDREW BOYER and SARAH my Wife have constituted and appointed our true and beloved freind, HENRY LEWIS, our true and lawfull Attorney for to see one Deed of Gift acknowledged and recorded in the Court of Rappa: acknowledged and given by me the sd ANDREW BOYER and SARAH my Wife by Deed of Gift given unto MARY CAPER and THOMAS her Son all which I the said BOYER and SARAH my Wife doth require the said LEWIS as wee were then and theire present As Witness our hands and Seales this 6th day of August 1687
Teste XPHER ASCOUGH, ANDREW marke BOYER
WM. MARKERS SARAH marke BOYER

pp. April Court 1689
9- TO ALL XPIAN PEOPLE I RALPH WHITTON of Rappa. County in the Colony of Vir-
10 ginia send Greeting. Know yee that I the sd RALPH WHITTON being of a good
and perfect mind without fraud or deceit for diverse and good causes and considerations me hereunto moving and more especially for the love and affection I beare to my well beloved Wife, ELIZABETH WHITTEN, by these presents do give grant and confirm unto WILLIAM FITZHARRIS for the use of my said Wife, ELIZABETH WHITTON, her heirs or assigns all my Plantation and divident of land whereon I now live lying and being in Rappa. County with all the houses orchard fences and other appertenances thereunto belonging and all my goods and Chatels implements household stuff servants stock of Cattle horses and hogs Debts bills bonds accts. necessary and other things whatsoever as well moveable as immoveable of what nature or kind soever they be or in whose hands custody or places they be or may be found To have and to hold leavy prceive use receive and enjoy all and singular the aforementioned premises with all and singular the appurtenances unto sd WM. FITZHARRIS for the proper use of my aforesaid Wife, ELIZABETH WHITTON her heirs or assigns for ever freely and quietly

without any manner of reclaime challenge of conditions of the said RALPH WHITTON my heirs or assigns or any other persons by any means in any manner of wise and without any account reclaiming or answer wherefore to me or any in my name to be given rendered or done in time to come that either I the said RALPH WHITTON my heirs or any other persons whatsoever by us for us or manner or in the name or names of us or any of us at any time or times hereafter may claime challenge or demand in or to the premises or any part thereof any right title interest use or possession both from all action of right title Claime Interest rise or possession and demand thereof, Wee and every of us to bee utterly excluded and for ever debarred by these presents, and I the said RALPH WHITTON my heirs all the sd goods land and other things above mentioned with the appurtenances unto the said WM. FITZHARRIS for the proper use of my said Wife as abovesaid against all people will warrant and defend by these presents of which goods chattels and lands and other things aforementioned I the said RALPH WHITTON have put the sd Mr. WM. FITZHARRIS in peaceable possession for the use aforesaid by the delivery of Six pence which I have paid and delivered to said WM. FITZHARRIS the day of the date hereof In Witness whereof I have hereunto sett my hand and affixed my Seale the 10 day of March 1688

Signed Sealed and Delivered in the presence of

JOHN COLLEYVOWE, RALPH WHITTEN
THO: + LOOPSELL,
WM: FITZ JEFTETH

Recognit in Cur Court Rappa 3 die Aprilis Ano 1689

Mr. JAMES BOUGHAN I do hereby desire you and do give you full power licence and authoritie to appeare for me at the next Court held for Rappa. County then and their to acknowledge a Deed of Guift unto Mr. WILLIAM FITZHARRIES for the (blank) of my Wife, ELIZABETH WHITTON all my Estate both personally and Reall bearing date with these presents for yr. so doing this shall be your sufficient Warrant Witness my hand and Seale this 1st day of March 1688

Recordr. RALPH WHITTON

p. 11 THIS INDENTURE made the 31st day of January in year of our Lord 1688 Between HUMPHREY BOOTH of County of Rappa., Planter, of one part and SAMUEL GRIFFIN of the same County, Ship Wright, of other part Witnesseth that said HUMPHREY BOOTH for diverse causes and valuable considerations and especially for and in consideration of the full sum of Twenty two pounds Sterling money of England and one Boat Twelve foot by the Keele to be compleatly made and finished with Keels and Oares well and truely paid whereof the sd HUMPHREY BOOTH doth hereby acknowledge the Receipt whereof and himself to be fully satisfied and paid before the Sealing and delivery of these presents and thereof doth clearly discharge the said SAMUEL GRIFFING and his heirs by virtue of these presents doth bargain and sell unto SAMUEL GRIFFING and his heirs one ISLAND lying and being on the South side of RAPPA; RIVER in the County of Rappa: situate before the Plantation of Capt. BOOTH deced, containing Eighty acres be the same more or less withall woods waters profitts and appertinances thereunto belonging unto him the sd SAMLL. GRIFFING his heirs and I HUMPHREY BOOTH for myself my heirs do covinant promise to and with sd SAML. GRIFFING his heirs to save and keep harmless sure and indemnified the sd SAML. GRIFFING that he said GRIFFING may have liberty to make use of what White Oake trees he shall think fitt for his use on the divident of land belonging to the sd BOOTH and lastly I the sd BOOTH do hereby promise to ratifie and confirm the above bargained premises with sufficient warrant and assurance by acknowledgement in the County Court of Rappa: to the use and be-

hoofe of the sd SAMUEL GRIFFING his heirs and assignes forever as Witness my hand and Seale the day and yeare first above mentioned
Signed Sealed and Delivered in the presence of us
ARTHUR FORBES, HUMPHREY BOOTH
CHAS. marke ~ ATKINSON
Recognitr in Cur. Court Rappa 3 dai Aprilis Ano 1689

pp. TO ALL &c. I FRAN: LORD HOWARD, Baron of Effingham, his Maties Lieut. &
11- Governr. Genll. of Virginia &c. Whereas &c. Now Know yee &c. give and grant
12 unto EDWARD ADCOCK one hundred and forty two acres of land lying and being
in County of Rappa: according to the most antient and lawfull bounds thereof formerly granted to RANDOLPH PETER of sd County deced and was lately found to be Escheat to his Sacred Maties as by an Inquisition recorded in Mr. Secretary's Office under the hand and Seale of Colo. ISAAC ELLERTON, Escheator of the sd County, and a Jury sworn before him for that purpose dated the 15th day of 8ber 1685 may appear as is since granted to the sd Mr. EDWARD ADCOCK who hath made his Composition according to Law To have and to hold &c. To be held of our Sovereign Lored the King &c., yeilding and paying &c.
EFFINGHAM

KNOW ALL MEN by these presents that I EDWARD ADCOCK of the County of Rappa. do assigne conveigh and make over from me and my heirs forever the contents of this within mentioned Patent unto JOHN BROOKES of the aforesd. County to him and his heirs forever and do warrant the same from me or any by me from the claime of any person or persons whatsoever As Witness my hand and Seale this 10th day of Janry. 1688
Witness DANLL. DOBYNS, EDWARD ADCOCK
ELIZA. DOBYNS
Recognitr. in Cur Court Rappa. 3 die Aprilis Ano 1689

KNOW ALL MEN by these presents that I ELIZABETH ADCOCK have for a valuable consideration in hand reced of and from JOHN BROOKES do with free will and consent assigne and sett over unto the sd JOHN BROOKES and his heirs forever all my right of Dower of land assigned by my Husband, EDWARD ADCOCK, unto the sd BROOKES holding myself fully satisfied for the same and per these presents and utterly barred from any claime or right to any part or parcell of the land above mentioned In Witness whereof I have hereunto sett my hand and Seale the 5th day Febry. 1688
Signed Sealed and Delivered in the presence of
ELIZA: DOBYNS, ELIZA. ADCOCK
ABRAH: A DEPREE; HENRY ADCOCK

KNOW ALL MEN by these presents that I ELIZABETH ADCOCK do by these presents ordaine and constitute my loving friend Mr. DANLL. DOBYNS my true and lawfull Attorney for me and in my name and place to acknowledge my right of Dower to a Patent One hundred and forty two acres of land assigned by my Husband, EDWARD ADCOCK, unto JOHN BROOKS ratifying and confirming what my said Attorney shall do act or cause to be done in the premises as if I were in presents In Witness whereof I sett my hand and Seale this first day of February Ano One thousand Six hundred and Eighty eight
Signed Sealed and Delivered in the presents of
ELIZA: DOBYNS, ELIZA: ADCOCK
ABRAH: A DEPREE, HEN: ADCOCK

KNOW ALL MEN by these presents that I EDW: ADCOCK of County of Rappa: and Colony of Virginia, Planter, am held and firmly bound and indebted unto JOHN BROOKES of the same County and Collony, Planter, his heirs or assignes in the sum of Six thousand pounds of good sound Merchantable Tobb: and Caske to be pd. convenient to landing in the aforesd. on all demands which payment well and truely to be made and don I bind myself my heirs firmly by these presents. Sealed with my Seale this 4th of February 1688

The Condicion of this obligation is such that if the above named JOHN BROOKS his heirs or assigns shall and may from hence forth forever peaceably and quietly have and enjoy all that parcell of land conteying One hundred forty and two acres being in the County of Rappa. according to the most antient and lawfull bounds thereof formerly purchased by RANDOLPH PETERS of the sd County deced and was found to Escheat to his Matys as by Inquisition recorded in Mr. Secretary's Office under the hand of Colo. ISAAC ELLERTON, Escheator of the sd County and Jury sworn before him for that purpose dated the 15th of October 1688 and is since granted to said EDWARD ADCOCK as by Patent bearing date the first day of February 1686/7 and by the above bound EDWARD ADCOCK assigned to the above named JOHN BROOKES as by then assigner bearing date the 10th day of Jany. 1688 may appeare with all the appertanances without the lett trouble eviction or contradiction of the above bound EDWARD ADCOCK his heirs or assigns or any other person whatsoever having or pretending to have any manner of claim or demand of in or to the said Divident of land and premises aforesaid or to any part or parcell thereof by from or under the sd EDWARD ADCOCK his heirs or assignes or any other persons whatsoever then the above obligation to be void and of none effect otherwise to remain in full force power and virtue. Witness my hand and Seale this 4th day of February One thousand Six hunmdred and eighty eight

ELIZA: DOBYNS, EDWARD ADCOCK
ABRAH: A DEPREE, BEN: ADCOCK

p. 14 KNOW ALL MEN by these presents that I NICH. FRANKLIN of County of Rappa. in the Parish of Sittenburn do for a valuable consideration in hand reced give grant sell and by these presents for me my heirs confirm unto JOHN HACKLEY of County and Parish aforesaid his heirs a parcell of land by estimation Seventy acres more or less being in County of Rappa. and Parish of Sittenburn on the South side of the River and OCCUPACON RUN beginning at a red Oake being a corner tree of EDWARD MOSELEYs, thence South by a line of marked trees of ED. MOSELEY to a Pok Hickory by a branch side, thence down the Branch to a Spanish Oake on the West side of the Branch, thence Westerly crossing the Ridge by a line of marked trees to a white Oake by a small Branch, thence down the branch to OCCUPACON RUN, thence by and upon the Run to the red Oake first mentioned the said parcell of land with all its rights and priviledges To have and to hold from me the sd NICHOLAS FRANKLIN my heirs to him the said JOHN HACKLEY his heirs in as large and ample manner to all effects as may be collected out of the Patent without the hindrance or interruption of me the sd NICHO. FRANKLIN my heirs or any person claiming the premises or any part thereof the sd JOHN HACKLEY paying and discharging the Rights and services from henceforth to grow due and of right accustomed In Witness whereof I have hereunto sett my hand and Seale this Fourteenth Novemr. 1688

Signed Sealed and Delivered in the presents of
FRAN: SLAUGHTER, NICHO. FRANKLIN
LELAND LOUIS, MARGARET SLAUGHTER
Recognitr in Cur Comt Rappa 3 die Aprilis Ano 1688

pp. 14-15 KNOW ALL MEN by these presents that we JOSEPH TAYLOE and BARBARA his Wife for diverse good causes and considerations us hereunto moving and especially for the love and affection the sd BARBARA TAYLOE bears to BARBARA ROBINSON being her the said BARBRA TAYLOR's God Daughter by these presents fully and freely give unto sd BARBRA and her heirs one young Mare between a Roane and a Sorrel, two Wall eyes four white feet branded on the neere buttock with the brand S B with all her future increase with warranty of the sale of the sd Mare from the claime of any person whatsoever and furthermore we the said JOSEPH TAYLOE and his Wife do desire Mr. WM. COLSTON to record this our Deed of Guift for the use of the sd BARBARA ROBINSON as aforesaid in Testimony of which Gift and order for recording we have hereunto sett our hands and Seales this Eighth day of March 1688/9
Signed Sealed and Delivered in the presents of us

DEN: MACCARTY, JOSEPH TAYLOE
ELIZ: CAREY, OWEN DERMOTT BARBARA TAYLOE

pp. 15-16 KNOW ALL MEN by these presents that I BENJA. GOODRICH of JAMES CITTY COUNTY and Admirst. of the Will annexed of JOHN FRY late of NEW KENT COUNTY deced do by virtue of an order of the Genll. Court dated the 28th day of 8ber ano. Dom: 1688 giving me the same power and authoritie as Mr. GEO: MORRIS had in and by the last Will and Testament of the sd FRY to acknowledge such lands as was by him sold before his death and it appearing to me that the sd JOHN FRY had sold layed out and received satisfaction of Mr. JAMES OSBURNE of the County of NEW KENT for two hundred and fifty acres of land but had made no acknowledgment of the same before his death, I the sd BENJA: GOODRICH therefore being qualified as aforesd. made by virtue thereof do assigne settle and make over unto Mr. JAMES OSBURNE abovesd. Two hundred and fifty acres of land scituate and being in County of Rappa. and on the South side of RAPPA. RIVER being part of Five thousand one hundred acres of land formerly granted to HEN: AWBREY by Patent bearing date the 9th day of March 1677/8 and by him assigned over unto the sd JOHN FRY, the land is bounded Begining at a great Hickory by the MAINE SWAMP of HOSKINS CREEK & runing thence S. W. to a Poplar and Spanish Oake in the South side of a small Branch, thence N. W. to a Stake between a Spanish Oake and red Oake on a level, thence N. East to the aforementioned MAINE SWAMP to a white Oake by a great white Marsh and a little below the mouth of a Branch, and finally thence down alonge the MAINE SWAMP its windings and turnings to the first specified Station and do Warrant the sale of the abovesd. Two hundred and fifty acres of land from me my heirs &c. unto sd Mr. JAMES OSBURN his heirs and do warrant it from all persons claiming or to claime by or under me in as full and ample manner to all intents as it is assigned from Mr. HEN: AWBREY aforesaid unto said JOHN FRY and do oblige myself to acknowledge at any Court of Record when thereunto demanded. In Witness whereof I have hereunto sett my hand and affixed my Seale this 31st day of Jany. 1688
Signed Sealed and Delivered in the presents of us

PHILL: PENDLETON, BENJA. GOODRICH
WM. LEADER; RICHD. JONES

Recognitr in Cur Comt. Rappa 3 die Aprilis Ano. 1689

p. 16 This shall oblige me THO: HINES of County of Rappa., Planter, my heirs or assignes to pay or cause to be paid unto HENRY PICKETT in behalf of REBECCA STANFIELD, the Daughter of EBENEZAR STANFIELD deced, to the sd PICKETT his heirs the just sum of five thousand pounds of good sound tobb: and Caske to contain the same convenient in the above sd County before or upon the 10th day of 8ber next As Witness my hand this 10th day of December 1688

The Condition of the above obligation is such that if the above said THOMAS HINES his heirs give in securitie at the next Court held for this County on the South side to deliver unto the sd PICKETT his heirs in the behalf of the above said REBECCA STANFIELD two Cowes which was her said Father's which said Cows is run upon the said STANFIELD Plantation with all their encrease for the good and benefit of the sd REBECCA STANFIELD and I the sd HINES do for myself my heirs to do my utmost indeavour to look after the said two Cows and their encrease and in case the Cows dye before the sd Child comes of age or the day of her marrage I the sd HINES do oblige myself my heirs to make good or delivery unto the sd Child two Cows when she comes of age or upon day of Marrage and also to give in Securitie at the abovesd Court to pay or cause to be well and truely paid unto the above said Child when she comes of age or upon the day of Marrage the just sum of Seventeen hundred pounds of good sound Tobb: and Caske being the half of her Father's Estate in the abovesd. County and upon the unperformance of this sd obligation the above bond to be in full force and if performed the above bond to be void and of no effect as Witness my hand this 10th day of October 1688

Teste THO: WHELON, THO: Sig. T H HINDES
WM. JOHNSON

Recognitr in Cur Comt. Rappa. 3 die Aprilis Ano. 1689

p. 17 IN OBEDIENCE to an order of Rappa. Court bearing date the Sixth day of March 1688 have survayed the bounds of a certain Deed of Sale granted by Mr. WM. UNDERWOOD to THO: MEADES bearing date the 12th day of September 1683 .. According to the bounds therein expressed which by the above sd Survayr. makes appeare that it runneth Thirty perches in to the land sold by WALTER PAVEY unto Mr. JOHN RICE as the Platt denotes including no more then 678 acres

p WM. MOSELEY, Surveyer

pp. 17-18 TO ALL XPIAN PEOPLE to whom these shall come I DANIEL DOBYNS of the County of Rappa. in the Colony of Virginia send Greeting in our Lord God everlasting. Whereas I the said DANIEL DOBYNS for certain considerations by me reced before Mariage to ELIZABETH my now Wife as also out of the natural affection I beare unto HENRY SMYTH have given made over and sett unto sd HENRY SMYTH an estate as is here following in manner and forme expressed (Vizt) three young Cows and one three year old heifer being all of the sd HENRY SMITHs Fathers marke and one of the said Cows being red with a white tayle and known by the name of Coll, the other two Cows being of a black colour with some white about them, the one called Young Bacon the other Double Deeggs, the heifer being red and called Rose, wch said Cattle with their encrease male and female I give unto the said HENRY SMYTH and his heirs forever. Also I give unto the sd HENRY SMYTH one large feather bed and bolster, a pair of Blanketts, a Rugg answerable also I give unto sd H. SMYTH two good pewter dishes and six plates answerable, Two good silver spoons, six good leather Chairs, one Iron Kettle of fourteen gallons, one Iron pott of six gallons, two good Tables, one good Chest, one Gold Ring, one large Silver Tobb: box, ten ewes and a Ram, four Breeding Sows and four thousand pounds of good sound sweet sented Tobb: and Caske, all which said Cattle or Estate to be secured and delivered unto the said SMYTH my me the said DANIEL DOBYNS my heirs at the severall ages of the said SMYTH hereafter nominated (Vizt) the Stock of Cattle and hoggs with the household Stuff and the Ring and Silver Box be delivered to the said HENRY SMYTH at the age of Sixteen years; also that Two thousand pounds of Tobb: and Caske be delivered him at the same age; And that the said HENRY SMYTH be at liberty to act and do for himself at the age of Sixteen and to have the Plantation to himselfe whereon GEORGE SUGGETT now liveth when attayned to the age aforesd. And the other Two thousand pounds of Tobb: and Caske to be paid when the sd SMYTH atteyneth to the age of Twenty one alwais provided that the Estate all and singular rest and remaine on the old Plantation belonging to the said SMYTH until the delivery according to the true intent and meaning of these presents and that if any of these Cattle or their encrease becom so that be more advantage to the sd SMYTH to have them killed and a younger of the same kind put in lieu or the just value of Tobb: to pay unto the sd SMYTH for any beast so killed, Also that if it should so happen that the sd HENRY SMYTH decease before age or without heirs before age or willing his estate that then the whole right of this Estate return to ELIZABETH my now Wife and her heirs forever as being the only Auther thereof. Now Know yee that I the said DANIEL DOBYNS do by these presents Ratifie confirm and estate the aforesd. granted premises according as is above expressed and mentioned and acknowledge the same in Court As Witness my hand and Seale this 5th day of February 1689

Signed Sealed and Delivered in the presents of us

JOHN marke 𝒯 THOMSON, DANLL. DOBYNS

EDWARD ADCOCK

Recognitr in Cur Comt. Rappa 3 die Aprilis Ano 1689

pp. 18-21 TO ALL XPIAN PEOPLE to whom these presents shall come Wee WILLIAM COGWELL and JAMES COGWELL of CHARLES CITTY COUNTY in the Province of MERILAND, Planter, am possed of a parcel of land containing Five hundred acres being part of a Patent of one thousand acres as by the sd Patent relation thereunto had may more at large appeare. Now know yee that we the said WILLIAM COGWELL and JAMES COGWELL for a valuable consideration by us in hand already paid we thereunto moving have granted sold confirmed & by these presents do for us our heirs grant bargaine and sell unto JOHANNA HUDSON of the County and Place aforesaid, Widow, her heirs Two hundred and fifty acres of land being the half moiety or half part of the sd Five hundred acres aforesd. situating and lying at the head of PORTOBACO CREEK in Rappa. County in the Colony of Virginia which sd Two hundred and fifty acres adjoining with the Plantation comonly known or called by the name of COGWELLS PLANTATION which is now in the tenure of and occupation of the said JOHANNA HUDSON, Together with all housing fencing orchards gardens and all other priviledges profitts and comodities whatsoever belonging to the sd land granted by vertue of the sd Patent or any other ways or means whatsoever To have and to hold the said Two hundred and Fifty acres of land together with all the abovesd appurtinances priviledges whatsoever thereto belonging and of right any wise apperteyning to said JOHANNA HUDSON her heirs and the sd WM. COGWELL and JAMES COGWELL themselves their heirs do covenant and grant to and with sd JOHANNA HUDSON her heirs that said WM. and JAMES COGWELL shall forever renounce disclaime all right or interest that ever wee had or every may or can have whatsoever unto the sd Two hundred and fifty acres of land or any part thereof and we do most fully and absolutely warrant and confirm the sd land with all the afore recited premises from us the sd WM. and JAMES COGWELL our heirs and assigns and from all other persons whatsoever unto the sd JOHANNA HUDSON her heirs in as full and ample manner as any person doth or may enjoy his land by any Patent granted in this Colony and that said JOHANNA HUDSON her heirs shall from henceforth forever hereafter peaceably and quietly possess and enjoy the aforesd. land with all priviledges without the disturbance or interruption of us WM. COGWELL and JAMES COGWELL our heirs and we do further covenant that if at any time hereafter there shall arise concerning the land any molestation from us or any other persons whatsoever unto the sd JOHANNA HUDSON her heirs do hereby most fully and absolutely warrant assure and confirme the sd parcell of land from us or any other person whatsoever,

Furthermore wee the sd WM. COGWELL and JAMES COGWELL together with our Wives, SUSANNA and ANN, shall by ourselves or our certaine Attorneys acknowledge this present Deed of Sale in Rappa. County Court or before two of his Maties Justices of Peace in the said County aforesd. when thereunto required In Witness whereof wee the parties above mentioned have hereunto putt our hands and Seals this present day being the 27th of March 1689

Signed Sealed and Delivered in the presents of us

WM. FORD,	WM. COGWELL
ELIZA. marke ~ MUNFORD	JAMES COGWELL
EDMD. POTTER	

Recognitr in Cur Com Rappa 3 die Aprilis Ano. 1689

KNOW ALL MEN by these presents that we WM. COGWELL and JAMES COGWELL of CHARLES COUNTY in the Province of MARYLAND, Inholder, do assign over all our right and Interest of all our Stock of Cattle and hogs belonging to the Plantacon that now is in the possession of JOHANNA HUDSON in the County of Rappa. in the Colony of Virginia and likewise all our household goods only a flock bed and furniture and a sett of Tools unto JOHANNA HUDSON her heirs; Likewise a new (blot) I may take away the said JOHANNA HUDSON her heirs shall peaceably possess and enjoy the sd Cattle hogs and household goods from us the sd WM. and JAMES as aforesd. or from any other persons that shall or may lay claime to In Witness whereof wee the parties above mentioned have hereunto sett our hands and Seals this 26th of March 1689

Signed Sealed and Delivered in the presence of us

WILLIAM FORD,	WILLIAM COGHILL
ELIZA. Sig. ~ MUNFORD,	JAMES COGHILL
EDMD. POTTER	

Recognitr in Cur Comt. Rappa 3 die Aprilis Ano. 1689

TO ALL XPIAN PEOPLE to whom these presents shall come Wee the said WILLIAM COGWELL and JAMES COGWELL of CHARLES CITTY COUNTY in the Province of MARYLAND Together with our Wives, SUSANNA and ANN COGWELL send Greeting in our Lord God Everlasting. Now know yee that the said WM. and JAMES COGWELL with our Wives, SUSANNA and ANN, do hereby constitute and ordain our loving friend JAMES SMITHSON of Rappa. County our true and lawfull Attorney for us and in our names to acknowledge a certaine Deed of Sale for Two hundred and fifty acres of land sold to Mrs. JOHANNA HUDSON in Rappa. County Court or before two of his Maties Justices for the sd County and do by these presents absolutely give our sd Attorney full power and authoritie for us and in our names and to our use aforesd. Ratifying and confirming all and whatsoever our said Attorney shall do or cause to be done in the sd premises and as fully and amply to all intents and purposes whatsoever as if wee ourselves were then and there personally present. In Witness whereof we have hereunto sett our hands and seales this Twenty Seventh day of March 1689

Signed Sealed and Delivered in the presence of us

WM. FORD,	WM. COGHILL
ELIZA. MUNFORD	JAMES COGHILL
EDMO: POTTER	SUSANNA COGHILL

p. 21 SURVAYED and perfected for Colo. WM. LOYDE and ZACHARIA EFFORD a certaine parcell of land conteyning One hundred and nine acres and devided equally between them according to the demonstration of the above mentioned Plat lying on the North side of RAPPA RIVER and on the upper side of a small Creek which issues out of the said River above the now Plantation of RICHD. GREEN this 28th of

March 1689

pr WM. MOSELEY, Surveyer R. C.

pp. 21-22 KNOW ALL MEN by these presents that I RICHARD DUDLEY SENR. in the County of Rappa., Planter, do for a consideration of pay to me already received issue transfer and sett over unto my Son, THO: DUDLEY, Eighty acres of land which sd land I bought of ROBERT WILLIAMS and to begin his bounds as followeth (Vizt) at the which maketh the SPRINGS belonging to (blank) SHEARMANs Plantation joyning to his old field and so to run alonge by the sd SHEARMANs line up to the end of my land to a marked Dogwood tree and so to come through the Woods along my line down the Swamp called the GREAT SWAMP and so to run down the SWAMP untill he com to a branch called ENGLISH BRANCH and so alonge by the head of it to the place at the first beginning, And if the above bounds shall want of being Eighty acres of land then the said THO: DUDLEY is to take it towards the line belonging to Mr. RICHARD JASPER yeilding and granting from me my heirs and assigns the same to enjoy peaceable and quietly without any hindrance or any other way to disturb by me or my heirs granting him the said THOMAS his heirs to enjoy it forever and granting him the same power as I enjoy my land according to the Tenor of my conveyance with all priviledges thereunto belonging and further engage myself to ratifie and confirme this above expressed in open Court on demand. In Witness hereof I have hereunto sett my hand and Seale this 11th day of Apl. Ano. 1689

Signed Sealed and Delivered in the presents of us

ISAAC WRIGHT, RICHD. DUDLEY SENR.

RICHD RJ JASPER,

RICHD. my marke R DUDLEY

Recognitr in Comt. Rappa. 1 die Aprilis Ano 1689

KNOW ALL MEN by these presents that I RICHD. DUDLEY SENR. of TOTASKEY CREEK in the County of Rappa.; Plantr., do constitute and appoint my beloved Friend, JOHN JONES, of the County of Rappa. in TOTASKEY CREEK my true and lawfull Attorney for me and in my behalfe to acknowledge to my Son, THO: DUDLEY, Eighty acres of land according to the Tenor of a conveyance given him from under my hand and Seale bearing date this 11th day of Aprilis Ano 1689 at the next Court held for the County of Rappa. and what my said Attorney shall act and do therein I do hereby allow of in as full and larg manner as if I were personally present at the sd Court Given under my hand and Seale this 25th day of April Ano Dom. 1689

Witness RICHD. RJ JASPER, RICHD. DUDLEY

ABRAH. Marke A KIDMARE,

RICHD. R DUDLEY

p. 22 THOMAS JENKINS his marke a crop on the Right eare and a hole and underkeel on the left. Recordatr. Teste

pp. 22-24 THIS INDENTURE made the 24th day of December 1688 and in the 4th yeare of the Reign of our Sovereigne Lord the King the 2nd (by the Grace of God of England, Scotland, France and Ireland & King Defender of the faith &c.) between NATHANIEL CALE of County of Rappa. Gent., of the one part and JOHN TAVERNER of County aforesd. also Gent. of the other part Witnesseth that sd NATHANLL. CALE for and in consideration of Four thousand pounds of Tobb: to him paid or secured to be paid by JOHN TAVERNER the which is hereby acknowledged as for good causes him hereunto moving hath granted and confirmed unto JOHN TAVERNER his heirs One hundred acres of land part of a Devident of Six hundred scituate & butting on the North side of RAPPA.

RIVER in the Parish of FARNHAM and County aforesd. granted by Deed from Mr. WM. HODGSKINs and PHEBE his Wife unto SAMLL. SLANY which sd One hundred acres of land was excepted by them out of the Six hundred and afterwards bargained and sold by them unto GILES CALE, Father of the sd NATHALL. CALE, by writing under the hands and Seals dated the 1st day of May 1667; acknowledged by them and recorded among the records of the sd County; And all houses out houses profitts hereditaments and appertinances to the same are now in the Tenure and occupation of the sd JOHN TAVERNER To have and to hold the sd One hundred acres of land before hereby granted with all the premises rights and appertinances unto the sd JOHN TAVERNER his heirs from hence for ever and sd NATHALL. CALE for himself his heirs doth grant unto JOHN TAVERNER his heirs in form following that he the sd JOHN TAVERNER his heirs may peaceably and quietly enjoy the sd land and all the premises without the hindrance or interruption of sd NATHALL. CALE or any other persons whatsoever and also sd NATHALL. CALE and his heirs at the request of JOHN TAVERNER his heirs shall make and seale any conveyance and assurance (if need be) of the premises and acknowledge the same according to the true intent and meaning hereof. In Witness whereof the parties aforesd to these presents Indentures have sett their hands and Seales in the day and year first above written Signed Sealed and Delivered in the presence of

EWD. SUGGETT, NATHLL. CALE
ISA: WEBBE; DANLL. HORNBY

Recognitr in Cur Comt Rappa 1 die Maii Ano. 1689

Mem: The day and yeare within written menconed NATHLL. CALE entered into the Mancon House belonging to the land within granted and took possession thereof and afterwards delivered the same Turf and Twigg from the sd Land in name of Livery and Seizen & all and singular the premises within granted

in presence of JOHN SUGGETT, NATHLL. CALE
ISA: WEBB; DANLL: HORNBY

pp. 24-25 KNOW ALL MEN by these presents that wee ADAM WOFFENDALL of the County of Rappa. in Virginia and HONORIA WOFFENDALL for the valluable consideration of Three thousand two hundred and fifty pounds of Tobb: well and truely paid before the signing and sealing hereof the Receipt whereof sd ADAM WOFFENDALL doth hereby acknowledge himself therewith fully satisfied and paid and of every part and parcell thereof doth clearly acquitt and discharge WM. MARSHALL of County aforesd. his heirs by these presents hath granted sold and confirmed unto WM. MARSHALL his heirs One hundred acres of land being part of Two hundred and sixty acres of land taken up by ADAM WOFFENDALL lying and being in the County aforesd. on the North side of the River and in the Freshes thereof and beginning at a marked Pock Hickory standing in the line of Mr. FRANS. SLOUGHTER, from thence S. W. to a red Oake, from thence to a white Oake standing on the head of a small branch and runing down the sd Branch to a marked white Oake standing on the mane run being a corner tree of the aforesd. land from thence down the Maine Branch the severall Courses to the line of RALPH WORMLEY Esqr. and binding up on THO: HOPE and from thence runing in the line of Mr. SLOUGHTER to the place where wee first began To have and to hold the sd Land with all timber woods underwoods and appertinances thereunto belonging to him the sd WM. MARSHALL his heirs as also the priviledge of Timber of any other part of the sd land and now in possession of the aforesaid WOFEENDALL as the said MARSHALL have occasion for forever or his heirs &c. with their and every of their rights whatsoever to the only proper use of them the sd MARSHALL his heirs against the sd WOFFENDALL his heirs or any other persons laying any lawfull clame to any part thereof shall warrant from all persons whatsoever the sd MARSHALL his heirs paying from time to time all the rents and dues belonging to our Sovereigne Lord the King his heirs and lawfull Successors after the date of these presents As Witness our hands and Seals this 16th of February 1688/9

THO: marke HARVEY — ADAM WOFFENDALL
ANN Sig CARVER, — HONORIA WOFFENDALL
JOHN BATTALIE

Recognitr. in Cur Comt Rappa 1 die May 1689

KNOW ALL MEN by these presents that I HONORIA WOFFENDALL of the County of Rappa. do constitute and ordaine and appoint my well beloved friend, JOHN BATTAILE, to acknowledge my thirds of land which was bought of my Husband by WM,. MARSHALL and do ratifie and confirme as if I was in presence myself Witness my hand and Seale this 18th day of Febry 1688/9

THO: HARVEY, — HONORIA Sig. WOFFENDALL
ANN marke CARVER

pp. KNOW ALL MEN by these presents that I ROBERT PAYNE of County of Rappa. do
25- for and in consideration of a valuable sum of Thirteen thousand pounds of good
26 lawfull Tobb: in Cask according to Act by me in hand received the Receipt
whereof I the sd ROBERT PAYNE do hereby acknowledge theire with fully satisfield and paid and by these presents have granted sold and confirmed unto Mr. JAMES SCOTT of the aforesd. County his heirs a certain parcell or tract of land conteyning Twelve hundred acres being part of a Patent granted to my Father, ROBERT PAYNE deced, for 3141 acres dated the 27th of Aprill 1668, the said land lying and being in the Freshes of Rappa. and on the South side the River adjacent to the land adjacent to the said PAYNE to JOHN HILL (Vizt.) begining at a red Oake corner tree to the sd HILL which stands by RAPPA ROAD and extending thence along the sd HILLs line N. by E. to a corner Stake to the said HILL which stands in the line of JOHN MEADERS thence along the said MEADERS his line W. N. W. to another white Oake, thence W. by S. to a Gum by a branch of PORTOBACCO CREEK, thence S. S. W. by the sd Swamp over the sd HILLs W. to a Poplar neare a small branch of GUM SWAMP, thence S. by E. to a Stake, thence S. S. E. crossing the Maine Run of ALLENS CREEKE to a Stake, thence crossing the sd Run againe N. E. to the first mentioned red Oake by the Road side. I the sd ROBERT PAYNE do hereby grant convey and make over from me my heirs unto JAMES SCOTT his heirs To have and to hold use and enjoy the same with all its rights and priviledges of all woods waters water courses and whatsoever else peaceably and quietly without any hindrance or disturbance of me the sd PAYNE my heirs &c. to make what further assurance sd JAMES SCOTT or his Councell in Law shall require in that case and do further engage myselfe to acknowledge this my Deed before the Court of Rappa. there to be when thereunto lawfully called by the sd JAMES SCOTT or his heirs he or they paying all dues or impositions which shall be charged and for further confermation I have hereunto sett my hand and Seale this 27th day of Aprill 1689

Signed Sealed and Delivered in presents of us

WILLIAM CLAPHAM, — ROBT. PAYNE
JNO. MILBURNE, JNO. marke HILL

I KATHERINE PAYNE do hereby acknowledge unto JAMES SCOTT and his heirs and assigns all my right title and interest of every part of the land mentioned in the above said Deed of Sale with all the rights and appertinances thereto belonging as Witness my hand and Seale the day and year above mentioned

KATHARINE PAYNE

Recognitr in Cur Comt Rappa 1 die Maii 1689

p. 26-27 KNOW ALL MEN by these presents that I ROBERT PAYNE of the County of Rappa. do for and in consideration of a valuable sum of Five thousand pounds of good lawfull Tobb: in caske according to Act by me in hand received the Receipt whereof I do hereby acknowledge there with fully satisfied and paid and by these presents have given sold and confirmed unto GEO: ANDREWS SENR. and GEO: ANDREWS JUNR. both of the same County above said their heirs a certain parcell of land conteyning Two hundred acres being part of a Patent granted to my Father, ROBT. PAYNE deceased, for 3141 acres bearing date the 27th of April 1668, the said land lying and being in the Freshes of RAPPA. and on the South side the River adjacent to the land by me the sd PAYNE to Mr. JAMES SCOTT and to the land of Mr. GAINES (Vizt.) beginning at a white Oake corner to Mr. GAINES and extending thence along the sd GAINES line S. E. to a small Hickory, thence along another line of GAINES E:S:E: to a small black Oake (213) on a hill side neare a Great Run, thence crossing the sd Run S:W: to a Stake, thence N:E: to a Stake in the line of Mr. JAMES SCOTT, thence alonge the sd SCOTTs line (intersecting the aforesaid Run againe) to the first mentioned white Oake, I the aforesaid ROBERT PAYNE do hereby grant and confirm from me my heirs unto GEO: ANDREWS SENR. and GEO: ANDREWS JUNR. their heirs To have and to hold and to enjoy the same with all its rights of Woods, Water and Water courses and whatsoever else peaceably and quietly without any lett eviction or disturbance of me the sd PAYNE my heirs or any other persons whatsoever claiming to any part of the demised premises, Also I the sd ROBERT PAYNE do oblige myself my heirs to make what further assurance the sd GEO: ANDREWS SENR. and GEO: ANDREWS JUNR. or their Councell in Law shall require in that case and hereby further engage my Wife to acknowledge this Deed of Sale before the Court of Rappa. when thereunto lawfully required he or they paying all dues or impositions which are or shall be charged and in further confirmation hereof I have hereunto sett my hand and Seale this twenty ninth day of April 1689

Signed Sealed and delivered in the presents of us

ROBERT PLEY, ROBERT PAYNE

SAMUEL MARSH

I KATHARINE PAYNE do hereby acknowledge unto GEO: ANDREWS to his heirs and assigns all my title and interest of every part of the land mentioned in the abovesd. Deed of Sale with all the Rights thereto belonging as Witness my hand and Seale the day and year above written

KATHERINE PAYNE

Recognitr in Cur Comt Rappa 1 die Maii Ano 1689

pp. 27-28 KNOW ALL MEN by these presents that I ROBERT PAYNE of County of Rappa. do for and in consideration of one white Guilding already in hand received the Receipt of I the sd ROBERT PAYNE do hereby acknowledge therewith fully satisfied and paid and by these presents have given sold and confirmed fully and absolutely unto HENRY LONGE of the same County above said his heirs a Certaine parcell or tract of land conteyning Eighty seven acres and a halfe lying and being in the Freshes of RAPPA: and on the South side of the River adjacent to the land sold by me the sd PAYNE to WM. CLAPHAM, JOHN HILL and JAMS: SCOTTbeginning at a red Oak (by the MAIN ROAD) side Corner tree to JOHN HILL and runing thence South by West to a double line Oake in the Edge of a WHITE OAKE SWAMP, thence South East by South to a Spanish Oake in the edge of the sd SWAMP, thence N:E: to a Stake being a corner Stake of GEO: LAMBETH, thence along the said LAMBETHs line South East to a Hickory and small Oake corner tree to CLAPHAM, thence along the said CLAPHAMs line No. to a Stake by a small Hickory being a Corner tree to JOHN HILL, thence along the sd line of HILL North to the first mentioned red Oake I the aforesd. ROBT. PAYNE do hereby grant and make over from me my heirs to HENRY LONGE his heirs To have and to hold and enjoy the same with all its rights and priviledges of all woods and water courses and whatsoever else peaceably and quietly without hindrance from the said PAYNE my heirs or any other persons whatsoever claiming to any part of the demised premises, Also I the sd ROBERT PAYNE do oblige myselfe to make what further assurance the sd HENRY LONGE or his Councell Learned in the Law shall require and do hereby further engage myself to acknowledge the Deed of Sale before the Court of Rappa. when thereunto lawfully called by the sd HENRY LONGE or heirs, he or they paying all dues or impositions which shall be charged and for further confirmation hereof I hereunto sett my hand and seale this 29th day of Aprill 1689

Signed Sealed and Delivered in the presents of us

ROBERT PLEY, ROBERT PAYNE
SAMUEL MARSH

I KATHARINE PAYNE do hereby acknowledge unto HENRY LONG and unto his heirs all my right and interest of every part of the land mentioned in the abovesaid Deed of Sale with all the rights and appertinances thereto belonging as Witness my hand and seale the day and year above written

KATHERINE PAYNE

Recognitr in Cur Comt Rappa 1 die May Ano. 1689

pp. KNOW ALL MEN by these presents that I ROBERT PAYNE of County of Rappa. do
29- for and in consideration of a valuable sum of Six thousand pounds of good law-
30 full Tobb: in caske according to Act by me in hand received the Receipt whereof
I the sd ROBERT PAYNE do hereby acknowledge therewith fully satisfied and by these presents have given and confirmed fully and absolutely unto WILLIAM CLAPHAM of the abovesaid County his heirs a certain parcell of land conteyning Three hundred acres being part of a Patent granted to my Father, ROBT. PAYNE deced, for 3141 acres being dated the 27th of April 1668; the said land lying in the Freshes of RAPPA: and on the South side the River beginning at a white Oake in the line of Mr. GRAY and extending thence along the said GRAYs line S.S.E. crossing the Mane Run of a Creek to a small black Oake by the Creek side, thence down the said Creek its severall courses to a small Hickory by the said Creek side in HENRY LONGs cleared ground (Vizt.) South W. thence S:W. to a Stump being formerly a corner Red Oake, thence E. S. W. to a white Oake at the head of a small branch being in a line of GEO: LAMBETHs, thence along the sd LAMBETHs line W. to a Hickory and small Oake, thence W. to a Stake on the South West side of a Pocoson, thence crossing the sd Pocoson N. W. to a great white Oake, thence S. E. to a small white Oake by a small branch, thence N. E. to a Spanish Oake Stump in the line of JOHN MEADORs, thence E. to the first mentioned white Oake, I the sd ROBERT PAYNE do hereby sell and make over from me my heirs unto the sd WM. CLAPHAM his heirs To have hold and enjoy the same with all its rights of all woods waters and water courses and whatsoever else peaceably without any hindrance of me the said PAYNE my heirs or any other persons whatsoever claiming or pretending any lawfull claime to any part of the demised premises, Also I the sd ROBERT PAYNE do oblige myself my heirs to make what further assurance the sd WM. CLAPHAM or his Councell in the Law shall require in that case, and do further engage myselfe to acknowledge this my Deed of Sale before the Court of Rappa. to be enrolled when thereunto lawfully required by the sd WM. CLAPHAM or his heirs he or they paying all dues or impositions which are charged and for further confirmation I have hereunto set my hand and Seale this 27th day of April 1689

Signed Sealed and Delivered in the presents of
JAMES SCOTT, ROBERT PAYNE
JNO. MILBURNE, JNO. marke /\ HILL

I KATHARINE PAYNE do hereby acknowledge unto WM. CLAPHAM his heirs all my right and interest of every part of the land mentioned in the abovesd Deed of Sale with all the rights and appurtenances thereunto belonging Witness my hand and Seale the day and year above menconed

KATHERINE PAYNE

Recognitr in Cur Comt Rappa 1 die May 1689

pp. KNOW ALL MEN by these presents that I ROBERT PAYNE of County of Rappa. do
30- for and in consideration of a valuable sum of Six thousand and Nine hundred
31 pounds of good lawfull Tobb: by me in hand reced. the Receipt whereof I ROBERT PAYNE do hereby acknowledge theirwith fully satisfied and paid and by these presents have granted and confirmed unto JOHN HILL of the same County aforesaid his heirs a certain tract of land conteyning One hundred and Sixteen acres being part of a Patent granted to my Father, ROBERT PAYNE, for 3141 acres bearing date the 27th of April 1668 the sd land being in the Freshes of Rappa. and on the South side the River adjacent to the land sold by me the sd PAYNE to WM. CLAPHAM beginning at a white Oake corner tree to the sd CLAPHAM and extending thence along a line of JOHN MEADERS, W.N.W. to a Stake in the sd line, thence S. by W. crossing a great Pocoson to a red Oake by the Road side, thence S. E. to a small Hickory by a Stake in the line of CLAPHAM, thence along the sd CLAPHAMs line W. to a Stake on the S. W. of a Pocoson, N.N.E. crossing the Pocoson to the first mentioned white Oake, I the said ROBERT PAYNE do hereby grant and make over from me my heirs to JOHN HILL his heirs To have the same with all its rights of all woods waters and water courses and whatsoever else peaceably and quietly without any hindrance of me the sd PAYNE my heirs or any other persons claiming any lawfull claime to any part of the demised premises also I do oblige myself to make what further assurance he the sd JOHN HILL or his Councell in the Law shall require and do further engage myself to acknowledge this my Deed of Sale before the Court of Rappa there to be enrolled when lawfully called by the sd JOHN HILL or his heirs, he or they paying all the compositions which shall be charged and for further confirmation thereof I have sett my hand and seale this 29th day of Aprill One thousand Six hundred and Eighty nine

Signed sealed and delivered in the presents of
ROBERT PLEGE, ROBERT PAYNE
SAMUEL MARCH

I KATHARINE PAYNE do hereby acknowledge unto JOHN HILL and unto his heirs and assignes all my right and interest of every part of the land mentioned in the above Deed of Sale with all the rights and appurtenances belonging As Witness my hand and Seale the day and yeare above written

KATHARINE PAYNE

Recognitr in Cur Comt Rappa 1 die Maii Ano Dom 1689

pp. July Court 1689
31- TO ALL XPIAN PEOPLE to whom these presents shall come Greeting. Know yee
32 that I DAVID ROSIER of Sitternburne Parish in Rappa. County, Planter, and my Wife, SARA ROSIER, for and in consideration of Eight hundred pounds of good sound merchantable Tobb: and Caske to conteyne the same in hand already reced. of FRAN: JAMES of the sd Parish and County, Planter, have bargained and sold unto sd FRAN: JAMES his heirs all our right and Interest in a parcell of land formerly be-

longing unto PHILLIP SHEREWOOD deceased, the Father of my Wife, which whole Divident of land is scituate in said Parish of Sittenburne and County of Rappa. adjoining to the land of WM. JETT of the sd Parish of Sittenburne and County of Rappa. and is estimated to be about three hundred acres more or less Know yee therefore by these presents that wee the above DAVID and SARAH ROSIER do hereby assigne and make over all our right and interest in the said land above mentioned from us our heirs unto FRAN: JAMES his heirs and the same to warrant and defend unto FRANCIS JAMES from all persons by or from us our heirs and admrs. unto said FRANCIS JAMES his heirs In Witness whereof we have hereunto sett our hands and Seales this Twenty fourth day of November One thousand Six hundred and Eighty eight

Witness JOSEPH AMON, DAVID his marke ᑕ ROSIER
WM. HEATHER SARAH her marke ᒪ ROSIER

Acknow. in Rappa. Court the first day of May ano 1689 by SARA ROSIER and by DAVID ROSIER acknow. at a Court held for the said County the 3rd day of July and recorded the 10th said month and yeare

p. 32 BEE IT KNOWN unto all men by these presents that we LODOWICK ROWZEE and JOHN ROWZEE of County of Rappa. do for ourselves our heirs sell and sett over unto JEREMIA PARKER of sd County of Rappa. for the consideration of Four hundred and fifty pounds of Tobb: and caske according to Act to us in hand paid all the land containing Forty acres be it more or less that lyeth on the West side of OCCUPACIE CREEK between the line of the land that PARKER purchased of us the sd LODOWICK ROWZEE and JOHN ROWZEE and runing along the sd line from the first beginning tree a marked red Oake to a red Oke sapling and the mane Creek of OCCUPACIE which sd line of marked trees is his inward bounds and the sd Creek the "outward" bounds To have and to hold from us the said LODOWICK and JOHN ROWZEE and our heirs unto JEREMIA PARKER and his heirs and wee doe grant the sd JEREMIA PARKER quiett peaceable possession and enjoyment of the sd land and also to his heirs without the lett hindrance or ejection clame or clames of any persons that shall or may lay clame thereunto Witness our hands and seales this first day of June Ano Dom 1689

Signed and Delivered in presents of
ROBT. PAYNE, LODOWICK ROWZEE
EDMON Sig X CONELLOE JOHN Sig I ROWZEE

Recognitr in Cur Comt Rappa 3 die July Ano 1689

p. 32 KNOW ALL MEN by these presents that I KATHARINE PAYNE do constitute and appoint my friend Mr. JOHN DEANE my certaine Attorney and I do impower him in my place and stead to acknowledge in County Court of Rappa. all my right and Interest of several tracts or dividents of land according to Conveyances or Deeds of Sale and granted by my Husband Mr. ROBT. PAYNE (vist) unto Mr. WM. CLAPHAM, JAMES SCOTT, JOHN HILL, GEO: ANDREWS and HENRY LONG ratifying and confirming what my said Attorney shall do in the premises abovesaid as Witness my hand and Seale this Twenty second day of April 1689

Test JOHN MILBURNE Recordr. KATHARINE PAYNE

pp. 32-33 THIS INDENTURE made the 28th day of June Ano Dom 1689 Between SAMLL. BAYLY of the one part in the Parish of Farnham and in the County of Rappa. and RALPH WHITING of sd Parish and County of Rappa. of the other part Witnesseth that SAMUEL BAYLEY for and in consideration of Sixty six pounds Sterling to me in hand paid whereof I do acknowledge myself satisfied and contented have bargained and sold unto RALPH WHITING his heirs Two hundred and fifty acres of land sitaute and being in the County aforesd. on the North side of the River in the Freshes thereof on the West side of CHINGATEGUE CREEK and running up the Maine River its severall courses the full breadth of my land bought of Mr. THO: CHETWOOD being Eleven hundred twenty and five acres being at the lowermost part thereof together with all houses fencing and orchards and with the appurtenances thereunto belonging from him the sd BAYLEY his heirs to him the sd WHITING his heirs And from all or any other persons whatsoever by or under me nevertheless said WHITING subject to the Quitrents and services which from henceforth become due to be paid and performed for and in respect of the premises to the Kings Maties his heirs or Successors, Furthermore the sd BAYLY shall and will be ready to acknowledge the same in open Court and shall give possession when thereunto required and that my now Wife shall also acknowledge her rights therein for the confermation of which and every part thereof have hereunto sett my hand and Seale the day and year above written

Signed Sealed and Delivered in presents of

PHILLIP HUNNINGS, SAMLL. BAYLEY

JNO. GRIFFIN, ED: JONES

Recognitr in Cur Comt. Rappa. 3 die July Ano 1689

KNOW ALL MEN by these presents that I SARAH BAYLEY, the Wife of SAMLL. BAYLEY, in the County of Rappa. and Parish of Farnham have nominated and hereby do putt and constitute Mr. WILLIAM COLSTON of the County and Parish aforesaid my true and lawfull Attorney to acknowledge my right of Dower of a seat of land in the Freshes of Rappa. to Mr. RALPH WHITING and severall others and whatever my said Attorney shall act and do in the premises aforesaid I do hereby ratifie and confirme as if I was personally present to do the same. Witness my hand and Seale the second of July One thousand Six hundred and Eighty nine

Sealed and Delivered in the Presents of

WM. HARRISON, SARAH Marke S BAYLY

HANC. H JENKINS

Recognitr in Cur Comt Rappa 3 die July Ano 1689

p. 34 THIS INDENTURE made this 3d day of July Ano Dom 1689 Between SAMLL. BAYLEY of the one part in the Parish of Farnham & in the County of Rappa. and PHILLIP HUNNINGS of the said Parish and County of Rappa. of the other part Witnesseth that SAMLL. BAYLY for and in consideration of one third part of a VESELL or SHIP now called the *DOLPHIN* which I acknowledge to be fully satisfied and contented have bargained and sold unto PHILLIP HUNNINGS his heirs Four hundred and fifty acres of land scituate lying and being in the County aforesd. on the North side of RAPPA RIVER in the Freshes thereof on the West side CHINGATEAGUE CREEK begining at the head line of RALPH WHITINGs which is the breadth of Two hundred fifty acres from the Mane River side runing the full breadth of my land with its severall courses upon CHINGATEAGUE CREEK and so in to the woods untill he hath his full Foure hundred and fifty acres of land compleated together with all houses fencing orchards or out orchards whatsoever and with all other the appertenances thereunto belonging from himselfe the said BAYLY his heirs to him the said HUNNINGS his heirs and from all or any persons by from or under me or any other Nevertheless the said HUNNINGS subject to the Quitrents and services from henceforth shall grow due to be paid in respect to the premises to the Kings Maties his heirs and Successors, Furthermore the sd BAYLY shall acknowledge the same in open Court when thereunto required and that my now Wife shall also acknowledge her right thereof In Confirmation of which and every thereto have hereunto set my hand and seale the day and yeare above written

Signed Sealed and Delivered in the presents of
JOHN BROWNE, SAMLL. BAYLY
THO: LEWIS, RALPH WHITINGS
Recognitr in Court Rappa 3 die July 1689

pp. TO ALL TO WHOM &c. I Sr: WM. BERKELEY Kngt. Governor &c. send Greeting.
34- Whereas &c. Now Know yee that I the said WM. BERKELEY Knight Govr. accor-
35 dingly give and grant unto RICHD. GOODMAN Four hundred Twenty and foure
acres of land lying in Rappa. County on the North side of the River begining at a marked Corner marked Beech standing by a Swamp called the BRYERY SWAMP runing up the ROAD PATH North to a marked red Oake standing by the aforesaid ROAD PATH, thence N.E. along an old PATH called by the name of CHICKESEN PATH by the marked trees to a marked Corner of the TURKEY BRANCH, thence S. to a marked white Oake standing at the head of the aforesd. BRYERY SWAMP, thence down the sd BRYERY SWAMP several courses to the first mentioned tree the sd land being due &c. followeth Three hundred acres part thereof formerly granted to EDWARD WETHERBURNE and GERARD REYNOLDS and by them sold and assigned to the sd RICHD. GOODMAN and One hundred twenty foure acres residue is due by and for the Transportation &c. To have and to hold &c. Yielding and paying &c. Provided &c. Given under my hand and the Seale of the Colony this 20th day of November in the yeare of our Lord 1670
WILLIAM BERKELEY

KNOW ALL MEN by these presents that I <u>EDWARD</u> GOODMAN of the County of Rappa. in Virginia, Plantr., for and in consideration of the sum of Five thousand pounds of good Tobacco in hand paid and received of WILLIAM SMITH of the aforesaid County, Carpenter, the receipt whereof I do hereby acknowledge, do bargaine sell and make over unto sd WM. SMITH all my right and interest of the within mentioned Patent of land be the quantitie more or less To have and to hold the same to him the sd WM. SMITH his heirs or assigns without any lett or molestation from me my heirs or assigns or any persons whatsoever that may lay claime thereunto In Witness whereof I have hereunto set my hand and Seale this 28th day of June 1689
Signed Sealed and Delivered in the Presents of
SAMLL. GRIFFIN, <u>EDMUND</u> marke GOODMAN
Recognitr in Cur Comt Rappa 3 die July 1689

pp. KNOW ALL MEN by these presents that I THO: PARKER of the County of Rappa.
35- doe for me my heirs assigne and make over from me my heirs all my right title
36 and interest to the within mentioned Fifty acres of land be it more or less unto
Capt. WM. MOSELEY of the sd County his heirs Witness my hand and Seale this 21st day of May Ano 1689
Sealed and Delivered in presence of
ROBERT PLEY, THOS: PARKER
RICHD. LIGHTON ELIANOR marke 0 PARKER
ELIANOR PARKER on the 22d day of May 1689 signed and sealed this Assignment in presence of LODOWICK ROWZEE & WM. HARPER
Recognitr. in Cur Comt Rappa 3 die July 1689

(Five lines of Indenture from SAML. BAYLY to PHILLIP HUNNINGS repeated)

KNOW ALL MEN by these presents that I ELINER PARKER, Wife of THOMAS PARKER, of County of Rappa. do authorize and constitute EDWARD ROWZEE of the said County my true and lawfull Attorney for me and in my name to acknowledge unto Capt. WM.

MOSELEY of the said County all my right and interest of in and unto that Fifty acres of land be it more or less that my sd Husband sold by Assignment to Capt. WM. MOSELEY on the 21st day of May last past in the next Court held for the County of Rappa., ratifying and by these presents holding firm and stable whatsoever my said Attorney shall therein act and do as if I myselfe were then and there personally present Witness my hand and seale this 22d day of May Onel thousand Six hundred and Eighty nine
Sealed and Delivered in presence of
LODOWICK ROWZEE, ELIANER marke of D PARKER
WILLIAM HARPER Recordt. Teste

pp. 36-38 THIS INDENTURE made the 5th day of January Ano 1688/9 in the yeare of the Reigne of our Sovereigne Lord James the second by the grace of God of England Scotland France and Ireland, King Defendr. of the faith &c. Between HENRY LUCAS of Farnham Parish and County of Rappa:, Plantr., of the one part and JOHN BATTEN of the said Parish and County, Planter, of the other part Witnesseth that HENRY LUCAS for and in consideration of a certaine sume of mony to him in hand paid before the ensealing hereof, the receipt which the sd HENRY LUCAS doth hereby acknowledge and thereof doth discharge the sd JOHN BATTEN his heirs and every of them, by these presents & for other good causes him moving, have granted bargained and sold and confirmed unto JOHN BATTEN his heirs One hundred acres of land scituate lying and being in the Parish and County abovesd. on the North side of RAPPA RIVER being part of the sd LUCCAS Devident lying at the mouth of RICHARDSONS CREEK commonly known or called by the name of BUTTONS PLANTATION being at a marked (blank) standing at the mouth of a small branch between the sd Plantation and Mr. SAGER and from thence extending along the sd River towards the sd LUCASs Plantation to a marked (blank), thence S. E. to the first departure; To have and to hold the sd One hundred acres of land with all the hereditaments profitts and appertenances thereto belonging with all the woods and waters therein conteyned by the yearly rent due to his Maties his Successors or Rent Gatherers for the time being appointed unto the pper use and beehoofe of him the sd BATTEN his heirs And the sd LUCAS for himselfe and his heirs the 100 acres of land aforesaid with the premises and appertinances to him JOHN BATTEN and his heirs &c. against him the said HENRY LUCAS and his heirs &c. shall and will warrant and forever defend by these presents And further said HENRY LUCAS doth for himselfe and his heirs &c. promise and grant to JOHN BATTEN his heirs for and notwithstanding any act or thing done or suffered to be done that at the time of executing an estate of the Premises with appertinances to sd JOHN BATTEN his heirs &c. he is absolutely seized thereof as of fee simple to him and his heirs and full power to grant and convey the premises according to the intent and meaning of these presents and the said One hundred acres of land now are and may hereafter remane unto the sd JOHN BATTEN his heirs freely acquited from all manner of sales, dowers, wills and from all other titles or incumbrances made by him the sd HENRY LUCAS or by his assent or procurmt. the aforesd Quitrents due to his Maties his heirs &c. for the time to come only excepted and foreprized and that the said JOHN BATTEN may forever hereafter to him his heirs have and quietly enjoy the abovesd land without the lett of him sd HENRY LUCAS or any other persons lawfully claiming under him and also sd HENRY LUCAS will at all times forever at the request and cost of him the sd JOHN BATTEN make acknowledge and execute such further lawfull acts whatsoever for the better suretie and sure making of the said land unto the said JOHN BATTEN as by him and their Councell in the Law shall be devised and required In Witness whereof alll and singular the premises according to the true intent thereof the sd HENRY LUCAS hath hereunto sett his hand and affixed his seale the day and yeare first above written

Signed Sealed and Delivered in the presents of
GEO: SPENCER, HENRY LUCAS
ALEXR. SWAN
Recognitr in Comt. Rappa 3 die July 1689 pr HENRY LUCAS

pp. 38-40 THIS INDENTURE made the 29th day of June in year of our Lord God according to the Compatation of the Church of England 1689 Between THOS. LEWIS of the Parish of North Farnham in the County of Rappa., Planter, of the one part and HENRY WEBSTER of the Parish & County, Planter, of other part Witnesseth that THOMAS LEWIS for and in consideration of sum of Five thousand pounds of every way good sound Merchantable Tobb. the receipt whereof said THOMAS LEWIS doth hereby acknowledge and thereof doth acquitt and discharge the sd HENRY WEBSTER his heirs, by these presents hath bargained sold and confirmed unto HENRY WEBSTER his heirs all that peice or parcell of land lying and being in Parish and County aforesaid on the North side of a Creek called TOTASKEY CREEK beginning upon the side of the sd CREEKE at a Corner tree of one LEONARD JONES and so runing up the sd line in breadth and length the full quantitie of Seventy acres being part or parcell of a tract of land which sd THOMAS LEWIS formerly bought of JOHN (blot) as by Deed bearing date the 16th day of February in year of our Lord 1687 Relacon being there unto had more fully may appeare and now in occapation of sd THO: LEWIS or his assigns and the Reversion thereof with all Deeds wrightings touching and concerning the premises with all profitts and appertenances thereunto belonging or in any wise apperteyning, the Quit rents for the same from henceforth growing due to the Chief Lord or Lords the Reginory or Regniors only excepted To have and to hold the sd Seventy acres of land above hereby mentioned to be bargained and sold with the appertinances unto sd HENRY WEBSTER his heirs to the only proper use and behoofe of sd HENRY WEBSTER his heirs and THOMAS LEWIS for himself and his heirs the said Seventy acres above menconed with its appertinances unto HENRY WEBSTER and his heirs against him said THO: LEWIS and his heirs shall warrant and forever defend by these presents and the said THO: LEWIS for himselfe and his heirs doth grant to said HENRY WEBSTER his heirs by these presents that he upon the reasonable request and at the proper cost and charges in the Law of the said HENRY WEBSTER his heirs do make execute or cause to be made due acknowledged and suffered such further lawfull and reasonable act and acts and conveyances as by the Councell learned in the Law of the sd HENRY WEBSTER his heirs shall be reasonably devised or required and said THO: LEWIS for himselfe his heirs promise that he the said THO: LEWIS and MARY his Wife at some Court to be holden within Six months in County of Rappa. abovesd in open Court before the Justices then and there sitting acknowledge this present Deed and interest of Dower and thereof in and to the above menconed to be hereby bargained and sold unto HENRY WEBSTER his heirs In Witness whereof the said THOMAS LEWIS hath sett his hand and seale the day and yeare first above written
Sealed and Delivered in the presence of
THOMAS CLARK, THO: LEWIS
ANTHO: STEP; JAMES ELLIS
Recognitr in Cur Comt. Rappa 3 die July 1689
KNOW ALL MEN by these presents that I MARY LEWIS, Wife of the within named THO: LEWIS, do freely clearly and voluntarily give and acknowledge my assent and consent to the Deed within written and also do relinquish release and acquit claim all my title and interest of a Dower and third of in and to the said Land within mentioned to be sold with their appertenances unto the within HENRY WEBSTER his heirs Witness my hand the day and yeare first within written

Witness THO: marke X CLARKE MARY the marke of M LEWIS
ANTHO: STEP, JAS: ELLIS
Recognitr in Cur Comt Rappa 3 die July 1689

KNOW ALL MEN by these presents that I MARY LEWIS of County of Rappa and Parish of North Farnham do make and appoint my true and well beloved friend, HENR: LEWIS, of the aforesaid County my true and lawfull Attorney for me in my name giving him full power to acknowledge and grant unto HENRY WEBSTER of the aforesaid County and Parish his heirs all the Right and Interest I have in one parcell of land which said HENRY WEBSTER hath bought of my Husband, THO: LEWIS, scituate and being on the West side of TOTASKEY CREEKE which by Deed bearing date the 29th of June 1689 In Witness whereof I have sett my hand and seale this Third day of July 1689
Signed Sealed in the presence of us
DAVID LOYDE, MARY LEWIS
THOS: GAINES her marke

pp. 40-41 KNOW ALL MEN by these presents that we LODOWICK ROWZEE and JOHN ROWZEE and EDWARD ROWZEE of County of Rappa. for the consideration of Five thousand pounds of good sound merchantable Tobb. and Caske well and truely to us in hand paid by THO: PARKER of said County do grant and by these presents have sold from us our heirs and Successors unto THO: PARKER his heirs the full compliment and quantitie of Fifty five acres of land lying in the County of Rappa. on South side of RAPPA. RIVER on the Mane Creeke side comonly known by the name of OCCUPACEY CREEKE the sd Fifty five acres of land being part of a Devident of land bequeathed unto sd LODOWICK and JOHN ROWZEE by our Father, Mr. EDWARD ROWZEE, in his last Will & Testament and now in full and free tenure possession of us the sd LODOWICK ROWZEE and JOHN ROWZEE, the Fifty five acres of land by a true and lawfull survey made by a lawfull Surveyor beginith at a marked small red Oake close adjoining to their corner side of the clere ground of the Plantation of us the sd LODOWICK ROWZEE and JOHN ROWZEE whereon we now dwell and inhabitt and close on the Brim of the bank side of OCCUPACIE CREEKE and runing from thence East to a red Oake saplin, thence South East to a red Oake saplin, thence South West to a small white Oake by a great dead red Oake thence North West to a black Oake saplin, thence N. East to the first mentioned station, we the abovesd. LODOWOCK, JOHN and EDWARD ROWZEE do warrant the above said land with all the parts appurtinances and privilidges thereof from us our heirs unto sd THOMAS PARKER his heirs peaceably to him to have hold and enjoy without the hindrance of us the sd LODOWICK ROWZEE, JOHN ROWZEE, EDWARD ROWZEE or any other persons whatsoever that may lay any claim to within this Colony of Virginia, And we have also put him sd THOMAS PARKER into possession for himselfe his heirs forever in peaceable possession of the sd Fifty five acres of land by Livery and Seizen with Turf and Twigg acknowledging thereby to have quitted our claim in and unto the sd property and fee simple of the same to rest in and appertaining unto the sd THO: PARKER and his heirs In Witness whereof we have put our hands and seales this 21st day of May in year of our Lord 1689
Sealed and Delivered in presence of
ROBT. PLEY, LODOWICK ROWZEE
RICHD. LIGHTON JOHN I ROWZEE
EDWARD ROWZEE

Recognitr. in Cur Comt. Rappa p. LODOWICUM, JOHANNIM et EDWARDUM RAWZEE 3 die July 1689

pp. Augt. Court 1689
41- KNOW ALL MEN by these presents that we JOHN and MARY DYKE of County of
42 Rappa and of the Parish of South Farnham for a valuable consideration in hand received of and from HENRY WOODNOTT of the same County and Parish aforesd. whereof we the said JOHN and MARY DYKE are fully satisfied and contented hath granted and confirmed unto HENRY WOODNOTT his heirs that Thirty acres of land be the same more or less situate and being in Farnham Parish in Rappa County on the South side of RAPPA. RIVER and adjoining and connected with the lands of ANDREW DUDDING, JOHN CHANEY and the said WOODNOTT, sd land being a part of a Devident of land whereon sd JOHN and MARY now liveth which Thirty acres of land be the same more or less is conteyed within the several bounds following that is to say begining at a marked white Oake upon ADNREW DUDDINGS and runing down a branch to the Swamp where the sd Branch leadeth into Deviding this land from the mane Devident, this branch being the bounds on the N:W: side, the said Thirty acres of land then from the forke of the sd branch and Swamp up the sd Swamp his severall courses and distances alonge the land of JOHN CHANEY leading to the land of the sd HENRY WOODNOTT, then alonge sd WOODNOTTs land to the land of sd DUDDING and along the line of sd DUDDING to the first menconed white Oake upon the branch by ANDW. DUDDING; To have and to hold the aforesaid land with all rights whatsoever appertaining without the lett or trouble of us our heirs with further warranty from any persons whatsoever that shall lay any claim to the land and do further oblige ourselves our heirs at the request of sd WOODNOTT his heirs to make grant and suffer to be be made further Deeds conveyances for the more sure conveying and securing of the sd land as he the said WOODNOTT or Councell learned in the Law shall reasonably require and at the desire of the sd WOODNOTT his heirs to make acknowledgment hereof in the County Court held for Rappa In Witness whereof we the sd JOHN and MARY DYKE have unto these presents sett our hands and seales this 3d day of April 1689

Signed Sealed and delivered in presents of us

HENRY ⓗ MACKENY — JOHN DIKE
THO: LOUGH — MARY Sig X DIKE

Recognitr in Cur Comt Rappa 7 die August Ano 1689

pp. KNOW ALL MEN by these presents that I RICHARD WEST of County of Rappa. of
42- the Parish of Sittenburne do for my heirs for the sum of Two thousand Five
43 hundred pounds of Tobb: in caske give and confirme unto JOHN RICHEE his heirs a parcell of land containing Fifty acres more or less begining at a red Oake standing by HUCCLEBERRY SWAMP, thence by the sd Swamp side on the North side to a marked line Oake, thence through the Swamp by a line of trees to a marked Locust on the South side which parts the lands of VALENTINE ALLEN and RICHD. WEST bounding on the lines of said VALENTINE ALLEN by and with a great branch to a corner tree of MARTIN JOHNSON standing by the River thence by the River to the tree first mentioned to said JOHN RICHEE To have and to hold said land with all manner of priviledges upon the said land belonging as it to me is granted to the sole and proper use of him said RICHEE his heirs, he paying and discharging the rights and services due and of right accustomed, And further the said RICHARD WEST doth for his heirs grant with sd RICHEE his heirs &c. that sd RICHEE shall at all times hereafter quietly hold the aforesaid parcell of land as also the said JOHN RICHEE shall have quiet and peaceable use of so much Timber as will build the sd RICHEE a fence and Twenty foot Dwelling House and a Ten foot Milk house and as much Rail Timber as the sd RICHEE his heirs shall have occasion for fencing on his abovesd land from the land of the sd RICHARD WEST joyning upon the land of the sd RICHEE with every part and parcell of the abovesaid premises

without hindrance of me sd RICHARD WEST his heirs or any other persons whatsoever lawfully claiming the premises from or under me. As Witness my hand and seale this 20th day of July 1689
Signed Sealed and Delivered in the presents of us
FRAN: SLAUGHTER; RICHD. Sig. R WEST
ROBT. AD ADAMS
Recognitr in Cur Comt Rappa 7 die Augt. 1689

pp. 43-44 TO ALL TO WHOM &c. I Sr. WM. BERKELEY Knight Governor &c. send Greeting &c. Whereas &c. Now know yee that I the sd Sr. WM. BERKELEY Knight Governor &c. accordingly give and grant unto Coll. JOHN CATLETT Two thousand acres of land being on the North side of RAPPA RIVER and beginneth at a marked Beech by a small gutt over against a Ledge of Rocks on the South side of the River and is above three miles below the lowest FALL extending for breadth by or nigh the River side, N:W: to a red Oake, thence into the Woods E:N: East to a white Oake, thence S:S:E: and West of like distance and upon their opposite courses abovemenconed the sd land being due unto Collo. CATLETT by and for the Transportation of Forty persons into this Colony To have and to hold &c. yeilding and paying &c. provided &c. Given at JAMES CITTY under my hand and Seale of the Colony this 2d day of June Ano. 1666
WILLIAM BERKELEY

KNOW ALL MEN by these presents that I JOHN CATLETT, Son and heire to Collo. JOHN CATLETT late of the Colony of Virginia deced, for a valuable consideration to me in hand paid by Mr. JOHN WAUGH of STAFFORD COUNTY within the sd Colony, CLERKE, do grant and sett over unto the sd JOHN WAUGH his heirs and assigns forever all my right and demand of in and to the within menconed Patent and all the land appurtenances and Priviledges therein granted either in right of my said Deced Father or of my own right or otherwise howsoever And I do by these presents oblige myselfe and my heirs to acknowledge this present Deed at the next Court to be for this County of Rappa. Witness my hand and Seale this third day of June Ano Dom One thousand Six hundred and eighty nine Sealed and Delivered in the presence of
JOHN BATTAILE JOHN CATLETT
GERARD LOWTHER
Recognitr in Cur Comt Rappa 7 die Augt. 1689

pp. 44-46 THIS INDENTURE made the 19th day of June Ano Dom 1689 Between HUMPHREY BOOTH of Rappa County, Planter, Son and heir apparent of HUMPHREY BOOTH, late of sd County, Gent. deced; ROBT. BROOKES of sd County, Planter, and CATHARINE his Wife, Daughter also of the sd HUMPHREY BOOTH deced and heir entaile in Posin (blot) to the sd HUMPHREY, the Son of the one part and RICHARD STOKES of the said County, Planter, of the other part Witnesseth that said HUMPHREY BOOTH, ROBERT BROOKES and CATHERINE his Wife for sum of Two thousand one hundred and three pounds of Tobb: to them or one of them in hand at and before sealing and delivering hereof by sd RICHARD STOKES truly paid by these presents have and each and every of them hath bargained sold and confirmed unto RICHARD STOKES his heirs all that parcell of land containing Fifty nine acres and one quarter of an acre scituate and being in Parish of Cittenburne on the South side RAPPA RIVER in County aforesd lying runing and extending in manner following Beginning at a certaine Stake sett in the NEW FENCE Pasture of sd RICHD. STOKES and adjoining to the land of the edge of a Pocoson, thence S. West to a small red Oake saplin neere a Hickory, thence West to the first mentioned Stake and all woods underwoods timbers trees standing or being on the sd parcell of land and all houses edifices and buildings thereupon standing erected

or built all ways passages watters profitts and appurtenances whatsoever to the premises belonging and all the right they the sd HUMPHREY, ROBERT and CATHERINE or any of them now have To have and to hold the sd Fifty acres and one quarter of an acre of land and all the premises unto sd RICHARD STOKES his heirs to his own proper use and for none other and said RICHARD STOKES from henceforth forever peaceably and quietly have and enjoy the before menconed premises without the lawfull suit denial or interruption of any persons whatsoever and that they the sd HUMPHREY BOOTH, ROBERT BROOKE and CATHERINE his Wife shall and will within six months next ensuing in due form of Law acknowledge these presents before his Majties Justices of Peace for Rappa County and that they do suffer and execute such further and other lawfull and reasonable acts for the further conveying and assuring of the before bargained premises unto RICHARD STOKES his heirs as he sd RICHARD STOKES or their Councell learned in the law shall reasonably desire In Witness the sd parties to these Indentures have sett their hands and seales
Signed Sealed and Delivered in the presents of us
The marke of T THO: GRIFFIN, HUMPHREY BOOTH
SAMLL. THACKER, ROBT. BROOKE
JOHN ALMOND KATH. BROOKE
Recognitr p BOOTH, BROOKE & Exor BROOKE in Cur Comt Rappa 7 Augst ano 1689
KNOW ALL MEN by these presents that I KATHERINE BROOKE do hereby depute and authorize Mr. WM. MOSLEY my lawfull Attorney for me in my name before his Majesties Justices of Peace of Rappa County in open Court or otherwise to acknowledge one Indenture of Deed of Sale dated with these presents made between HUMPHREY BOOTH my Brother, RICHD. BROOKE my Husband & me, CATHERINE of the one part and RICHARD STOKES of the other part to ratifie and confirm all that my sd Attorney shall do in the premises. Witness my hand and Seale this 29th of June 1689
Signed Sealed and Delivered in the presents of us
THO: T GRIFFIN, KATH: BROOKE
JNO. ALMOND Recordatr. Teste

pp. 46-47 KNOW ALL MEN by these presents that I HUMPHREY BOOTH of County of Rappa. in Virginia, Planter, for divers good causes me thereunto moving more especially for Six pounds Ten Shillings, Four breeding sowes, two shoats and three barrels of Indian Corne in hand paid and secured have by these presents bargained sold and confirmed unto GARRAT EVANS of the aforesaid County in Virginia, Plantr., his heirs Eighty acres of land being in the County aforesd. and bounded begining with the MANE ROAD on the upper side of PRICES RUN from thence down the sd Run till it includes Eighty acres square, the sd land lying and being on the South side of the aforesd River To have and to hold the aforesd Eighty acres from me my heirs unto the aforesaid EVANS his heirs and from the clame to any part thereof and further do oblige myself my heirs to give unto the aforesd EVANS his heirs any other assurance as his or their Councell in the Law shall advise if this shall not be thought sufficient in Law and for the better assurance of this conveyance I bind myself my heirs unto said EVANS his heirs in the full and just sum of Twenty thousand pounds of legall Tobb: payable upon all demands in case the sd EVANS be disturbed or molested in the quiet and peaceable possession of the aforesd land. In Testimonie whereof I have hereunto sett my hand and Seale this (blank) day of May One thousand Six hundred and eighty nine Signed Sealed and Delivered in presence of us
GEO: LOYD, HUMPHREY BOOTH
JAMES FULLERTON
HENRY marke ⊙ NEWTON

Recognitr in Cur Comt. Rappa 7 die Augst 1689

pp. BE IT KNOWN unto all men by these presents that wee LODOWICK ROWZEE, JOHN
47- ROWZEE and EDWARD ROWZEE of the Parish of Sittenburne the County of Rappa-
48 hannock for and in consideration of the sum of Five thousand pounds of Tobb:
to us in hand paid have sold and confirmed THOS: CRIPPS his heirs all and wholy a certain tract of land containing Thirty acres be it more or less being in sd County of Rappa on the South side of RAPPA: RIVER and on a small branch or gutt that falleth into OCCUPACY CREEK and begineth at a small red Oake in a point by a great Marsh, it being the corner tree of the land of WM. HARPER and runeth from sd Corner tree N.W. along the line of WM. HARPER to a marked red Oake by a Deepe branch side from thence over the said Deep Branch still keeping the same course alonge the same line to a marked Pockhickory that standeth on the further side of a Deep Branch that falleth into the abovesd small gutt or branch of OCCUPACY CREEK and runing from the sd Pockhickory alonge the branch down the sd branch and into the abovesd small gutt or branch finally down the said branch including all the land between the sd branch and the aforemenconed line of WM. HARPERs land To have and to hold the sd parcell of land to him sd THO: CRIPS and his heirs with all the right thereof belonging from all and every of us our heirs and from the just claime of all persons that may lay any claime thereunto or to any part thereof and wee have this day for ourselves our heirs put sd THOS. CRIPPS free full and actuall possession of sd parcell of land by livery and seizen to the free and absolute behoofe and comoditie of him the sd THO: CRIPPS and his heirs and assigns forever Witness our hands and seales this 26th day of July 1689

Witness THO: PARKER SENR. ED. RAUZEY
JOSEPH JH HENLEY LODOW. RAUZEY
JOHN I RAUZEY

Recognitr in Cur Comt Rappa 7 die Augt 1689

pp. THIS INDENTURE made the 7th day of August One thousand six hundred Eighty
48- and nine and in the first yeare of the Reigne of our Sovereign Lord and Lady
49 WILLIAM and MARY by the grace of God &c. King and Queen Defender of the
faith &c. Between EDWIN THACKER of the County of MIDDLESEX in the Parish of CHRIST CHURCH, Survr: of the one part and JOHN MEADOR of the County of Rappa in the Parish of South Farnham, Planter, of other part Witnesseth that EDWIN THACKER for a valuable consideration in hand well and truely paid by JOHN MEADOR the said EDWIN THACKER doth acknowledge and absolutely release and by these presents I have given sold and confirmed unto JOHN MEADOR his heirs One hundred and five acres of land situate in County of Rappa. in the Parish of South Farnham being part of Fifteen hundred Sixty and three acres granted by Patent unto the abovesaid EDWIN THACKER dated the 20th of April Ano 1687, and bounded begining at a corner Hickory of JOHN EVANS his land in the sd MEADORs line and runing thence by EVANS line S: by W: to a corner Hickory and two red Oakes marked by it, thence S:W: to a marked line to a Stake by a red Oake and thence N:E: by E: by a marked line to the land of sd MEADOR to four Oake saplings on the South side of a hill and thence runing on the sd MEADORs land alongst his line to the first specified station the place it began And also all profitts and appertinances belonging unto the sd One hundred and five acres of land as all the right which sd EDWIN THACKER may claim by virtue of ye sd Patent or otherwise To have and to hold sd land and all premises with their rights unto JOHN MEADOR his heirs subject nevertheless to the Quit rents which from henceforth shall grow due unto their Maties their heirs and Successors and EDWIN THACKER for himselfe his heirs grant with JOHN MEADOR his heirs that he said EDWIN THACKER hath full right to grant and convey the

bargained land and that JOHN MEADOR shall peaceably enjoy the same without trouble of EDWIN THACKER or any other persons claiming under them In Witness the parties have hereunto sett his hand and seale the day and yeare above written
Signed Sealed and Delivered in presence of us
THO: EDMONDSON, EDWIN THACKER
JA: TAYLER
Recognitr in Cur Comt Rappa 7 die Augt 1689

pp. THIS INDENTURE made the one and twentieth day of Jany. in year of our Lord
49- one thousand six hundred eighty and eight and in the thirty fourth yeare of the
51 Reigne of our Sovereigne Lord James the second by the grace of God of England
Scotland France and Ireland &c. Between JOHN CURTIS of County of NORTHUMBERLAND Gent. of one partie and CHRISTOPHER ROBINSON of County of MIDDLESEX Gent. of other part Witnesseth that sd JOHN CURTIS for One hundred and ten pounds Sterling money to him in hand paid by XPHER ROBINSON before the sealing and delivery hath sold and confirmed firmly and absolutely unto CHRISTOPHER ROBINSON his heirs all that tract of land conteyning Two thousand Five hundred acres of land be the same more or less or the whole quantitie contained within the bounds of the Patent granted for the same to Mr. ABRAHAM MOONE bearing date the 6th day of September Ano 1684 and situate and being on the South side the Rappa River in the Freshes of the sd River being in Rappa. County and is commonly called or known by the name of MOON W(blot) Begining to be measured at the mouth of a Creek or Swamp commonly called HENSIN SWAMP adjoining to the lands now in the possession of Mr. JOHN or GEORGE HASLEWOOD and contayned within the severall bounds and distances in the said Patent menconed Together with all Plantations houses fences cleared ground woods waters privilidges and appurtinances to the same and all the right wch he the sd JOHN CURTIS might have to the above menconed bargained and sold premises which sd tract of land is lawfully descended and come to him sd JOHN CURTIS, he is Son and heire of ANN, Relict and Exx. of the before mencioned ABRAHAM MOONE, who did by his last Will and Testament devise the sd premises to the sd ANN and her heires forever Exc(blot) always out of the sd Tract of land Three hundred acres of land bargained and sold by JOHN CURTIS to ANDREW JACKSON to bee taken out of the lower side of sd Tract of land and runs backward the full bredth of the same according to the grant thereof to sd JACKSON To have and to hold to sd XPHER ROBINSON his heirs and sd CURTIS for himselfe his heirs doth grant that said Tract of land hath been already sufficiently seated according to the Law of this Country and the Condition of the sd Patent to save it from being forfited and that he is lawfully seized in a good fee simple without any condition and that it may be lawfull for the sd XPHER ROBINSON his heirs to hold and enjoy to his proper use (except as before excepted) without hindrance of any person whatsoever and that FRANCES, the Wife of sd JOHN CURTIS, shall freely and voluntarily acknowledge these presents at any Court held for County of Rappa. and relinquiseth all right of Dower & thirds to the sd recited premises and lastly sd JOHN CURTIS doth by these presents authorize and appoint Mr. HENRY AWBREY and Mr. WM. COLSTON or either of them to acknowledge these presents as the act and deed of sd JOHN CURTIS at any Court held for sd County of Rappa. In Witness whereof the parties have to these presents sett their hands and seales Sealed and Delivered in the Presents of us
WM. DARNELL, JOHN CURTIS
WM. MORGAN, PAUL THILMAN
Recognitr. p AWBREY et COLSTON in Cur Comt. Rappa 7 die August 1689
KNOW ALL MEN by these presents that I JOHN CURTIS of County of NORTHUMBERLAND Gent. am firmly bound unto XPHER ROBINSON of County of MIDDLESEX Gent. in the sum

of Two hundred and Twenty pounds of good and lawfull money of England to be paid unto XPHER ROBINSON to which payment to be made firmly by these presents Sealed with my seale and dated the 21st day of Jany. 1688

The Condicon of this obligation is that if the above bound JOHN CURTIS and his heirs do well and truly observe and keep all and every the covinants and agreements which ought to be observed menconed in a Deed bearing equal date with these presents between JOHN CURTIS of the one part and XPHER ROBINSON of other part for the sale of a certaine Devident of land conteyning Two thousand five hundred acres of land without fraud or covin then this present obligation to be void or else to remaine in force

Sealed and Delivered in the presents of JOHN CURTIS

RICHD. RADFORD, RICHD. BROOKES,
DANLL. WHITHORNE, WM. DARNELL, PAUL THILMAN

Recordatr in Cur Com Rappa. 15 die August 1689

pp. WHEREAS Mr. JAMES BEDLECOMB of County of Rappa. deced in his last Will and
51- Testament unto his two Children foure hundred and fifty acres of land lying
52 vizt. Two hundred acres of land upon the branches of TOTASKEY and JAMES
TRAPLEY who hath maryed the Daughter of Mr. BEDLECOMB to have Two hundred and fifty acres upon FARNHAM CREEK the sd TRAPLEY suffering their Mother to live there without puting her to her thirds to the intent she may not disturb her Son, JAMES BEDLECOMB, in and we do here declare under our hands and seales that the true intent and meaning of this writ is that this is and shall be a small Division and not henceforth disturbe each other except our Mother shall come to take her thirds out of the land here intended for JAMES BEDLECOMB and if so then JAS. BEDLECOMB to take out of the other Divident Fifty acres of land as his own right and that the heirs of the aforesd. persons be confined to this Division and wee do hereby oblige ourselves firmly by these presents that we will at all times hereafter secure each other in this Division as our Councell at Law shall devise to the true intent and meaning of this Instrument In Witness whereof we have hereunto sett our hands and seales this 20th of June 1689

Signed Sealed in the presents of us

WM. SLOUGHTER, JAMES Sig. +++ BEDLECUMB
JOHN RICE, ED: JONES JAMES Sig. I T TRAPLEY

Recordr. Cur Comt. 3 die August 1689

pp. KNOW ALL MEN by these presents that I WM. CLEATON in the County of Rappa.
52- and in the Parish of North Farnham doth for a consideration of Two thousand
53 pounds of good sound every way well conditioned Tobb: and caske to me paid
doth sell and make over unto ABRAHAM COOKE of the County and Parish all my right title and interest of Fifty acres of land the which land belongeth to my Mothers Plantation and (blot) hundred acres of land that she doth now live on and that my Father bought of WM. LANDMAN by Deed from under hand will more at large appeare and I the sd WM. CLEATON and MARY my Wife do warrant the sd land to sd ABRAHAM COOKE his heirs from us our heirs and further from all persons whatsoever under or by us with all rights whatsoever in as full and ample manner as the Law shall require and further to acknowledge this I the sd WM. CLAYTON and MARY my Wife do oblige ourselves in the penalty of Five thousand pounds of Tobb: and Caske to acknowledge in Rappa Court when said ABRAHAM COOKE shall require as Witness our hands and seales this 28th day of May 1689

Sealed and Signed and Delivered in the presents of us

ANGELL JACOBUS, WM. Sig. M CLEATON
THO: Mar: + DEDMAN MARY ++ CLEATON

Recognitr W. CLEATON et Uxor in Cur Comt Rappa 4 die 9bris ano 1689

pp. 53-54 TO ALL XPIAN PEOPLE. Know yee that I ROBERT PAYNE with the consent of KATHERINE my Wife have sold and made over and do for a valuble consideration which is secured to be paid unto me sd ROBERT PAYNE do bargaine sell and firmly make over unto LEONARD CHAMBERLANE and ROBERT COLEMAN their heirs or either of them all my right and Interest that I have to a certain tract of land lying on the South of RAPPA RIVER and joining to land of JOHN COX and runing for breadth up the River the sd being granted by Patent bearing date the 26th day of May 1650 as by the records of JAMES CITTY doth appeare unto my Grandfather, EPHISDITUS LAWSON, for Nine hundred acres of land. Now know yee that I ROBERT PAYNE and KATHEREINE my Wife for ourselves our heirs do for the future dissun and disdane all and every part or parcell title or titles in or unto the land above menconed enjoyning ourselves our heirs or any from or under us that LEONARD CHAMBERLANE and ROBERT COLEMAN their heirs shall peaceably enjoy and possess the above land and all the appurtenances thereunto belonging from the claime of us or any under us Also engageing myselfe with my Wife to assigne over unto sd CHAMBERLANE and COLEMAN or either of them the Patent that was granted to my abovesaid Grand Father deced and also give them what further assurance of my right shall be thought fit but no further then our right now is and do engage my selfe and my sd Wife to acknowledge this our act and deed in the County Court of Rappa when there unto required as Witness our hands and seals this 22nd day of January 1688

Signed Sealed and Delivered in the presents of us

JNO. mark W WOOD, ROBERT PAYNE
SAMLL S GRIFFIN KATHERINE PAYNE

Recognitr R. PAYNE in Cur Comt Rappa 4 die 7bris 1689

pp. 53-54 TO ALL PEOPLE to whom these presents wrighting shall come MICHALL SCURLOCK of Parish of North Farnham in Rappa County, Planter, send Greeting. Know yee that wee sd MICHALL SCURLOCK as well for and in consideration of the natural love and affection which I have and beare unto my Sons, THOMAS SCURLOCK and EDWARD SCURLOCK as also for and in consideration of the sum of Five Shillings of lawfull English money to me in hand by the sd THOMAS and EDWD. well and truely paid the receit whereof I do hereby acknowledge and for divers other good causes and considerations have granted and by these presents do sell and confirm unto sd THOMAS SCURLOCK and EDWARD SCURLOCK and their heirs all that parcell of land containing One hundred and three acres in Rappa County bounding in the lands now in the severall occapacons of THO: TAYLER, JNO. HILL and JNO. OVERTON and all Gardens, pastures, meadows, woods, timber and trees standing upon the hereby granted land and all houses, barns, stables, edefices and buildings whatsoever hereupon standing or built and all ways passages water courses rights whatsoever to the said land belonging and all Patents Wrightings and evidences whatsoever concerning the premises or any part thereof all which hereby granted premises were given and bequeathed unto me the sd MICHAELL SCURLOCK by DAVID BURKE late of the County aforesd. deced in and by his last Will and Testament and are parte and parcell of a Devident of Three hundred and three acres of land granted to sd DAVID BURKE by Patent dated the 17th day of 9ber Ano Dom 1660 To have and to hold all the said land and all the premises hereby granted unto sd THO: SCURLOCK and EDWARD SCURLOCK and their heirs from the day of the date to their use forever to be held of our Sovereigne Lord the King his heirs and Successors in fee and of the manner of East Greenwich in the County of Kent I the sd MICHAELL SCURLOCK and my heirs and all the before granted land and premises unto THOMAS

SCURLOCK and EDWARD SCURLOCK and their heirs will warrant and defend (the yearly rents from henceforth growing due to be paid the Chief Lord of the Fees only excepted) In Witness whereof I sd MICHAELL SCURLOCK have hereunto sett my hand and seale the fifteenth day of Septemre. 1687
Signed Sealed and delivered in the presents of us
THO: GLASSCOCK, MICHAL SCURLOCK
THO: OCKLEY, JNO. ALMOND
Recognitr in Cur Comt. 4 die 7bris 1689

pp. 54-55 KNOW ALL MEN by these presents that I THO: ARNOLD of the County of Rappa. GRACE my Wife have sold land made over unto HENRY GOING of sd County a certaine parcell of land being in the County abovesd. and the North side thereof containing by estimacon Fifty acres more or less and bounded begining at spreding white Oake standing on the West side of the Mane Branch of GINGOTEAGE and runing West to the line of PROSSER and up the sd branch to a marked Hickory To have and to hold the sd parcell of land with all its rights and privilidges whatsoever from me my heirs or assignes unto the sd HENRY GOING his heirs in as ample manner as I myself hold and enjoy, sd GOING paying to our Sovereigne Lord the King the usuall rents which are due unto him. In Witness whereof we the sd THOMAS and GRACE have set our hands and seales this third day of June in year of our Lord 1689
Signed Sealed and Delivered in the presents of
JOS. RUTTER, THO: ARNOLD
WM. Mar: /M\ TAYLER GRACE ARNOLD
Recognitr in Cur Comt Rappa a 4 die 7ber ano 1689
KNOW ALL MEN by these presents that I GRACE ARNOLD, Wife of THOS: ARNOLD, of St. Marys Parish in Rappa. have appointed my trusty and well beloved friend, JOSEPH BUCKLEY, my true and lawfull Attorney to acknowledge in Court in my name my interest of a tract of land sold unto HENRY GOING according to a Deed made by my Husband and myselfe as Witness my hand this 3d of September 1689
Witness prsent JOS. RUTTER GRACE ARNOLD
JOHN BOULWERE

pp. 55-57 THIS INDENTURE made the 27th day of Aprill in year of our Lord 1689 Between Mr. JOHN FOSAKER of St. Marys Parish in County of Rappa. Gent. of one part and JOHN BARTHOLOMEW and CHARLES FLEMING of the same Parish and County of other part Witnesseth that JOHN FOSSAKER for Five thousand pounds of Tobb: and caske there being Two thousand seven hundred and fifty paid before the sealing and delivery of these presents and the rest to be paid the ensuing year in October next being the one halfe sweet scented by sd JOHN BARTHOLOMEW and CHARLES FLEMING or either of them their heirs and for the receipt of the aforesd sum received I sd JOHN FOSSAKER do hereby acknowledge and thereof the aforesd sum received release and discharge sd JOHN BARTHOLOMEW and CHARLES FLEMING and sd JOHN FOSSAKER hath granted sold and released unto JOHN BARTHOLOMEW and CHARLES FLEMING a tract of land formerly belonging to Mr. JOHN & GEORGE MOTT containing Three hundred acres of land and by them sold unto PETER GALLEN and by sd GALLEN sold unto THOMAS CLAPHAM who sold the same unto JOHN FOSSAKER, who married one of the heirs of the aforesaid MOTT and now selleth the same to JOHN BARTHOLOMEW and CHARLES FLEMING the said land being in the Parish and County abovesd with all houses buildings gardens fences trees water and all other the premises with appertinances thereunto belonging To have and to hold all the sd land for so many acres of land as aforesd with all the appertinances to the same unto JOHN BARTHOLOMEW and CHARLES FLEMING and their

heirs to be hold forevermore cleare and freed from all incumbrances the Quitrents to be henceforth to his Maties only excepted And that JOHN FOSAKER and ELIZABETH his Wife will at any time acknowledge in open Court either to be held at our County Court or at the Genll. Court this conveyance unto the sd JOHN BARTHOLOMEW and CHARLES FLEMING their heirs and assignes when thereunto required and at the cost and charge of said JOHN BARTHOLOMEW and CHARLES FLEMING their heirs such further assurance of the sd premises and JOHN FOSAKER do oblige myselfe to warrant the sd land from all persons or to pay unto JOHN BARTHOLOMEW and CHARLES FLEMING or either of them Ten thousand pounds of Tobb: or according as Judgment shall be given of the Case and damage they shall sustayne thereby and for sure performance of this Indenture of Sale of land I the above named JOHN FOSAKER have hereunto sett my hand and seale
Signed Sealed and Delivered in the presents of
THOMAS PARKER, JOHN FOSAKER
THOMAS TRIP ELIZ: FOSAKER
Recognitr in Cur Comt Rappa 4 die 7ber 1689
KNOW ALL MEN by these presents that I ELIZABETH FOSAKER for divers causes and considerations do constitute and appointe my well beloved friend, Mr. JAMES HARISON, to be my true & lawfull Attorney to acknowledge a parcell of land I say my thirds in a parcell of land sold to JOHN BARTHOLOMEW and CHARLES FLEMING giving unto my sd Attorney full and ample power as though I were personally present As Wittness my hand this 2nd of September 1689/9
Teste ALEXR. DONIPHAN ELIZABETH Sig × FOSAKER
TO: GLENINING

pp. 8br. Court Rappa. Vide 195
57- Whereas ARTHUR SPICER of sd County purchased a certaine tract of land of Capt.
59 ARTHUR GRANT of Citty of Bristoll, Mariner, scituate and being in the Freshes of Rappa River and on the North side thereof and abuting and bounding on a Plantation of sd ARTHUR SPICER comonly called and knowne by the name of POPLAR NECK and on the land of JOHN PAYNE and from thence on a Swamp called IRELAND on the sd land of JAMES TRENT and from thence up the head branches of CHARLES BEAVER DAM wch sd land is to the Neighbourhood generally knowne and called by the name of WARRENS LAND and for as much as sd land was by sd GRANT conveyed together with Deeds Patents Pachmts. Wrightings bonds and all other evidences relating thereto and Capt. THO: COOPER (by virtue of a well authenticated Power of Attorney from sd GRANT) was in May in year 1688 duly acknowledged and executed according to the Stat of Enrolment by power authorizing him sd COOPER thereunto and for as much as it is evidently knowne to the Court and Mr. WM. COLSTON, the Clerk thereof, that what is above written is truth and that sd COLSTON did at the time of executing the sd Deed and Conveyance (accdg. to Law) all the sd Deeds and papers above expressed in to his Custody in order to the recording of the same at his Office at his own house but it pleased God it so happen that his House with many of the Records and papers therein were in the Night burned to ashes by which means all the afore menconed Deeds Evidences were so as aforesd by fire consumed and distroyed This Court therefore at the special Instance and request of sd ARTHUR SPICER and WM. COLSTON, Clerke, order this writing to be put upon the Records that it may be as an evidence of the Truth per Memorian

At a Court held for Rappa County the 2nd day of 8ber 1689

Present	Mr. HEN: AWBREY	Capt. SAMLL. TRAVERS	
	Mr. JAMES HARISON	Capt. WM. MOSLEY	Justices
	Capt. GEO: TAYLER		

This Court at the Instance of ARTHUR SPICER and WM. COLSTON above named have ordered the above writing to be entered of Record as also the within Depositions of Mr. JOHN TAVERNER, Capt. GEO: TAYLER and the sd WM. COLSTON. Signed by the Order of the Court Teste WM. COLSTON Cl Cur

JOHN TAVERNER aged 48 years or there abouts being sworn sayeth that he saw the within specified conveyance and other Parchments at a Court held for this County in May Ano 1688 in order to be then acknowledged and further sayed not
Sworn in Rappa County Court by JOHN TAVERNER the 2nd day of 8ber 1689
Teste WM. COLSTON Cl Cur

Capt. GEO: TAYLER made oath upon the Holy Evangelists that he saw within specified conveyance acknowledged by Capt GEO: COOPER in Court ano 1688 held for this County was was lawfully impowered thereunto by Capt. ARTHUR GRAUNT
In Rappa County Court the 2d 8ber 1689
Mr. COLSTON made oath upon the Holy Evangelists that the within specified conveyance was duly acknowledged at a Court held for this County in ano 1688 by Capt. GEO: COOPER who was lawfully impowered there unto by Capt. ARTHUR GRAUNT and that the sd conveyance with other evidences concerning the land were delivered to him in order to be recorded Teste WM. COLSTON Cl Cur

pp. 59-60 TO ALL TO WHOM these presents shall come I JOHN HARPER of the Parish of Farnham in County of Rappa. send Greeting in our Lord everlasting. Now know yee that I sd JOHN HARPER for divers good considerations me thereunto moving before the ensealing of these presents wherewith I acknowledge myselfe well and truly satisfied do by these presents give and confirm unto ROBERT CADE of County and Parish aforesd. all my right title and possession which I have to a part of a tract of land being in County and Parish and being part of a greater Devident formerly granted unto THOS. HARPER being by estimation Two hundred acres and One hundred acres part thereof conveyed by sd HARPER unto sd CADE by Sale dated the 7th day of March 1672 and the other hundred acres sold by JOHN HARPER, Son and heir of the sd THOMAS HARPER, unto sd ROBERT CADE and bounded begining at a marked Hickory on a point by the Manc Swamp of PISCATAWAY CREEKE at the mouth of the middle branch in Forke Between them and thence runing up the sd Branch to the land of FRANCIS BROWNE to a Stake between a white Oake and line thence by his South to a small white Oake, thence South to an old white Oake stump and Spanish Oake marked by a small branch corner of JOSEPH GOODRICH land, thence by his line W. to a red Oake on the brow of a hill where the head of the sd small branch in the line thence by a line of marked trees West to the sd Maine Swamp, thence down the sd Swamp to the place it first began To have and to hold the aforesd Two hundred acres of land to him sd ROBERT CADE and his heirs in as large manner to all intents and purposes as it is granted to me sd JOHN HARPER by Patent engaging myselfe my heirs that the sd ROBERT CADE shall peaceably possess every part and parcell of the sd land according to bounds without molestation from any peson that shall lay any clame thereof the sd ROBERT CADE paying yearly and every yeare the Kings Rents and farther I sd JOHN HARPER do oblige myselfe my heirs to acknowledge this sale of land in Rappa Court unto the sd ROBERT CADE his heirs when thereunto required In Testimony whereof I have hereunto afixed my hand and seale this first day of (blank) One thousand Six hundred and Eighty nine
Signed Sealed and Delivered in the presents of
JOHN GATEWOOD, JOHN HARPER
JOHN Mar: I EVANS

These presents shall oblige me LIDIA HARPER, Wife to JOHN HARPER the above named, to acknowledge all my right and title in the above menconed premises unto the above named ROBERT CADE Witness my hand and seale the day and yeare above written

LIDIA HARPER

Recognitr in Cur Comt. Rappa 2 die 8bris 1689

pp. THIS INDENTURE made the 28th day of September in yeare of our Lord 1689 Be-
60- tween JOHN BATTAILE of the one part and ROBERT THOMAS of other part Wit-
62 nesseth that JOHN BATTAILE for Four thousand pounds of good sound sweet sented Tobb: and caske to him in hand paid by sd THOMAS whereof sd JOHN BATTAILE doth hereby grant and confirm unto ROBERT THOMAS One hundred & twenty six acres & half of land scituate and being in County of Rappa. on South side of the River and in the Freshes thereof begining on the Northwest side of CEDAR CREEK at the top of the Point being low ground and extending by the River side North West to two small scrubby Oakes, thence South West crossing over a great bite of the sd Creek and over the MANE ROAD to a Hickory by a small branch, thence S. E. to a Spanish Oake, thence W. crossing the said Creeke to the first menconed Station and all houses buildings gardens fences trees and all other the premises and all right of him said JOHN BATTAILE and CATHERINE his Wife To have and to hold said land for so many acres of land as aforesd with all and singular appertenances to the same belonging unto said ROBERT THOMAS and his heirs free and cleare from all former sales and all other demands and incumbrances whatsoever the quitrents henceforth to be due to his Maties only excepted by the said JOHN BATTAILE and that said JOHN BATTAILE and CATHERINE his Wife will at any time acknowledge in open Court either to be held at the County Court or at the Genll. Court In Witness whereof the parties firzt mentoned have set their hands and seales Signed Sealed and delivered in the presents of us

WM. TAYLOE, JOHN BATTAILE
REES EVANS CATH: BATTAILE

Recognitr in Cur Comt. Rappa 2 die 8br 1689

These are to authorize and impower Mr. EDWARD JONES in my behalf to acknowledge to ROBERT THOMAS a Deed of Sale bearing date with these presents as Witness my hand this 2d day of October 1689

Test WILLIAM TAYLOE, CATHERINE Mark X BATTAILE
REES EVANS

p. Vide Fol. 104. KNOW ALL MEN by these presents that I JOHN BATTAILE of County
62 of Rappa and St. Marys Parish do hereby assigne and make over to JOHN POWELL of the sd County and Parish all my right and interest of the within menconed Deed of Sale from me my heirs and assigns &c. To him his heirs in as full and ample manner as it is made to me by the within menconed Deed. In Witness whereof have sett my hand and seale this 18th of July in the year of our Lord one thousand Six hundred and Eighty sixth seventh

Signed Sealed delivered in presents of us

JOHN SIZE JOHN BATTAILE
GEO: MACKOANALL

Recognitr in Cur Compt. Rappa 1d die 8ber ano 1689

p. TO ALL TO WHOM these presents shall come I FRAN: LORD HOWARD Baron of
62 Effingham his Maties Lieut. Governr. of Virginia send Greeting. Whereas &c. Now Know yee that I the sd FRANCIS LORD HOWARD &c. accordingly give and grant unto HENRY WOODNUTT Two hundred and fifty acres of land lying and being in

County of Rappa. according to the most antient and lawfull bounds thereof formerly granted to FRAN: THEDFORD of County aforesd and lately found to escheat unto his most sacred Maties as by an Inquisition recorded in Mr. Secretarys Office under the hand and Seale of Col. ISSAC ALLERTON, Escheater, of the sd County and a Jury sworn before him for that purpose dated the 15th day of 8ber 1685 may appeare and is since granted to sd HENRY WOODNOTT who hath made his composition according to Law; To have and to hold &c. yeilding and paying &c. Given under my hand and Seale of the Colony this first day of February Ano One thousand six hundred and Eighty 6/7

EFFINGHAM

KNOW ALL MEN by these presents that I HENRY WOODNOTT and ELIZABETH WOODNOTT of County of Rappa do in the behoofe of me my heires or assignes sett and make over unto ELIZABETH WHITTON her heirs the contents of the within menconed Patent and to acknowledge the same in Court as witness my hand this 15th of March 1686/7

Teste DANLL. DOBYNS, HENRY WOODNOTT
JOHN COLLEYVOW ELIZABETH WOODNOTT

Recognitr p WOODNOTT in Cur Comt. Rappa 2d die 8ber 1689

p. 63 KNOW ALL MEN by these presents that I ELIZABETH BONNER of County of Rappa and Parish of Farnham for severall good causes me thereunto moving do give unto my Son, JAMES BONNER, a young Mare about two years old and of a bright Bay with a sar in her forehead and all her encrease male and female to him and his heirs forever And I give unto my Daughter, CATHERINE, one young Mare of a younger age with all her encrease to her and her heirs forever by these presents give and confirm the above Mares unto my abovesd Son and Daughter being now in my Widowhood and free from the incumbrances of Debts with warranty from any person that shall lay any claime unto as Witness my hand this day and yeare above written

Being present CHARLES DODSON, ELIZABETH Mark O BONNER
CHRISTR. PUTLEY

Recordr. Cur Comt. Rappa. 16 die 8bris 1689

p. 63 I PATRICK CAMMELL do give to JOHN ROBERTS SENR. one Cow calfe with one crop on the left eare and a slit in the right eare and an over keele to him and his heirs forever and all her encrease

Teste DAVID WILSON PATRICK Sig P CAMMELL

Recordr. in Cur Comt Rappa 16 die 8bris 1689

pp. 63-65 TO ALL XPIAN PEOPLE to whom these presents shall come We EVAN DAVIS of County of Rappa and JUDITH my Wife send Greetings in our Lord God everlasting Know yee that wee sd EVAN DAVIS and JUDITH my Wife for divers good causes and valuable considerations thereunto moving and especially for the sum of One thousand pounds of Tobb: in Cask have granted unto THOMAS WILLIAMSON of sd County his heirs all that parcell of land conteyning Three hundred acres more or less being in sd County on South side of Rappa River and begining at a marked Gum at the mouth of a branch lying upon RALPH WHITTON, thence alonge the land of JOHN COLLEYVOWE, thence alonge a branch called the SPRING BRANCH that devidith the land from the land THO: HUNTLEY liveth upon then from the first mentioned marked Gum up the MYREY BRANCH joyning on the land formerly JOHN MATTYSON and up the sd Branch so far as that deviding line shall compleat the complemt. of Three hundred acres of land from a greater tract of land of sd EVAN DAVIS & JUDITH his Wife, this being the lower part of the Devident of one thousand acres of land; To have and to hold the sd land and premises with all rights of hunting hawking fishing and fowling woods waters Mills milseats edifices orchards gardens fences and buildings with all appertenances whatsoever thereunto to him the sd THO: WILLIAMSON his heirs paying yearly unto our Sovereigne Lord the King his heirs and Successors all such rents and services as shall hereafter be due and sd EVAN DAVIS and JUDITH for themselves or assignes promise with THO: WILLIAMSON his heirs that sd land free from all former grants and incumbrances and will warrant and defend the said Sale to him sd THO: WILLIAMSON his heirs from all persons who shall clame any right in any part thereof and will make further Deeds as he sd THO: WILLIAMSON or his Councell learned in the Law shall reasonably require. In Witness whereof EVAN DAVIS and JUDITH my Wife have hereunto sett our hands and seales this 6th day of July One thousand Six hundred and eighty nine and in the first yeare of the Reigne of our Sovereigne Lord William of England France and Ireland Signed Sealed and Delivered in presents of us

WILLIAM COVINGTON, EVAN marke ††† DAVIS
LEONARD WILLIAMSON, EDWD. ADCOCK JUDITH Sig + DAVIS

Recognitr in Cur Comt Rappa 2 die 8ber 1689

KNOW ALL MEN by these presents that I JUDITH DAVIS, Wife of EVAN DAVIS in the County of Rappa do hereby authorize and appoint my well beloved true and trusty friend, JAMES BOUGHAN, my true and lawfull Attorney for me and in my name to acknowledge a Deed of Sale of land to THO: WILLIAMSON in the aforesd County to acknowledge the same in Rappa. County Court which sale from under our hands and seales will appeare bearing the same date whatsoever my lawfull Attorney shall do I will stand to Witness my hand this 6th day of July 1689

Teste RICHD. COVINGTON, JUDITH Mark + DAVIS
ELIZA. Mark E WHITTON

pp. 65-68 THIS INDENTURE made the 30th day of September in yeare of our Lord 1689 and in the first yeare of the Reigne of our Sovereigne Lord and Lady William and Mary King and Queen &c. Between JOHN MOSLEY of County of Rappa in Colony of Virginia, Carpenter, of one part and EDWARD THOMAS of the same County and Colony, Mercht., of other part Witnesseth that JOHN MOSLEY for and in consideration of Three hundred acres of land already in his possession and secured by conveyance bearing date with these presents whereof the sd JOHN MOSLEY doth by these presents have granted and confirmed unto EDWARD THOMAS his heirs all that tract of land containing One hundred and fifty acres it being part of a Devident of land formerly purchased of Mr. RICHD. JONES quantitie Three hundred and fifty acres by WM. WILLIAMSON deced and by his last Will and Testament bequeathed to his Sister, ELIZABETH, her heirs, who was late Wife of me the sd JOHN MOSLEY situate and being on the South side of Rappa County back in the woods bounded S. E. on the land of sd EDWARD THOMAS which he purchased of JOHN BROCK and whereon the sd THOMAS doth now live, S. W. on the DRAGON SWAMP, N. W. on a tract of land commonly called JACKMANS COD and N. E. on the remaining part of the aforesd Devident of Three hundred and fifty acres including the aforesd quantitie of One hundred and fifty acres Together with all the woods underwoods timber trees standing growing lying and being To have and to hold sd parcell of land with all profitts to the same belonging to the only proper use and behoofe of him sd EDWARD THOMAS his heirs that the sd JOHN MASSEY now hve full power to grant the before bargained premises and doth promise that sd EDWARD THOMAS shall from henceforth hold the bargained premises against him the sd JOHN MASSEY his heirs In Witness whereto sd JOHN MASSEY by these presents hath hereunto sett his hand and fixed his seale

Signed Sealed and Delivered in the presents of us
THOMAS NORMAN, JOHN MASSEY
ANTHO: BELL
Recognitr in Cur Rappa 2 die 8bris 1689

KNOW ALL MEN by these presents that I JOHN MASSEY of County of Rappa., Carpentr., am firmely bound and indebted unto EDWARD THOMAS of same County, Mercht., his heirs in sum of Two hundred pounds Sterling good and lawfull money of England to be paid by good sufficient Bills of Exchange drawn payable on Sight in the Citty of LONDON on all demands the payment which truly do I bind myselfe my heirs dated this 30th of September 1689.

The Condition of the above obligation is that if above named EDWARD THOMAS his heirs shall from henceforth peaceably and quietly use all that parcell of land conteyning 150 acres it being the S. Wt. part of a Tract of land conteyning Three hundred and fifty acres formerly purchased by Mr. WILLIAMSON deced of Mr. RICE JONES SENR. deced, as by a Deed of Sale bearing date 23d July 1666 may appeare and by sd WILLIAMSON bequeathed unto ELIZ. his Sister her heirs and late Wife of the above bound JOHN MASSEY as by the Will may appeare situate on the South side Rappa County back in the woods with all the appurtenances without trouble of the above bound JOHN MASSEY his heirs or any other persons whatsoever pretending to have any manner of clame in any part thereof and the above bound JOHN MASSEY his heirs at the reasonable request of the above named EDWARD THOMAS his heirs do give such further and better assurance of the sd tract of land as he shall require by his Councell learned in the Law and that the above bound JOHN MASSEY when his Son, JOHN MASSEY JUNR., shall attayne to the age of one and twenty years shall procure assignmt. of his right the premises that then the above obligation to be void otherwise to remain in full force Witness my hand and seale this 30th day of Septr. 1689
Signed sealed and delivered in the presents of us
THO: NORMAN, JOHN MASSEY
ANTHO: BELL
Recordr. in Cur Rappa. 17 die 8bris 1689

pp. THIS INDENTURE made the Thirtieth day of September in the year of our Lord
68- God 1689 and in the first yeare of the Reigne of our most Sovereigne Lord and
70 Lady William and Mary King and Queen of England &c. Between EDWARD THOMAS of County of Rappa in Colony of Virginia, Mercht., of one partie and JOHN MASSEY of same County and Colony, Carpenter, of the other party Witnesseth that EDWARD THOMAS for and in considertion of One hundred and fifty acres of land already in his possession secured by Deed of Sale bearing date with this present Instrumt. of Wrightin to him delivered and paid before the ensealing and delivery of these presents by sd JOHN MASSEY whereof sd EDWARD THOMAS doth grant and confirm unto sd JOHN MASSEY his heirs all that parcell of land conteyning Three hudnred acres, Two hundred part thereof being part of a tract of land which EDWARD THOMAS pruchased of Mr. JOHN BROOCK, the other sd acres being part of a tract of Seven hundred and fourteen acres granted to EDWARD THOMAS as by Patent bearing date 23 April 1688 scituate and being in Rappa on the South side back in the woods bounded the South Easterly parts of it on the severall courses of THO: TOSLEYs line, North Easterly one the abovesd tract of six hundred and fourteen acres belonging to sd EDWARD THOMAS, N. Westerly on the land of sd JOHN MASSEY and S. Westerly on the land whereon sd JOHN THOMAS doth now live including the aforesd quantitie of Three hundred acres according to Survey made by Mr. EDWIN THACKER the 16th day of 8ber 1689, Together with all the woods timber standing lying and being To have and to hold sd parcell of land and every part thereof

with the Comodities and advantages belonging unto sd MASSEY his heirs and EDWARD THOMAS his heirs warrant and grant with sd JOHN MASSEY his heirs shall from henceforth forever peaceably hold the bargained premises against all manner of persons lawfully claiming In Witness whereof EDWARD THOMAS to these presents hath hereunto set his hand and fixed his seale
Signed Sealed and Delivered in the presence of us
THO: NORMAN, EDWARD THOMAS
ANTHO: BELL
Recognitr. in Cur Comt. Rappa 2 die 8bris 1689
KNOW ALL MEN by these presents that I EDWARD THOMAS of County of Rappa do ow and am firmly bound unto J. MASSEY of same County his heirs in sum of Two hundred pounds Sterling good and lawfull money of England to be paid by sufficient Bills of Exchange payable on sight in the Citty of LONDON which payment to be truly made I bind myselfe my heirs by these presents Sealed with my Seale this Thirtieth day of September One thouand Six hundred and eighty nine.
The Condition of the above obligation is that if the above named JOHN MASSEY his heirs may from henceforth peaceably and quietly enjoy the parcel of land containing Three hundred acres part thereof the N. Easterly part of that tract whereon the above bounded EDWARD THOMAS now lives the other hundred acres being part of a devident of Seven hundred and Fourteen acres granted to sd THOMAS by Pattent bearing date the 23d of Aprill 1688, the quantity of three hundred acres being bounded on the S: East the severall courses of THOMAS TOZLEYs line, N. E. in the remaining part of the sd EDWARD THOMAS seven hundred and fourteen acres, N. W. on the sd MASSEYs land and S:W on the land whereon EDWARD THOMAS doth now livewith all the appurtenances without the trouble of the above bounden EDWARD THOMAS his heirs or any other person under sd THOMAS whatsoever and that the above bound EDWARD THOMAS his heirs at the reasonable request of JOHN MASSEY his heirs do give better assurance of the sd tract of land as he or his learned Councell in the Law require then this present obligation to be void or to remain in full force Witness my hand and Seal this 30th day of September 1689 Signed Sealed and Delivered in the presents of us
THOMAS NORMAN, EDWARD THOMAS
ANTHO: BELL
Recognitr in Cur Comt. Rappa 2 die 8bris 1689

p. Two crops two holes and two under keele is the mark wch is given to all the
70 Cattle and Stock in Genll. belonging to Mr. JOHN GEBBINS

pp. 9ber Court Ano Dom 1689
70- THIS INDENTURE made the 4th day of 8ber 1689 Between RICHARD KING of the
73 Parish of Farnham and County of Rappa., Planter, of one part and EDWARD JONES of the Parish and County aforesd, also Planter, of the other part Witnesseth that RICHARD KING in consideration of Fifteen thousand and nine hundred pounds of good and merchantable Tobb: by sd EDWARD JONES paid unto RICHARD KING hath sold and confirmed unto EDWARD JONES his heirs Three hundred acres of land one part of which are the houses & Plantation of sd RICHARD KING and late in the occupacon or holding of Mr. JOHN BERTRAND being part of the land granted unto sd RICHARD KING being therein thus expressed (Vizt) Five hundred ninety and one acres of land scituate on the North side of Rappa River begining at a Branch or a marked red Oake the branch bearing East and runing thence South to a marked red Oake, thence E. to a red Oake at the head of a branch of FARNHAM CREEK, thence N. to the land of JOHN WILLIAMS to a marked white Oake, thence N. by the sd land of JOHN WILLIAMS to a marked white Oake

thence N. by the sd land of JOHN WILLIAMS and lastly S. W. to the place whence it began and likewise all houses edifices and buildings upon the sd Three hundred acres of land hereby granted and also all other the hereditatments and right of said RICHARD KING by virtue of the said Patent (Except and always reserved unto the sd RICHARD KING out of this present grant all the land with every of the appertenances heretofore granted him unto MARTIN HAMMON and JOB HAMON and to either of them their heirs) To have and to hold the sd Three hundred acres of land and all other premises hereby granted with every of their rights (except as excepted) unto sd EDWARD JONES his heirs Subject to the Quit rents due for the premises and sd RICHARD KING his heirs will warrant and defend against all persons clayming or pretending to claim the same forever by these presents and moreover it is agreed that all the land that shall be over and above the sd Three hundred acres hereby granted is in this provisoe and further condicon that sd EDWARD JONES his heirs shall pay for every hundred acres of such land Three thousand pounds of good merchantable toba: in Cask and so after the same rate for a greater or lesser quantitie than One hundred acres after the same shall be Surveyed and ascertained which is to be had and don within one yeare after the date hereof otherwise the granted hereby of what land is above the said Three hundred acres to be void and of non effect the sd RICHARD KING for himselfe his heirs doth promise with sd EDWARD JONES his heirs that sd EDWARD JONES his heirs shall have sd Three hundred acres of land with the houses and appertenances belonging and all other the lands and premises hereby granted (except as excepted) from the hindrance or interruption of him the sd RICHARD KING his heirs, And sd RICHARD KING doth further promise for himself and SARAH his Wife and her heirs he and she shall not only acknowledge these presents in form of Law but also he she and his heirs shall acknowledge all such further Deeds which shall be thought fitt by the sd EDWARD JONES his heirs or Councell In Witness whereof the parties have sett their hands and seales
Signed Sealed and Delivered in the presence of us

JAMES SAMFORD, RICHARD KING
HUGH Sig H HARRIS, SARAH KING
THO: T B BAYLIS, JOHN TAVERNER

Memoran: the 5th day of Novr. 1689 The above named RICHARD KING entered into the Capital Messuage and took possession thereof and also took Turff and Twigge on the above ground granted and then presently after delivered possession and delivered thereby of all and singular the Plantacon land and premises menconed according to the Tenure of this present Deed of Bargaine and Sale unto said EDWARD JONES Witness his hand the day and yeare hereby expressed in the presence of

JAMES SAMFORD, RICHARD KING
JOHN TAVERNER

Recognitr in Cur Comt Rapp 6 die 9ber 1689

KNOW ALL MEN by these presents that I SARAH KING, Wife of RICHARD KING of the Parish of Farnham and County of Rappa, Planter, have nominated and in my place put JOHN TAVERNER my true and lawfull Attorney to appeare before the Worshipfull Court of Rappa and acknowledge my full assent and consent to the passing away all my right and interest of Dower unto certaine lands houses and appertinances sold unto EDWARD JONES of sd Parish and County in and by a certaine Indendure bearing date with these presents and therefor I do remise and forever quit claim all my right and interest of Dower to the sd land and premises and every part and parcell As Witness my hand and seale the 4th day of Novr. ano Dom 1689
Sealed and Delivered in the presents of

DAVID LOYD, HUGH Mark H CONNER SARAH KING

pp. 73-76 THIS INDENTURE made the 15th day of 8ber in year of our Lord God 1689 Between SAMLL. BAYLY of County of Rappa. Gent. of one part and PHILLIP HUNNINGS of sd County and Parish of other part Witnesseth that sd SAMLL. BAYLY for a valuable consideration to him paid by PHILLIP HUNNINGS hath granted unto sd PHILLIP HUNNINGS his heirs all that Devident or parcell of land conteyning Foure hundred and fifty acres being part of a greater quantitie, and scituate and being in County of Rappa. on the North side of RAPPA RIVER upwards of a mile back upon CHINGATEAGUE begining at a stake by a red Oake being a corner to RALPH WHITING extending thence N. Easterly to a small white Oak corner tree of JAMES MATHEWS, thence E. crossing the main run of CHINGOTEAGUE to a saplin red Oake, thence S. to the line of Esqr. WHITING, thence along the same W. to a small red Oake corner tree to the sd Esqr: thence along another line of the sd Esqrs: S. by W. to an Hickory on a point neere CHINGOTEAGUE, thence W. to the first mentioned Station, Together with all houses plantations, fences woods waters and appertinances whatsoever to the same belonging To have and to hold the sd Four hundred and fifty acres of land and all premises unto sd PHILLIP HUNNINGS his heirs and that sd PHILLIP HUNNINGS his heirs shall at all times quietly and peaceably occupie the sd parcell or devident of land without trouble of sd SAMLL. BAYLY his heirs or assigns or any persons claiming any right under him and that his now Wife shall freely and voluntarily relinquish all right and clame of Dower and Third the before recited premises In Witness whereof sd parties have sett their hands and seales

Sealed and Delivered in the presents of us

LENARD ⒭ ROBINSON, SAMLL. BAYLY
THO: T SMITH SARAH BAYLY

Recognitr in Cur Comt Rappa 6 die 9ber 1689

KNOW ALL MEN by these presents that I SAMLL. BAYLY of County of Rappa am firmly bound to PHILLIP HUNNINGS of said County in the just sum of One hundred pounds of lawfull money of England to be paid to which payment I bind myself firmly by these presents Sealed with my Seale dated this 14th day of 8ber 1689

The Condicon of this obligation is that if the above bound SAMLL. BAYLY his heirs at all time hereafter truly observe and keep all the agreements in a Deed of Sale bearing equall date between the above named SAMLL. BAYLY on the one part and PHILLIP HUNNINGS on the other part and that in all things according to the meaning of the same that then this obligation to be void otherwise to be in full force

Sealed and delivered in presence of us

LEONARD ⒭ ROBINSON, SAMLL. BAYLY

These presents witnesseth that wee PHILLIP HUNNINGS and ELIZ. HUNNINGS now Wife of the aforesaid PHILL: HUNNINGS do assigne and make over all the right and interest of all and singular the premises conteyed in the within Deed for us or either of use unto JOHN GRIFFIN his heirs for a valuable consideration already reced In Witness whereof we have hereunto sett our hands and seals this 18th day of 8ber 1689

Teste JOHN CARYLL PHILL. HUNNING
JOHN RICE ELIZ: Mar: L HUNNING

Recognitr in Cur Comt. Rappa 6 die 9br 1689

These presents witnesseth that wee JOHN GRIFFIN and ELIZABETH GRIFFIN the now Wife of the aforesd JOHN GRIFFIN do assigne and make over from us and either of us all our right and interest of all and singular the premises contained in the sd written Deed unto PHILLIP HUNNINGS his Exrs. or assigns forever for a valuable consideration already reced as Witness our hands and Seales this 16th day of 8ber 1689

Teste JOHN CARRELL JOHN GRIFFIN
ELIZ. GRIFFIN

Signed Sealed and Delivered by JOHN GRIFFIN in the presents of JOHN RICE
Recognitr in Cur Comt Rappa. 6 die 9bris 1689

KNOW ALL MEN by these presents that I ELIZABETH GRIFFIN, Wife of JOHN GRIFFIN, of Rappa County do make and appoint Mr. JAMES BOUGHAN of the aforesd County my lawfull Attorney to acknowledge in my name all my rights of all that parcell of land my Husband bought of PHILLIP HUNNINGS of the aforesd County lying upon TOTASKEY CREEKE unto the above said HUNNINGS and his heirs In Confirmacon whereof I have hereunto sett my hand and Seale this 3rd day of 7ber 1689

Teste HENRY Sig H PICKETT ELIZ. W GRIFFIN
JOHN CARYLL

p. 76 THIS INDENTURE made this 5th day of November Ano Dom: 1689 Between SAMUEL BAYLEY of County of Rappa of one party and JOHN EASTER of County aforesd of the other part Witnesseth that SAMUEL BAYLEY have sold unto sd JOHN EASTER his heirs &c. all that parcell of land conteyning One hundred Twenty and three acres lying and being on the Freshes of Rappa. and on the North side thereof nere a small creek called CHINGATEAGUE begining at a black Oake som two miles and half back in the woods neare a small branch and extending N. Eastly to another black Oake thence East crossing the Mane Run of CHINGATEAGUE to a red Oake, thence S. to a Stake a Spanish Oake, thence W. to the first station, being for satisfaction to me in hand paid and will warrant the sale of the aforesd parcell of land from me the sd SAMLL. BAYLEY his heirs from any other persons whatsoever to sd JOHN EASTER his heirs they paying the Rent thereof to whom it shall be due To which I do hereunto sett my hand and seale this day and yeare above written

Signed Sealed and Delivered in the presents of
JOHN MACKENNEY SAMLL. BAYLEY
JOHN Mar: 王 RENNOLDS,
LEO: R ROBINSON
Recognitr in Cur Com 6 die 9bris 1689

pp. 76-77 THIS INDENTURE made the fifth of November Ano Dom 1689 Between SAMLL. BAYLEY of County of Rappa of one part and JAMES MATHEWS of County aforesd of other part Witnesseth that sd SAMLL. BAYLEY have bargained and sold unto JAMES MATHEWS his heirs all that parcell of land conteyning one hundred acres being in the Freshes of Rappa and on the North side thereof neer a small Creek called CHINGATEAGUE begining at a small Hickory tree to PHILLIP HUNNINGS and extending thence N. to a black Oake corner tree to JOHN EASTER, thence E. crossing the Mane Run of CHINGATEAGUE to a Stake by a Spanish Oake, thence S. to a saplin red Oake, thence W. to the first menconed Hickery being some two miles back in the woods, all which being for satisfaction to me in hand paid whereof I hold myself fully satisfied and do further warrant the sale of the aforesd tract from me the sd SAMLL. BAYLEY my heirs or from any persons whatsoever under me the sd JAMES MATHEWS his heirs paying thereof to whome it may appeare to be due at all times hereafter which I hereunto sett my hand and seale

Sealed and Delivered in presents of
JOHN MACKENNEY, SAMLL. BAYLEY
JOHN 王 REYNOLDS, LEO: R ROBINSON
Recognitr in Cur Comt. Rappa 6 die 9bris 1689

p. 77 To Mr. LEROY GEORGE one black heyfer about a year & halfe old marked a cropp and two slitts in the right eare, a crop in the left eare with a small nick underneath. For LEROY GEORGE one black pide of the same marke

For Mrs. MARGARET GEORGE one red pyed heyfer about two yeares and a halfe marked in the right eare a crop and a hole and now on the left eare a crop & two slitts

For Mrs. MARGARET GEORGE one black heifer about one year and a halfe marked on the right eare a crop and a hole and now in the left eare a crop and two slitts

pp. 77-78 THIS DEED INDENTED in the year of our Lord God according to the computation of the Church of England 1689 Between ABRAHAM COOK of County of Rappa. and THOMAS GLADMAN of the aforesaid County Witnesseth that sd ABRAHAM COOK for and in consideration of the sum of Two thousand and Foure hundred pounds of Tobb. in Caske paid hath sold unto THOS: GLADMAN fifty acres of land being on the West side of TOTASKEY CREEK it being the half of one hundred acres of land lately bought WILLIAM CLEATON with all houses buildings upon the sd land and all other rights thereunto belonging which sd land I the said ABRAHAM COOKE do warrant to him sd THO: GLADMAN from the claime of any persons and furthermore I sd ABRAHAM COOKE and MARTHE my now Wife will in due forme of Law at Next October Court held for Rappa County before his Maties Justices of the Peace for the sd County in their open Court sitting acknowledge this present Deed also their right to the sd land mentioned both of Dower and Thirds or otherwise which sd land I ABRAHAM COOKE do warrant from me my heirs to him sd THOMAS GLADMAN his heirs forever In Witness whereof above ABRAHAM COOKE have sett our hand and seale this 28th day of September 1689
Signed Sealed and Delivered in presents of

GEO: *lo* CAKFORD, ABRAH: Mar: *G* COOK
THO: LEWIS MARTHA *M G* COOKE

Recognitr in Cur Com Rappa 6 die 9bris 1689

pp. 78-79 KNOW ALL MEN by these presents that I GEO: LAMBETH of County of Rappa do for Seven hundred and Sixty pounds of Tobb. already in hand reced sell unto HENRY LONGE of the same County his heires a certain parcell of land conteyning Thirty (blot) acres more or less lying and being in the Freshes of Rappa. and on the South side of the River adjacent to the land which the sd LONGE bought of ROBT. PAYNE, I the aforesd GEO: LAMBETH do hereby grant and make over from me my heirs unto HENRY LONG his heirs To have and to hold the same with all its rights peaceably and quietly without any lett of sd LAMBETH my heirs or any other persons Also I the sd GEORGE LAMBETH oblige myselfe my heirs to make what further assurance sd HENRY LONGE or his Councell learned in the Law require in that case and further ingage myselfe to acknowledge this my Deed of Sale before the Court of Rappa to be enroled when there unto lawfully called by the sd HENRY LONGE or his heirs he or they paying all dues and impositions which shall be charged and for further confirmation I have hereunto sett my hand and Seale this 18th of Febry. 1688/9
Signed Sealed and Delivered in the presents of us

THO: *T* THARP, GEO: his *G L* LAMBETH
JOHN GRAY

Recognitr in Cur Comt Rappa 6 die 8bris 1689

p. 79 KNOW ALL MEN by these presents that I JAMES ORCHARD of County of Rappa., Planter, for sum of Foure hundred and Thirty pounds of Tobb: and Caske have sold to JAMES JACKSON of sd County, Plantr., his heirs a certain parcell of land conteyning about Ten acres more or less scituate and being on the North side of Rappa.

River being on the N. E. line of MARTINs Patent and beginning at a marked Hickory standing in the SPRING BRANCH of the said JACKSONs and runing thence up the sd Branch by a line of marked trees to a small Ridge, then crossing the small Ridge by a line of marked trees to a marked Hickory in a Branch of the Mane Swamp, thence down the said branch by a line of marked trees to a white Oake in the sd N: E: line of MARTON againe thence alonge the sd line towards the River side to the first menconed Hickory, To have and to hold the sd land to him the sd JACKSON his heirs without the interruption of me sd ORCHARD my heirs or other persons whatsoever only the sd JACKSON his heirs is not to hinder the said ORCHARD his assigns for to go to his back land with his or their horse or Cart through the sd land aforemenconed In Confermation whereof I have sett my hand and fixed my Seale this 3rd day of November 1689
Signed Sealed and Delivered in the presents of us

CHARLES SEPOO, JAMES ORCHARD
FRAN: ⌶ T TAYLER

Recognitr in Cur Com Rappa 8 die ano 1689

p. 79 Memoran: To be recorded for SARAH CANNEDY, Daughter of JOHN and SARAH CANNEDY one Cow named Cherry marked on the left eare with a crop the right eare whole with her male and female increase for her. Given by ANDREW HARRISON and his Wife TOMZIN
Recordatr Teste THOMASIN Mar: O HARRISON

pp. 79-80 KNOW ALL MEN by these presents that I JOHN OWEN and REBECCA my Wife of St. Marys Parish in Rappa County in the Colony of Virginia, Tayler, have and do by these presents make over all my right of a certain parcell of land being in the aforesd Parish and County and by estimation Fifty acres of land more or less bounded begining at a white Oake standing in a branch and thence Westward alonge the line of Mr. FRAN: HALE and then unto a red Oake on the East side of a Run and then runing Northward along the branch unto the line of JAMES LAMB and runing alonge the line of JAMES LAMB unto a Branch which is the corner tree of EVAN WILLIAMS and runing Sotherly alonge the said EVAN WILLIAMS unto the white Oake at the first begining unto EVAN WILLIAMS his heirs for Two thousand pounds of Tobb: in hand received by me JOHN OWEN I sd JOHN OWEN do release and discharge the sd EVAN WILLIAMS and do warrant the Sale of the sd land from claime of any persons whatsoever And in confirmation of we have hereunto sett our hands and affixed our Seales this twenty sixth day of July 1689. This Deed of Sale to be acknowledged in Rappa. County Court Signed Sealed and Delivered in presence of us

JOSHUA DAVIS, JOHN Sig. I OWEN
FRAN: Marke FH HALE REBECCA OWEN
RICHARD Marke R SMITH

Recognitr in Cur Com Rappa 6 die 9bris 1689

pp. 80-81 THIS INDENTURE made this 21st day of October in yeare of our Lord 1689 Between WM. THACKER and ALICE his Wife of Parish of Christ Church in County of LANCASTER, Planter, of one part and ABRAHAM MARSHALL of Parish of Farnham in County of Rappa., Blacksmith, of other part Witnesseth that WM. THACKER and ALICE his Wife for a valuable consideration grant unto ABRAHAM MARSHALL his heirs a certain parcell of land conteyning one hundred acres being in the Parish of Farnham in County aforesd being part of a Devidend of land belonging to sd WM. THACKER and ALICE his Wife bounding on the Plantation of CHARLES DODSON on the Mane Branch of TOTASKEY with all the appertenances thereunto belonging which sd land

came to WM. THACKER by ALICE his Wife as being heiress of WM. MATHEWS, her Father, being part of a Devident of land granted unto WM. MATHEWS conteyning 1148 acres as by his Patent bearing date the 18th November 1662, relation being thereunto had may appeare. To have and to hold the sd bargained premises with all the appertenances unto sd ABRAHAM MARSHALL his heirs and I sd WM. THACKER and ALICE my Wife the above bargained premises against us or any of us our heirs and all other persons claiming the same In Witness whereof the above WILLIAM THACKER and ALICE his Wife have hereunto sett our hands and seales
Signed Sealed and delivered in the presents of

WM. LAWRENCE, WM. THACKER
JOHN ⅋ SERGAN, AN. + BURRELL ALICE Sig. Λ THACKER

Acknow: by WM. THACKER in Rappa. County Court the 6th day of 9ber 1689 and by ALICE the 4th day of December Foll. and recorded the 16th

pp. 81-82 KNOW ALL MEN by these presents that wee HAWKINS SNEAD, FRANCIS TAYLER and ELIZABETH TAYLER my Wife all of the County of Rappa. do for a valuable sum of Two thousand Three hundred pounds of good lawfull Tobb. in Cask by us received have granted unto BENJA: POWE of same County his heirs a certaine parcell of land conteyning One hundred acres being part of a Patent granted to CHARLES SNEAD deced for 1933 acres being dated the 20th of October 1686 the sd land being in the aforesd County and on the North of the River back in the Woods, Begining at a black Oake and extending thence North to a red Oake corner tree to the 800 acres and thence the same to a small Hickory, thence S. E., thence N. E. to the first menconed black Oake. HAWKINS SNEAD, FRAN: TAYLER and ELIZABETH TAYLER his Wife hereby sell unto sd BENJA. POE his heirs To have occupie and enjoy the same with all its rights of all woods waters and water courses without any hindrance of sd HAWKINS SNEAD, FRAN: TAYLER and ELIZA. TAYLER or any of our heirs or any other persons and do further engage ourselves to acknowledge this our Deed of Conveyance fore Court of Rappa thereto be enroled when thereunto lawfully called by sd BENJA: POWE, or his Father, CHARLES POWE, he or they pay all dues which shall be charged and further for confirmation the said parties have sett our hands and seales this third of Septr. Ano. 1689 Signed Sealed and Delivered in the presents of us

JAMES ORCHARD, HAWKINS SNEAD
THOS. Sig. T SNEAD FRAN: FT TAYLOR
ELIZABETH Sig. O TAYLOR

Recognitr in Cur Comt Rapp (blot) die 9bris 1689
KNOW ALL MEN that I ELIZABETH TAYLER authorize and impower Mr. JAMES ORCHARD my lawfull Attorney for me and in my behalfe to acknowledge and confirm unto BENJA: SPOWE all right and interest to a parcell of land conteyning One hundred acres according to a Conveyance Given under my hand and seale this 3rd day of 7bris 1689
Teste HAWKINS SNEAD, ELIZA. TAYLER
THOMAS T SNEAD

pp. 82-83 THIS INDENTURE made the 5th day of January Ano Dom 1688 in the fourth yeare of the Reigne of our Sovereigne Lord James the Second &c. Between JOHN PECK of Parish of Farnham in County of Rappa., Planter, of one part and WILLIAM RICHARDSON of County of NORTHUMBERLAND of the Parish of Mattapony of other part Witnesseth that sd JOHN PECK for Three thousand Five hundred pounds of Tobb: in cask to be paid by WM. RICHARDSON doth sell unto WM. RICHARDSON all that parcell of land of what quantitie soever it be lying on the left hand of the PATH leading from the Plantacon of Mr. ROBERT BAYLEY hold unto FARNHAM CHURCH and it is part of

Two hundred Forty and four acres of land held by JOHN PECK and purchased by JOHN PECK's Father Senr., deced, scituate two miles from TOTASKEY CREEKE in the Parish of Farnham in County of Rappa., begining at a little red Oake corner to & joyning upon JOHN PATRIDGEs line neere his fence, thence runing a straight Course over a bottom to a live red Oak corner tree on the left hand of the aforesd PATH, thence a straight line along the PATH side to a little red marked Oake upon JOHN PATRIDGE line, thence a straight line to the place of begining, and all profitts appurtaining to the hereby parcell of land and all the rights subject nevertheless unto the Quit rents and services which from henceforth shall become due And sd JOHN PECK doth promise WM. RICHARDSON his heirs shall peaceably and quietly hold sd land without trouble of sd JOHN PECK his heirs or any other persons and further JOHN PECK will acknowledge these presents in forme of Law for the better confirmacon thereof. In Witness whereof the parties have sett their hands and seals

Signed Sealed and Delivered in the presents of us

MATTHIAS WALKAREN JOHN Sig. ‡ PECK

JOHN PATRIDGE

Recognitr in Cur Comt Rappa 6 die 9br 1689

pp. 84-85 THIS INDENTURE made the 4th day of November in yeare of Reigne of our Sovereign Lord Wm. the Third by grace of God &c. Ano Dom: 1689 Between JAMES ORCHARD of Parish of Sittenbourne in County of Rappa., Plantr., and MARY his Wife of one part and DAVID STERNE of aforesaid Parish and County, Plantr., of other part Witnesseth that JAMES ORCHARD and MARY his Wife for divers good causes but more especially for the sum of Eight thousand pounds of Tobb: and caske to them in hand truely paid have granted unto DAVID STERNE his heirs all that tract or devident of land conteyning just Survey made thereof by Mr. WM. MOSELEY, Surveyor, (blot) hundred acres scituate and being in Parish and County aforesd. neere and adjoining to the sd River side begining at a Pine where formerly stood a white Oake corner tree to Capt. JOHN WEIRE and extending thence alonge the sd WEIREs line N. E. to a Gum, corner to the sd WEIRE, thence W. to the land of SNEAD being to a Stake by a Hickory on ye Mane Road side, thence SW to a red Oake in a point by the River side, thence to the first menconed Pine, the sd land being formerly granted to JOHN MARTIN in the yeare 1663 and afterwards by sd MARTIN Escheated in the year of our Lord 1670 as by their grants more at large appeare and now in possession of JAMES ORCHARD as by Deed dated the 4th day of December in year of our Lord 1688; To have and to hold the sd parcell of land and all appurtenances unto DAVID STERNE his heirs And sd JAMES ORCHARD and MARY his Wife for themselves their heirs &c. the sd tract of land conteyning Three hundred acres as aforesd and all other the premises unto sd DAVID STERNE his heirs against them their heirs and any other persons will warrant and forever defend, the sd JAMES ORCHARD and MARY for themselves grant and agree that upon the reasonable request at the cost and charges of DAVID STERNE make such further acts and assurances for the further better conveying the before premises unto DAVID STERNE his heirs as by sd DAVID STERNE his heirs or by his Councell learned in the Law shall be reasonably required (Excepting Thirty seven acres out of the abovesd bounds which joineth upon the sd JAMES ORCHARD and on the N: E: lines In Witness whereof the parties have sett their hands and seales

Sealed and Delivered in the presents of

JOHN DEANE, JAMES ORCHARD

JOHN ⁄ WARD MARY ORCHARD

Recognitr in Cur Comt Rappa 6 die 9br 1689

KNOW ALL MEN by these presents that I MARY ORCHARD, Wife of JAMES ORCHARD, do by these presents appoint FRAN: TAYLOR to be my true and lawfull Attorney for me and in my name to make acknowledgment in Rappa. Court of a certain parcell of land sold and conveyed to DAVID STERNE by my Husband, JAMES ORCHARD, confirming the same by these presents In Witness whereof I have hereunto set my hand and seal the 5th day of 9br 1689

Teste JAMES JACKSON, MARY Sig M ORCHARD
CHA. SEPOO

pp. 86-87 TO ALL XPIAN PEOPLE to whom these presents shall come, I JACOB LUMPKIN of County of NEW KENT send Greeting. Know ye that I JACOB LUMPKIN for good causes and valuable consideration and especially for the sum of Fifteen Thousand pounds of Tobb: in caske have granted unto STEPHEN BENBRIDGE of County of Rappa. all that parcell of land conteyning by estimacon Three hundred and odd acres as will more or less appeare by Survey made by virtue of an Extent granted Colo. MATHEW KEMP and Colo. WM. COLE by the Kings (blot) the land of JOSIAS PICKS and by the sd Colo: MATHEW KEMP and Col: WM. COLE the extend assigned to me said JACOB LUMPKIN more or less being in Rappa County and bounded on the back by WM: YOUNGs land likewise touching on ANTHO: SMYTHs land being the upermost bounds of and the land of JOHN LASTREE being the lowermost bounds To have and to hold the aforesd land and premises with all rights of hunting hawking fishing and all woods waters mills milseat houses building with all other the profitts belonging to him sd STEPHEN BENBRIDGE his heirs in as full manner as sd JACOB LUMPKIN hath in the land from COL. MATHEW KEMP and Colo: WM. COLE, paying all rights and services as are or shall become due and I the sd JACOB LUMPKIN do for myself promise to deliver unto the sd STEPHEN BENBRIDGE all such Patent Papers or order as is assigned by Colo. MATHEW KEMP to me sd JACOB LUMPKIN from all former gifts granted by me and further I promise to acknowledge this Deed in the County Court of Rappa and I sd JACOB LUMPKIN hath all the Right of this land as far forth I sd JACOB LUMPKIN hath from the abovesd Colo. MATHEW KEMP and Colo. WM. COLE. In Witness whereof I have sett my hand and seale this 2nd day of August One thousand Six hundred and Eighty (blot)
Signed Sealed and Delivered in presents of us
EDWARD ADCOCK, JACOB LUMPKIN
HEN: ADCOCK
Recognitr in Cur Com Rappa 4 die 10br Ano 1689

pp. 87-88 TO ALL XPIAN PEOPLE to whom these presents shall come, I JACOB LUMPKIN of County of NEW KENT in Virginia Gent. send Greeting. Whereas JOSIAS PICKES, Mariner, being Indebted to Coll: MATHEW KEMP, Attorney of EDWARD FLETCHER of LONDON, Mercht., Eighteen thousand pounds of Tobb: and caske and to Colo. WM. COLE Two thousand pounds of Tobb. and they the sd MATHEW KEMP and WM. COLE obtained Judgmt. in the Genll. Court for their severall debts with costs and at a Genll. Court the second day of May 1668 (the same Judgmt. being to me assigned), I obtained writs of Elegitt against the land of the sd PICKES as by the records of the said Court appear pursuant whereunto the sd Writs issued I paid and the Sheriff of County of Rappa. (in which was the lands of the sd PICKES) with ten able jury of Free holders assisted by a Surveyor found the sd PICKES seized of Three hundred Forty two acres of land situate on the South side of Rappa. River granted to him by Patent dated the 28th of March 1667 and accordingly the lands were extented and delivered to me sd JACOB LUMPKIN by Inquisition and proceedings of the sd Sheriff and Jury with the Surveyors Platt thereof may appeare, by virtue I JACOB LUMPKIN became possessed of the sd lands

and being in possession did by a certain Deed or Writing under my hand and seale dated the 2nd day of August 1686 granted unto STEPHEN BENBRIDGE of sd County of Rappa. the sd lands granted to sd PICKES contayining Three hundred Forty two acres according to the bounds expressed in the sd Deed with all my right and title by virtue of these extents as by the sd Deed relation thereto being had more fully appeare. Soon after which (vizt) on the 8th of January 1686 sd STEPHEN BENBRIDGE did assigne and make over the sd Deed with the land and appertinances menconed to PHILLIP LIGHTFOOT became possessed of and entered into sd lands and the same now is in his poasession. Now Know yee that I JACOB LUMPKIN for sum of Three thousand Five hundred pounds of good sweet sented Tobb: and Caske to me in hand paid by PHILLIP LIGHTFOOT being the remainder of the purchase money or consideration he was to pay for the sd land do hereby release and confirm to PHILLIP LIGHTFOOT Three hundred Forty and two acres of land according to the survey thereof with all my right and demand to the same to this day and also confirm the sd Bargaine and Sale by me formerly made to sd BEN-BRIDGE to sd PHILLIP LIGHTFOOT To have and to hold the same during the terme and time yet to come (he or they paying the quitrents due for the same) And I JACOB LUMPKIN promise with PHILLIP LIGHTFOOT his heirs that I will warrant the sd land according to the Survay the residue of the time of the sd extents against all persons whatsoever and that sd PHILLIP LIGHTFOOT his heirs shall peaceably and quietly have the same free and clear from all other troubles and will execute all such further and better assurances for confirmacon of the land for the remainder of the time yet to come of the sd extent as shall be required In Witness whereof I have hereunto sett my hand and Seale this twenty first day of 9br One thousand Six hundred and eighty nine
Sealed and delivered in the presents of

WM. SHERWOOD, JACOB LUMPKIN
WM. TODD

Recognitr Rappa 4 die 10br 1689

Vide Fol. 194. I STEPHEN BENBRIDGE of Farnham Parish in Rappa. County for a valuable consideration to me in hand paid by PHILLIP LIGHTFOOT of Peth Parish in GLOCESTER COUNTY assign and sett over all my right of the within menconed parcell of land purchased of Mr. JACOB LUMPKIN and do further oblige myselfe my heirs to make to him whensoever he shall ask or demand a firme Deed of the said land and sign deliver to him all and every Paper or other concerns about the sd land now in the hands of Mr. JACOB LUMPKIN and also whenever demanded to acknowledge the sd land in Rappa. Court as to make what sale for the sd land he the sd LIGHTFOOT or his Attorney shall see fitt for the securing of the same to him. As Witness my hand and seale this 8th of January 1686
Signed Sealed and Delivered in the presents of us

JOHN CLAYBURNE, STEPHEN BENBRIDGE
JOHN TRIGGS, GEO: 6 STANFORD

p. Vide Fol. 180 & 181.
89 Capt. TAYLER and loving freind after my love and Remembrance Remembered unto you with all the rest of our Friends in Genll. which doth desire to aske after my well fare &c. Sr. these will give you an acct. that I have received the mony for my land of Mr. SPICER and doth desire for him to give you many thanks for ye care therein and in token of love I have sent you by Mr. COOPER, Comander of the *VIRGINIA* in one box one good Castor Hat and band and six pare of Wash leather gloves which I desire yr. acceptance and if it doth ly in my way to serve you here you shall find him both ready and willing who is yr. loving friend and Servant to comand

Brittale January the 30th 1688 ARTHUR GRAUNT
To GEO: TAYLER Esqr. in the Freshes of Rappa.
Virginia by Capt. COOPER, Comandr. of the *NANCOME* L.D.C.
Recordr. Cur Comt Rappa 17 die 10br 1689

p. 89 THIS INDENTURE made the 4th day of 10br ano dom 1689 Witnesseth that GEO: WARD of Parish of South Farnham in County of Rappa. hath sold unto EMANUEL HAM his heirs all that parcell of land bought by the sd GEO: WARD of RICHARD WARSDALL and by the sd RICHARD WARSDALL made over and conveyed to sd GEO: WARD make over and convey sd land unto EMANUEL HAM his heirs To possess and enjoy said land with all rights waters woods orchards gardens belonging to sd land and being upon the Plantation of sd GEO: WARD with all the hoggs belonging and runing in the mark of sd GEO: WARD (his Chest Bedd Gunn and working Tools excepted) To have and enjoy sd land and premises without the hindrance of sd GEO: WARD or any person from him In Witness whereof sd GEO: WARD hath sett his hand and seale
Signed Sealed and Delivered in the presents of

THO: HUELESCOTT GEO: Sig. X WARDE
BARBARA ALLEN

Recognitr in Cur Comt Rappa 4 die 10br 1689

pp. 89-90 Vide Fol. 136
KNOW ALL MEN by these presents that the within menconed RICHARD HALE doth by these presents fully and absolutely signe and sett over unto JOHN GATEWOOD his heirs all his Estate and interest of this within specified bargain and sale for Two hundred acres of land and further sd RICHARD HAIL to and with ye sd JOHN GATE-WOOD his heirs that he and they shall forever hold and enjoy sd Two hundred acres and every part thereof without the trouble of sd RICHARD HALE his heirs or any other persons claiming under him being for a valuable consideration reced in hand In Witness whereof the partie hath sett his hand and seale this 4th day of December ano 1689
Signed Sealed and Delivered in presence of

EDWIN THACKER, RICHD. HAILE
THO: NEW

Recognitr in Cur Comt 4 die 10br 1689

p. 90 THIS INDENTURE made this 6th day of August Ano Dom 1689 Between WM. LOYD of one part and GRIFFIN CARTER of other part Witnesseth that sd WM. LOYD for a valuable consideration in hand received from GRIFFIN CARTER have granted unto GRIFFIN CARTER his heirs One hundred acres of land being part of a Patent of a Devident making its begining upon the corner tree of RICHARD WOOD that is next to COL. STONE in Mrs. PRICEs land and taking for breadth on the sd PRICE line W. just be breadth of a hundred acres and is bounded by sd RICHD. WOODs line a full mile by just Survey together with all woods and underwoods and all other the appertinances belonging To have and to hold sd one hundred acres unto GRIFFIN CARTER his heirs with warranty from me WM. LOYD and my heirs from all other persons In Witness whereof I have hereunto sett my hand and seale
Sealed and Delivered in the presents of

GEO: TAYLER WM. LOYD
SAMLL. THACKER

Recognitr in Com Rappa 4 die 10br 1689

pp. 91-92 THIS INDENTURE made this 5th day of 8br in year of our Lord 1689 Between HUMPHREY BOOTH, ROBERT BROOKE and KATHERINE BROOKE of the County of Rappa: of the one partie and THO: DAVIS of said County of the other partie Witnesseth that sd HUMPHREY BOOTH, ROBERT BROOKE and KATHERINE BROOKE hath for a valuable consideration already in hand received sold unto THOMAS DAVIS and his heirs one parcell of land conteyning One hundred acres being on South side of Rappa: River being part of a greater tract of land the sd One hundred acres to be bounded Beginning at the Run comonly called by name of PRICES RUN where the Mane Road goeth over and from thence extending itself up the sd Run or Branch as far as sd HUMPHREY BOOTH goeth up that course and from thence for its breadth along the sd BOOTH line which runeth W. and by E. and from thence directly down to the said Mane Road to sd PRICES RUN where it first began, Together with all profits and appertenances whatsoever belonging and all right that sd HUMPHREY BOOTH, ROBT. BROOKE and KATHERINE BROOKE have To have and to hold to him sd THO: DAVIS his heirs And it is hereby further covinanted upon by sd HUMPHREY BOOTH and THOMAS DAVIS that as they both shall live if in case the sd THOMAS DAVIS shall want Timber upon sd One hundred acres of land for to build such convenient housing as shall want that sd HUMPHREY shall and is hereby bound to find him Timber from his own land always provided that sd THOS. DAVIS make no waste of his own Timber In Testimony whereof the parties have put their hands and affixed their seals the first day of 8br One thousand Six hundred and Eighty nine

Signed Sealed and Delivered in the presents of

THOMAS DRANE — HUMPHREY BOOTH
THOMAS Sig T GRIFFIN — ROBT. BROOKE
KATH: BROOKE

Recognitr in Cur Court Rappa 4 die 10br 1689

KNOW ALL LMEN by these presents that I KATHERINE BROOKE of County of Rappa do by these presents appoint Capt. WM. MOSLEY of the same County my true and lawfull Attorney to acknowledge certain parcell of land scituate on PRICES RUN in sd County unto THOMAS DAVIS and his heirs hereby confirming what my sd Attorney shall do in the premises In Testimony whereof I have put my hand and seal this 4th day of xber 1689

Teste THOMAS DRANE, — KATH: BROOKE
THO: Sig. T GRIFFIN

p. 92 KNOW ALL MEN by these presents that I FRAN: SUTTLE of County of Rappa. do give unto MARY PRAGUE one young sorrel mare branded with I C on the far buttock with Warrant from any person that shall lay any claim to the same As Witness my hand and seale

Test THO: T SUTTLE, — FRAN: SUTTLE
FRAN: Mar: F SUTTLE

pp. 92-94 Vide Fol. 198

TO ALL XPIAN PEOPLE to whom this present writing shall come, I DANLL. SWELLIVANT of County of Rappa., Plantr., send Greeting in our Lord God everlasting this 6th day of September in year of our Lord 1689 Know yee that I sd DANIEL SWELLIVANT for sum of Eighteen thousand three hundred pounds of Tobb: paid by JOHN NEWTON of WESTMORELAND COUNTY in Colony of Virginia Gent. do by these presents sell unto JOHN NEWTON his heirs one tract of land conteyning Three hundred and fifty acres being part of a Devident of land granted to my Father, DANLL. SWELLIVANT by Patent bearing date the 2d of February 1663, part thereof being by my sd Father given and bequeathed to me by his last Will and Testament bearing date the 1st day of December 1673; and the other part coming and descending to me by the death of my Brother, DENNIS SWELLIVANT, as by the sd Patent and Will doth appear the sd land being in Parish of Farnham in County of Rappa butted and bounded beginning at a Mill Dam at the head of TOTASKEY CREEKE from thence alonge a PATH or ROAD comonly called or known by the MILL ROAD unto a line of marked trees that is on the outside of the sd SWELLIVANTs land and right unto the corner of a small Plantacon where one FRAN: ELMORE, Soyer, liveth thence along the sd line to a great Swamp or run down the sd run to DENNIS, his Cove, from thence up TOTASKEY CREEKE to the place where it first began with all and singular its rights Together with all houses gardens orchards pastures and appertenances belonging To have and to hold for the proper use and behoofe of sd JOHN NEWTON his heirs And I sd DANLL. SWELLIVANT will warrant from the clame of any manner of person whatsoever and said JOHN NEWTON shall peaceably and quietly hold sd land with all its rights forever without any lawfull trouble of me sd DANLL. SWELLIVANT my heirs or assigns In Witness whereof I have hereunto set my hand and fixed my seale

Signed Sealed and Delivered in the presents of us

SARAH JOPLING, DANIEL SWELLIVANT
JOHN FRONIELL, ROBT. X GOWRE

Recognitr in Cur Comt Rappa 1 die Jany. 1689

KNOW ALL MEN by these presents that I DANLL. SWELLIVANT of Rappa County in Virginia do ow and stand indebted unto JOHN NEWTON of WESTMORELAND COUNTY in Virginia in ye full sum of Thirty and six Thousand six hundred pounds of Tobb: to be pd. unto JOHN NEWTON and to the true performance whereof I bind myself my heirs In Witness whereof I have sett my hand and fixed my seale the day and year written

NOW KNOW yee that whereas I DANLL. SWELLIVANT of County of Rappa. have by Deed bearing date by these presents have sold to JOHN NEWTON a tract of land lying in Farnham Parish on TOTASKEY CREEKE conteyning Three hundred fifty acres Now if sd DANIEL SWELLIVANT his heirs do truely keep the agreements in sd Deed and that the Deed be acknowledged at the first Court held on the North side of Rappa. River then this obligation to be void otherwise to remain in full force

Signed Sealed and Delivered in the presents of

SARAH JOPLING, DANLL. SWELLIVANT
JOHN FRONIELL, ROBT. X GOWRE

pp. 94-96 THIS INDENTURE made the 9th day of February in the fifth yeare of the Reigne of our Sovereigne Lord James the Second ano Dom 1688/9 Between WM. CRIMES of the Parish of Petso in County of GLOCESTER of one party and JOHN SCOTT of Parish of Abington and County aforesd, Tanner, of other part Witnesseth that WM. CRIMES for sum of Fifteen thousand and five hundred pounds of good and sound sweet sented Tobb: and caske and for divers other causes hath granted unto JOHN SCOTT his heirs all that plantacon and Devident of land together with all houses orchards gardens and appertinances to the same belonging all which sd land and appertinances being on the River of Rappa. and which were conveyed unto sd WM. CRIMES his heirs by Deed indented the first day of 9br 1686 together with all rights and demands of him sd WM. CRIMES his heirs to sd land To have and to hold all and singular the sd lands and premises to sd JOHN SCOTT his heirs forever And sd WM. CRIMES doth for himselfe his heirs agree at the time of ensealing he hath good Estate in fee simple unto the lands and hath full power to sell so that it shall be lawfull for sd JOHN SCOTT his heirs quietly and peacably to have and enjoy the above granted lands and lastly WM. CRIMES doth promise to acknowledge all such further lawfull Deeds as by sd JOHN SCOTT shall be required In Witness I have sett my hand and Seale

Sealed and Delivered in the presents of us after WM. CRIMES
each parties were consented that the sd
SCOTT should have absolute possession of the sd land in 9ber next provided always that Mr. CRIMES have liberty of finishing his Crop on the sd Plantacon within specified
JOHN LEWIS, ROBT: THURSTON, PHILL. MAY
Recognitr in Cur Comt Rappa 4 die 10br 1689

KNOW ALL MEN by these presents that I WM. CRIMES of Parish of Petso and County of GLOCESTER Gent. am bound unto JOHN SCOTT of Parish of Aniton and County of Gloucester, Tanner, in the sum Thirty one thousand pounds of sweet sented Tobb. and cask I do hereby bind myself my heirs Witness my hand and seal this 9th day February 1689

The Condicon of this present obligation is that if WM. CRIMES his heirs at all times forever keep all the agreements in one Deed of Bargain and Sale bearing date with these presents which ought to be kept and the sd Deed is between the sd CRIMES of the one part and the sd JOHN SCOTT of the other part and that without any fraud or covin else to remain in full force and virtue

Teste JOHN LEWIS, WM. CRIMES
ROBT. THURSTON, PHILL. MAY

pp. 96-98 TO ALL XPIAN PEOPLE to whom these presents shall come we WM. HODGSON of County of Rappa and REBECCA my Wife send Greeting in our Lord God Everlasting Know yee that we WM. HODGSON and REBECCA my Wife for divers good causes and especially for and in consideracon of a Horse and sum of One thousand pounds of Tobb: in caske have sold unto THOMAS DAY of aforesaid County his heirs One hundred acres of land being part of a parcell of land conteyning Three hundred and Fifty six acres being in Rappa County on the South side of Rappa. River and bounded Begining at a corner white Oake by a branch and runing thence N. to DAVIS his land alonge his line N. W. thence E. over certain branches by land of EVAN DAVIS S. E. deviding the land from the land of THO: RICKETT to the first menconed branch it first began as by Patent bearing date the 24th of Febry. 1666 To have and to hold said land with all rights of hunting hawking fishing woods houses and buildings with all appertinances belonging to THO: DAY his heirs paying our Sovereign Lord the King such rents as shall be due and WM. HODGSON and REBECCA his Wife do warrant and defend the sd land from claime of any person whatsoever and to acknowledge the same In Witness whereof I the sd WM. HODGSON have set my hand and seale this 25th Jany. 1687/8

Signed Sealed and Delivered in the presence of
DANLL. DOBYNS, WM. W HUDSON
JEAN LANNY
Recognitr in Cur Comt Rappa 4 die 10br 1689

To the Worshipfull Bench held for Rappa County on the South side I REBECCA HUDSON do make my Husband, WM. HUDSON my lawfull Attorney for to acknowledge unto THO: DAY One hundred acres of land being part of her rights according as the conveyance specifieth As Witness my hand and seale this 4th day of 10br 1689

In the presence of RICHD. BROOKE REBECCA Mar: R HUDSON
REBECCA BROOKE

p. 98 Vide Fol. 171.
KNOW ALL MEN by these presents that I HENRY WEBSTER of County of Rappa. within menconed do assigne and make over unto the within menconed THO. LEWIS all my right of the within menconed Deed of Sale with all thereunto belonging Together with the House of fe(blot) from me my heirs to him sd THO: LEWIS his heirs

with the same warrante as he sd THO: LEWIS made to me In Witness whereof I sett my hand and Seale this 9th day of 10br 1689
Signed Sealed and delivered in the presents of us
WM. DAVIS, HENRY Mar: H WEBSTER
ELIAS YATES
Recognitr in Cur Comt Rappa 1 die Jany 1689

pp. TO ALL XPIAN PEOPLE to whom this present writing shall come I THOMAS SHORT
98- for the sum of Sixteen thousand pounds of Tobb: pd. by JOHN NEWTON of WEST-
100 MORELAND COUNTY in Colony of Virginia Gent. by these presents have sold unto JOHN NEWTON his heirs one tract of land conteyning One thousand acres granted by Patent to MICHAELL HUGILL and THO: SHORT, my Father, bearing date the 26th day of May 1666 the whole coming and ending to my Father, THO: SHORT, as Surveving the sd MICHAELL HUGELL and to me the sd THO: SHORT, his Son, as heire to my deced Father, being in the Freshes of Rappa. on the North side begining at a marked red Oake and runing S. & E. to a marked red Oake, thence E. N. E. into the Woods, thence West to the place it began being One thousand acres be the same more or less with all woods profitts and appertinances to the same belonging To have and to hold sd tract of land with all the rights to JOHN NEWTON his heirs and I THO: SHORT my heirs will warrant from the claime of any persons whatsoever and sd JOHN NEWTON peacably and quietly have sd tract of land to his own proper use without lett of me sd THO: SHORT my heirs and I do oblige myself to perform such other deeds as the Councell learned shall require at any time within seven years and the cost of him the sd JOHN NEWTON In Witness I have sett my hand and seale
Signed Sealed and Delivered in presents of
BENJA. BLANCHFLOWER, THOMAS SHORT
BENJA. NEWTON
Recognitr. in Cur Comt Rappa 1 die Jany. 1689

Xber the 23rd 1688 KNOW ALL MEN by these presents that I THOS: SHORT of Rappa. County in Virginia do stand indebted unto JOHN NEWTON of County of WESTMORELAND in Virginia in quantitie of Thirty two thousand pounds of Tobb. to be pd. unto sd JOHN his heirs & to the true performance whereof to be done and performed I do hereby bind myselfe my heirs firmly by these presents In Witness I have sett my hand and seale the day and year above written

Know yee that Whereas I THO: SHORT of County of Rappa have by Deed under my hand and seale bearing date with these presents have sold unto JOHN NEWTON of WESTMORELAND COUNTY one tract of land lying on the North side of Rappa River conteyning One thousand as by relation to sd Deed Now if sd THOS: SHORT his heirs do well and truely keep all the covinants in the sd Deeds which ought to be performed then this obligation to be void otherwise remain in full force
Signed sealed and delivered in the presents of
BENJA. BLANCHFLOWER, THOMAS X SHORT
BENJA. NEWTON

p. KNOW ALL MEN by these presents that wee JAMES CLAYTON and JOAN CLAYTON
100 the last Widow and relict of DANIELL SULLIVINT, late of Farnham Parish in Rappa: do by these presents make over unto JOHN NEWTON of WESTMORELAND COUNTY all our right either in right of Dower or any other ways to a certain messuage or tract of land conteyning Three hundred and fifty acres sold to abovesd JOHN NEWTON by Deed bearing date with these presents and situate in Parish of Farnham aforesaid

by DANLL. SWILLIVANT, Son of the aforesd. DANLL. SWILLIVANT Witness our hands this 6th day of December 1689

JOHN CLAUGHTON, JAMES CLEATON
ROBT. ROBINSON JOAN I CLEATON

1689 Recognitr Rappa 21 die Jany. 1689

pp. 100-101 KNOW ALL MEN by these presents that I JOHN FRYER with consent of my Wife, ROSAMOND, by a good consideracion moving us thereunto already in part received of THOS: CRAIN wee the sd FRYER and Wife do by these presents have sold parcell of land in Rappa. County conteyning One hundred and twenty five acres to enjoy it peacably with all privilidges and do oblige ourselves our heirs to defend the sd Sale of certin parcell of land from us our heirs and assigns forever In Witness whereof I have in behalf of my Wife sett my hand and seale this 11th July 1689

Teste WM. HANCECOME JOHN Sig: F FRYER
WM. BRIDGES

Recognitr in Cur Comt Rappa Janry 1st die 1689

KNOW ALL MEN that I ROSAMOND FRYER do hereby give my full consent to my Husband, JOHN FRYER, to acknowledge my name to a parcell of land lying in Rappa. County conteyning One hundred twenty five acres more or less sold to THO: CRAINE and I sd ROSAMUND FRYER do give my consent to the acknowledging of the sd land from me my heirs As Witness my hand and seal this twenty ninth day of 10ber 1689

Teste THO: THOMSON, ROSAMUND sign ? FRYER
JOHN WRIGHT, WM. ∓ MACKENEY

pp. 101-103 THIS DEED INDENTED of EXCHANGE made this second day of November in year of our Lord God 1689 Between THOMAS LEWIS of Parish of North Farnham in County of Rappa., Ferryman, of the one part and WM. DAVIS of the same Parish and County, Plantr., of other part Witnesseth that THO: LEWIS for a valuable consideration paid by WM. DAVIS as also for and in consideration of another tract of land in Exchange by sd WM. DAVIS assured unto sd THO: LEWIS and his heirs wherewith sd THOMAS LEWIS doth hereby acknowledge have granted unto WM. DAVIS and his heirs all ye peices of wood land ground being in Parish and County abovesd. on South side of a Swamp or a Beaver Dam issing and runing into a Creek there called TOTASKEY CREEK begining at the line of one JONES at the head of sd Swamp & so runing down sd Swamp and adjoining to the land of DAVIS conteyning Forty acres more or less being part of a tract of land which sd THO: LEWIS heretofore purchased of one JOHN OVERTON as by the Deed relation being had To have and to hold the parcell of wood land ground abovesd and sold in Exchange with all the appertenances to the same belonging unto sd WM: DAVIS his heirs and assigns and rents growing due to the Cheif Lord of the Sovereigns thereof only excepted To hold and quietly enjoy without the interruption of sd LEWIS or his heirs or any other person In Witness whereof the above named THO: LEWIS to this present Indenture of Exchange hath sett his hand and seale

Sealed and Delivered and Peacably and quietly possession of premises within written was had and taken by the within named THO. LEWIS and imediately by him delivered unto the within menconed WM. DAVIS the purchas of THO: LEWIS

THO: Mark T FRESHWATER,
JA: ELLIS

Recognitr in Cur Comt Rappa 1 die Janry 1689

Memo: that I MARY LEWIS, Wife of within named THO: LEWIS hereby without compulsion consent to the Deed within written and also release all my right and interest of

Dower and thirds to the sd within menconed to be bargained and sold to WM. DAVIS his heirs and assigns forever Witness my hand the day and year within written
Witness THOS: FRESHWATER, MARY LEWIS
JA: ELLIS
Recognitr and Recordr.
KNOW ALL MEN by these presents that I MARY LEWIS, Wife of THOMAS LEWIS, of County of Rappa., Ferryman, do hereby appoint my very good Friend, RICHARD HAM, my true and lawfull Attorney for me before their Majties Justices of peace for County of Rappa abovesd in open Court siting to acknowledge my assent to a certain Deed indented of Exchange bearing date with these presents made between my Husband, THOMAS LEWIS, of the one part and WILLIAM DAVIS and also in my name to relinquish all my right to the land menconed In Witness my hand and seale this 2d day of November 1689
Signed sealed and delivered in the presents of
THO: Ŧ FRESHWATER, MARY Mar: M LEWIS
JAMES ELLIS

pp. 103-105 THIS INDENTURE INDENTED of EXCHANGE made this 2nd day of Novembr. 1689 Between WILLIAM DAVIS of Parish of North Farnham in County of Rappa., Plantr., of one part and THO: LEWIS of same Parish and County, Ferryman, of the other part Witnesseth that WM. DAVIS for a valuable consideracon to him in hand paid by THO: LEWIS and in consideracon of another parcell of land in Exchange by sd THO: LEWIS conveyed to sd WM. DAVIS wherewith the sd WM. DAVIS doth grant in Exchange all that his peice of land being in Parish and County abovesd on North side of a Swamp or Beaver Dam issuing and runing into a Creek called TOTASKEY CREEK neere unto the FERRY and runing by the sd Creek & adjoining to the land of sd THO: LEWIS contayning Forty acres more or less which said Land being part of a tract of land purchased by WM. DAVIS of JOHN DE YOUNGE and THO: FRESHWATER deced, with all houses buildings orchards and marsh ground unto the same belonging the quit rents hence forth growing due to the Cheif Lord or Lords of the Signiery in respect of the premises only excepted To have and to hold the parcell of land above menconed and sold in Exchange with their appertinances unto THO: LEWIS his heirs and assigns forever In Witness whereof the above named WM. DAVIS to this Indenture of Exchange hath sett his hand and seale
Signed and Delivered and peaceable and quiet possession WM. DAVIS
and seizin of the land was had and taken by the within named WM. DAVIS and imediately by him delivered unto the within sd THO: LEWIS in the presence of THO: Mark Ŧ FRESHWATER, JAMES ELLIS
Recognitr in Cur Comt Rappa 1 die Jany 1689
Memo: That I ELIZ. DAVIS, Wife of the within named WM. DAVIS, do hereby without any compultion whatsoever freely give my consent to the Deed within written and relinquish all my right in the land within menconed unto the within sd THO: LEWIS his heirs and assigns forever Witness my hand the day and year first above written
Witness THO: Ŧ FRESHWATER, ELIZ: Mar: ☉ DAVIS
JAMES ELLIS
KNOW ALL MEN by these presents that I ELIZABETH DAVIS Wife of WM. DAVIS of County of Rappa. Plantr. do hereby appoint my good friend, RALPH WHITING, my lawfull Attorney for me before the Maties Justices of ye Peace for the County of Rappa. abovesd in open Court sitting to acknowledge my assent to a certain Deed of Exchange made between my Husband, WILLIAM DAVIS, and one THO: LEWIS and to relinquish all my right to the land Witness my hand & seale this 2d day of 9ber 1689
Signed sealed and delivered in the presents of us

THO: Mar: ₣ FRESHWATER, ELIZ: the marke of ʘ DAVIS
JAMES ELLIS

pp. 105-107 THIS INDENTURE made the 27th day of September 1689 Between HENRY BERRY of Rappa. County, Planter, and SARAH his Wife, WM. BERRY of the same place, Cordwainer, and MARGRETT his Wife of the one part and ROBERT PECK of the same place, Planter, of other part Witnesseth that HENRY BERRY and SARAH his Wife and WM: BERRY and MARGRETT his Wife for sum of One thousand pounds of Tobb: and one Mare in hand already satisfied and paid by ROBT. PECK unto them have sold unto ROBERT PECK his heirs and assigns all that One hundred acres of land being part of a Devident that WILLIAM LIPPETT formerly lived upon at the Eastermost extend of the sd land binding upon the sd LIPPETTs land line thence to a corner tree of Mr. SAVAGEs, thence to a corner tree to sd HENRY BERRY, thence runing along the line of sd HENRY BERRY to a Spanish Oake which is a corner tree with all their right together with all appertenances all which premises are situated on North side in the Freshes of Rappa To have and to hold sd land and premises hereby granted unto sd ROBERT PECK his heirs In Witness whereof the parties to these presents their hands and seals have sett Signed sealed and delivered by the within named HENRY BERRY, SARAH his Wife & WM. BERRY in the presents of us

THO: ABINGTON, HENRY BERRY
WM. Mar: M HEAD, SARAH MB BERRY
JOHN BERRY WM. BERRY
MARGRETT BERRY

Recognitr in Cur Comt Rappa 1 die Janry 1689

KNOW ALL MEN by these presents that wee HENRY and SARAH BERRY do by these presents appoint our loving friend Mr. JOSHUA DAVIS to be our true and lawfull Attorney to acknowledge in the Worshipfll. Court of Rappa. the sale and conveyance for certain parcell of land sold by my Brother, WILLIAM BERRY, and myself bearing date December <u>the 12th 1682</u> unto ROBERT PECK & heirs &c. and what my said Attorney shall do ratified and confirm As Witness my hand and Seale Decembr. the 20th 1689

JOS. RUTTER, HENRY BERRY
CHRISTR. SMITH his mark ß SARAH AB BERRY

KNOW ALL MEN by these presents that I WILLIAM BERRY, Cordwayner, do by these presents appoint my loving friend Mr. JOS. DAVIS, to be my lawfull Attorney to acknowledge in the Worshipfull Court of Rappa. the sale of a certain parcell of land sold by my Brother, HENRY BERRY, and myself bearing date <u>10ber the 12th 1682</u> to ROBERT PECK his heirs &c. and what my Attorney shall act in these presents do by these ratifie and confirm As Witness & Seale Ano 1689 December 17th
Sealed in the presents of us

JOHN BERRY, WM. BERRY
FRAN: DAUGHTY

pp. 107-108 To All &c. FRANS. MORYSON, Esqr. Governr. & Capt. Genll. of Virginia &c. Now know ye that I sd FRAN. MORISON Esqr. accordingly give unto LEONARD JONES Two hundred acres of land lying on the Westward side of TOTASKEY CREEK in County of Rappa. about three miles up the sd Creek and begining at a red Oake standing on a point by the aforesd Creek side called MATCHY MOP QUARTER, thence extending its breadth by the sd Creek side to and over a small gut that issues of the sd Creek and from the aforesd marked red Oake runing into the woods by a line of marked trees W. by S. to a marked Oake at the head of a branch or Vally thence its due breadth again N. by W. being the parallell course to TOTASKEY CREEK to another Spanish Oake thence back again to another marked Oake which is above the northward of the same gutt above menconed the sd land being due to sd JONES &c. To have & to hold &c. To be held &c. Yeilding and paying &c. Provided &c. Given at JAMES CITTY under my hand and the seale of the Colony this 19th day of July 1682 and in the 14th yeare of the Reigne of our Sovereigne Lord King Charles the 1nd &c.

Record 10th Junii 1665 FRAN. MORISON
Teste PHILL. LUDWELL C. C. Clff. THO: LUDWELL

KNOW ALL MEN by these presents that I the within named LEONARD JONES do hereby assigne unto RICHARD BRAMHAM of Parish of North Farnham in County of Rappa Virginia all my right to the Patent within written to the land therein menconed to be granted with appertenances unto sd RICHARD BRAMHAM his heirs and assigns to the only use and behoofe of sd RICHARD BRAMHAM his heirs forever Witness my hand and seale 19th day of October in yeare of our Lord God 1689

Signed Sealed and delivered in the presents of
WM. WB BUTLER, LEONARD Mark L JONES
JOHN Mark N LORD

9br the 30th 1689

Memo: that on the day and yeare abovesd WM. BUTLER and JOHN LORD witnesses to the above Assigmt. and Sale of land conteyned in the above Patent personally appeared before me and took their Corporall oath upon the Holy Gospell of God that they saw LEONARD JONES signe seale and deliver the above Assignmt. to RICHARD BRAMHAM the Assignee as his act and deed Given under my hand the day and yeare above written
RICHD. LEE Written

Recognitr in Cur Comt Rappa 1 die Jany 1689

KNOW ALL MEN by these presents that I LEONARD JONES of the RIVER MANTICOCCK of the Province of MARYLAND, Plantr., by these presents appoint in my place and stead my beloved Friend, THO: LEWIS, of Parish of North Farnham in County of Rappa. Virginia my true and lawfull Attorney for me in my name at some Court to be holden for the sd County of Rappa. within six months after the date hereof before his Majesties Justices of the peace then and there sitting to acknowledge for me a certaine Assignmt. bearing date the 19th day of 8br instant and all my right and interest of the Patent and land there menconed granted to one RICHD. BRAMHAM of Parish of North Farnham his heirs and I do hereby ratifie and the same to be as firm and stable as if I had been there present and done the same Witness my hand & seale this one and twentieth day of October One thousand Six hundred and Eighty nine

Signed sealed & delivered in the presents of us
WM. WB BUTLER, LEONARD L JONES
JOHN mark N LORD

Mr. That on the 30th day of November 1689 WM. BUTLER and JOHN LORD witnesses to the above Lettr. of Attorney personally appeared before me and took their Corporall Oaths upon the Holy Gospell of God that they saw the above LEONARD JONES signe and seale the above said Lettr. of Attorney Given under my hand the day and yeare above written
RICHARD LEE
Recordtr. Teste written

p. 109 Fol. 51). I RICHARD WEST for a valuable consideracon of Six thousand pounds of Tobb: do assigne over all my right and interest of the within menconed land from me my heirs forever As Witness my hand and seale this 21st of Janry 1689

Signed Sealed and Delivered in the Presents of

GEO: PLEY, RICHARD R WEST
GEO: Mar: K KING his mark
Recognitr in Cur Com Rappa 5 die Martii 1689

p. 109 TO ALL XPIAN PEOPLE to whom these presents shall come sendeth Greeting. Now Know yee that I WILLIAM UNDERWOOD for divers good causes but especially for Three thousand pounds of Tobb: to me in hand already received have sold unto WM. WHEELER One hundred acres of Woodland ground being bounded Begining at the corner tree of NATHAN POPEs land next to the land of JOHN PIPER and so alonge that line the length as shall contain the sd Hundred acres square for which sd sum of Tobb: before specified I sd WILLIAM UNDERWOOD do hereby grant the sd Hundred acres of land being in my full power without any limitation to alter or change the same unto WILLIAM WHEELER his heirs To have and to hold and quietly and peaceably to enjoy forever with warranty against me sd WM. UNDERWOOD my heirs or any persons whatsoever In Witness whereof I have hereunto set my hand and Seale this 4th day of 10br Ano Dom 1689
Sealed and Delivered in the presence of us
ANTHO: WALLIS, WM. UNDERWOOD
JOS: HEMINGS
Recognitr in Cur Com Rappa 5th die Martii 1689

pp. 110-112 TO ALL XPIAN PEOPLE to whom this present writting shall come Know yee that I ADAM WOFFENDALL of County of Rappa in Colony of Virginia, Planter, send Greeting in our Lord God writing the 15th day of February in yeare of our Lord 1689. Now know yee that I ADAM WOFFENDALL for sum of Four thousand pounds of Tobb: in caske do forever acquitt and discharge WILLIAM MARSHALL and have sold unto sd WM. MARSHALL his heirs one tract of land scituate and being in St. Marys Parish in the aforesd County containing Sixty seven acres more or less as by the Platt under Capt. MOSLEYs hand, Surveyor of the County, bearing date 15th of Febry. 1689/90 and bounded as followeth lying and being on the North side of Rappa River upon the East side of CHINGATEAGUE and begining at a red Oake corner tree of Mr. FRAN: SLAUGHTER and extending alonge Mr. SLAUGHTERs line to an Hickory in the sd line S. W. to a Stake at the angle of a white Oake and a black Oak in the line of Mr. SAMLL. BAYLY, thence alonge the sd SAMLL. BAYLYs line to the land sold by sd SAMLL. BAYLY to PHILLIP HUNNING, JAMES MATHEWS and JOHN EASTER, W. to a white Oake neere a small branch, thence S. E. to the first mentioned red Oak with all its members and appertinances woods mines Quarrys water and all other advantages To have and to hold said tract of land with all the premises unto WM. MARSHALL his heirs and will warrant and forever defend from the claimes of any persons whatsoever and ADAM WOFFENDALL do consent to make such further conveyance as their Councell shall advise and also with his Wife acknowledge this Deed in the County Court of Rappa. In Witness whereof he sd ADAM WOFFENDALL have sett his hand and seale
Sealed and Delivered in the presents of us
JOSH. DAVIS, ADAM WOFFENDALL
ISAAC I D DUNE, DEN Mar: D MURFY
I the sd ADAM WOFFENDALL do sell and add more to the conveyance of said Thirty acres of land unto WM. MARSHALL his heirs and assigne forever begining at a white Oake standing in the line of JNO. EASTER and extending East unto WM. BROWNEs corner tree and thence South alonge the ROAD to a marked Hickory standing on the line of Mr. SLAUGHTER unto the first station menconed this making void all former conveyance acknowledged unto WM. MARSHALL by ADAM WOFFENDALL

Memorandum This 26th day of February Livery & Seisin within parcell of land was delivered to WM. MARSHALL by possession delivery of the sd land by turff and twigg upon part of sd land by ADAM WOFFENDALL
In presence of us Test JOS: DAVIS
Recognitr in Cur Com Rappa 5 die Martii 1689
I do hereby authorize JOSHUA DAVIS my Attorney to acknowledge a conveyance of land unto WM. MARSHALL and this shall be his warrant for so doing As Witness my hand and seale this 26th day of Febry. 1689/90
Sealed and Delivered in the presents of us
DANNIS Mar: D MURFREY ADAM WOFFENDALL
ISAAC I D DUN
I do hereby authorize and impower JOSHUA DAVIS my Attorney to acknowledge my third for tract of land unto WM. MARSHALL and this shall be his warrant for so doing as Witness my hand and seale this 26th day of February 1689/90
Sealed and Delivered in presence of us
ELIZ. WOFFENDALL HONORIA H WOFFENDALL
KNOW ALL MEN by these presents that I ADAM WOFFENDALL of County of Rappa in Parish of St. Marys doe acknowledge myself to stand bound unto WM. MARSHALL of aforesd County and Parish in the just sum of Ten thousand pounds of good sound Merchantable Tobacco and Caske on my now Dwelling Plantation or convenient in the Parish aforesd. and for the true performance thereof I bind myself unto sd WM. MARSHALL and for the more further assurance of the true payment of the aforesd sum of Tobb. in Caske I do make over all my right of my now Dwelling Plantacon and One hundred acres of land thereunto belonging with all houses orchards and inclosures & other hereditaments unto WM: MARSHALL his heirs and do warrant the premises aforesd from me my heirs and in confirmation I have sett my hand and seale this 25th day of February 1689/90. The sum is Ten Thousd.
The Condicon of this obligation is the above bound ADAM WOFFENDALL his heirs shall at all times hereafter secure the abovesaid WM. MARSHALL in a quiett and peacable possession and enjoyment of a parcell of land bought of sd ADAM WOFFENDALL and save harmless and indemnified then this obligation to be void else to remain in full force In Witness hereof sd ADAM WOFFENDALL have put my hand and seale
Signed sealed and delivered in the presence of us
JOSHUA DAVIS, ADAM WOFFENDALL
ISAAC Mar: I D DUNN

pp. 113-114 TO ALL XPIAN PEOPLE Know yee that wee JOHN PHILLIPS and ADAM WOFFENDALL both of Parish of Sittenburne in County of Rappa., Planters, for divers good causes by us already received have granted both joyntly and severally unto WM. BROWNE of the sd Parish and County, Carpenter, his heirs & assigns all that certain parcell of wood land ground being in the Parish and County aforesd being part of a certain parcell of land which was surveyed by us sd PHILLIPS & WOFFENDALL the 26th day of May in year 1673, and being part of the land where the said PHILLIPS now liveth and taken up of Mr. KERTON, Trustee of the late Lords of the Neck of land being all that land belonging to sd PHILLIPS and WOFFENDALL adjoining to the Eastermost side of the Maine Branch of CHINGOTEAGUE CREEK and so from thence extending itself down the line of sd WM. BROWNs his marked trees said BROWNE paying yearly such quit rents and services as shall become due And furthermore it is covinanted between all the parties that sd WM. BROWNE his heirs &c. may quietly possess the sd land without any trouble of either of them In Witness whereof sd PHILLIPS and WOFFENDALL have sett our hands and fixed our seales this 12th day of February in year 1674

JOHN PHILLIPS
ADAM WOFFENDALL

The True intent of this Deed is no otherwise then to warrant the title of the sd land from us and our heris to sd BROWN & his heirs
Signed sealed and delivered in the presence of
JOHN HEARBERT, ELIAS YATES
Recorded at the Instance of sd WM. BROWNE this 18th of Mar. 1689

pp. 114-116 TO ALL XPIAN PEOPLE to whom these presents shall come JAMES ORCHARD of the County of Rappa and MARY his Wife send greeting. Know yee that we the sd JAMES ORCHARD and MARY his Wife for sum of Nine thousand Eight hundred pounds of tobb: and caske in hand paid have granted certain tract of land contayning One hundred fifteen acres being in the County of Rappa and on the N. W. side of a Creek comonly called CHEST CREEKE One hundred fifteen acres unto sd GEO: LUKE his heirs begining at the head of the sd Creek and extending up the same according to its severall courses to corner tree standing at the Marsh of Mr. JAMES HARRISON Spring Branch, from thence extending W. to line of marked trees to a small red Oake corner tree standing by the River, from thence South by the mouth of the sd Creek where it first began the said land being part of a Patent of Three hundred acres granted to Capt. JOHN WEIRE bearing date the last of March 16(blot) and by him sold unto WALTER WEIRE by Deed bearing date the 26th day of June 16(blot) and by him devised to his Relict, MARY WEIRE, as by his last Will and Testament in writing bearing date the 3d day 7ber 1673 sufficiently provided in due forme of Law and also one other Plantacon and tract of land conteyning fifty acres being in the County aforesd begining at an Oake corner tree standing at the head of Mr. JAMES HARRISONs Spring Branch being the same corner tree above menconed extending W: S: to above menconed small red Oake by Rappa. River from thence extending up the said River North West to the line that devides this land and the land of Mr. JAMES HARRISON finally down the sd line S. E. to the first begining Oake the same being part of a tract of land conteyning 250 acres taken up by the above menconed Capt. JOHN WEIRE and by him sold to above menconed WALTR. WEIRE and by the sd WALTR. WEIRE sold to Mr. GEO: JONES as by Deed bearing date the 12th of May 1677 and by sd GEO: JONES sold to the above menconed JAMES ORCHARD by Deed bearing date the 12 of September 1682, as by the severall above recited Deeds appeare To have and to hold the sd Tenement and Plantation and tracts of land with all houses buildings gardens marshes woods and hereditaments to same belonging unto GEO: LUKE his heirs and that they the said JAMES and MARY shall during their naturall lives and at the request and proper cost of him the sd GEO: LUKE make such further assurances in the land as he or his Councell learned in the Law advise In Witness whereof the sd JAMES and MARY have sett their hands and seales this fifth day of March ano dom 1689/90
Signed Sealed and delivered in the presence of

ROBT. BRENT, JAMES ORCHARD
HAWKINS SNEAD MARY sig: M ORCHARD

Recognitr in Cur Com Rappa 5 die Martii 1689
TO ALL XPIAN PEOPLE &c. MARY ORCHARD sends greetings Know yee that I the within menconed MARY ORCHARD hereby appoint in my name and stead and depute you Mr. ROBERT (blot)ENT to be my true and lawfull Attorney to acknowledge the within Deed unto Mr. GEO: LUKE and to act as if I myselfe were present and I do hereby confirm whatsoever you my Attorney shall act and do as Witness my hand and Seale this 5th day of March 1689/90

Signed Sealed and delivered in the presence of
HAWKINS SNEAD, MARY sig: M ORCHARD
ELIZA. S CAMPIAN

pp. 116-118 TO ALL XPIAN PEOPLE to whom these presents shall come I HAWKINS SNEAD of County of Rappa send Greeting. Know yee that I sd HAWKINS SNEAD for divers good causes and full and just sum of Two thousand and Two hundred pounds of good sound Tobb: & cask to him in hand paid have sold unto GEO: LUKE his heirs a certain parcell of land containing Eighty acres being in the County of Rappa and on the North side of Rappa. River begining at a red Oake standing by the MAIN ROAD extending thence South by East to a small Oake in line of WM. WEST the same being a corner tree thence extending alonge the sd WESTs line E. to the line that divides this eighty acres of land and One hundred acres sold out of the same devident to BENJAMIN SPOE by sd HAWKINS SNEAD and said 180 acres being devised to sd HAWKINS SNEAD by the last Will and Testament of CHARLES SNEAD deced, Father of sd HAWKINS SNEAD, as by the last Will and proved in due form of Law, the Eighty acres extending alonge the sd Deviding line to a small Hickory Corner tree to this land and of the sd SPOEs land, from thence South to the first beginning To have and to hold the sd Eighty acres of land with all rights to the sd GEO: LUKE his heirs with all woods waters pastures marshes sufficiently freed from all former grants In Witness whereof the sd HAWKINS SNEAD hath set his hand and Seale this 5th day of March 1689/90
Signed Sealed and Delivered in the presents of
ROBT. BRENT, HAWKINS SNEAD
JAMES ORCHARD
Recognitr in Cur Com Rappa 5 die Martii 1689

p. 118 March the 25th 1689/90. Yor: Petionr: DANIEL DOBYNS humbly craves a record for the marke of his hoggs and Cattle being as followeth (vizt) crop in both ears a like with a hole in the right and a slitt in the left Eare and shall pray &c.

pp. 118-120 THIS INDENTURE made the 24th day of August Ano Dom 1689 in the first yeare of the Reigne of our Sovereignes William & Mary &c. Between HENRY LUCAS & JANE his Wife of Farnham Parish and County of Rappa, Planter, of ye one part and JOHN BATTIN of the Parish and County, Plantr., of other part Witnesseth that sd HENRY LUCAS for sum of tobb: to him in hand pd. and for other good causes have sold unto JOHN BATTIN his heirs One hundred acres of land being in the Parish and County abovesd and on the North side of Rappa. River being part of the sd LUCASes Devidend (lying at the mouth of RICHARDSON CREEK) comonly called by the name of CLAPHAM PLANTACON Begining at ye mouth of a gutt on ye rivers bank at a small white Oake standing thereon and runing North West a small distance from ye River to a Stake by a great black river Oake, then North East to a Stake twixt two Dogwood trees, then South East to a stake by a Hickory and then South West to the place it began To have and to hold the sd One hundred acres of land with all appertinances belonging to the proper use and behoofe of him ye said JOHN BATTIN his heirs and assigns forever To have and to hold &c. ye aforesd land with appertinances without the lett of sd HENRY LUCAS or any other persons whatsoever and further HENRY LUCAS and JANE his Wife shall make acknowledgment before their Majesties Justices of the Peace for County of Rappa according to Law in that case provided In Witness of all and singular the premises thereof ye sd HENRY LUCAS and JANE his Wife hereunto set their hands and seales
Signed Sealed and Delivered in ye presence of us

JOHN Ī B BOWLES, HENRY LUCAS
ALEXANDR. SWAN,
ISABLE Mark ⊘ HERMANES
Recognitr in Cur Compt Rappa 2 die Aprill 1690

pp. 120-122 THIS INDENTURE made the 11th day of January 1689 and in the first yeare of ye Reigne of or: Soveraigne Lord and Lady William and Mary &c. Between Mr. HUMPHREY BOOTH and PHEBE his Wife of County of Rappa in Virginia of one part and HENRY NEWTON of sd County of other part Witnesseth ye sd HUMPHREY BOOTH and PHEBE his Wife for valuable consideracon in hand already received have sold unto HENRY NEWTON his heirs all his right whatsoever he have unto a certaine parcell of land conteyning One hundred acres of land included within the bounds hereafter mentioned (That is to say) begining upon a Gravely Run at a certain ROAD called by ye name of the CHURCH ROAD in Sittinburne Parish on ye South side ye River in ye County of Rappa. just where JERRED EVERS line crosses over the sd ROAD and so up along ye sd line till you meet with THOMAS DAVIS tree and then up along the uppermost line of sd HUMPHREY BOOTH to the land of RICHARD STOKES and down line of sd STOKES crossing ye said MAIN ROAD to his lower corner tree and from thence alonge the line of the sd lower till you meet with the sd CHURCH ROAD and so long the sd ROAD to the sd Gravelly Hill where you first began To have and to hold the land and every part there unto the sd HENRY NEWTON his heirs In Witness whereof the sd parties have sett their hands and fixed their seales
Signed sealed in the presents of us
THO: NEW, FRANCES NEW HUMPHREY BOOTH
SAMUEL his mark ⊹ GRIFFIN, JERRED EVERS PHEBE BOOTH
Recognitr in Cur Comt Rappa 2 die Aprill 1690
KNOW ALL MEN by these presents that I PHEBE BOOTH, Wife of HUMPHREY BOOTH of Rappa County in Virginia have made JOHN ALMOND my true and lawfull Attorney for me to acknowledge before Justices of the Peace sitting in Court for the County of Rappa one Deed of bargaine and Sale bearing date with these presents between sd HUMPHREY BOOTH and myself, PHEBE, of ye one part and HENRY NEWTON of the other pt. and also to relinquish all my right of dower to the sd land giving my sd Attorney full power and confirming whatsoever my said Attorney shall do In Witness I have hereunto set my hand & seale the 11th day of Janry. 1689
Signed Sealed and Delivered in ye presents of
JERRED EVERS, GEORGE LOYDE PHEBE BOOTH
GEORGE his mark ⨯ MURRELL

pp. 122-124 TO ALL XPIAN PEOPLE to whome these presents shall come Know yee wee EVAN DAVIS of County of Rappa. and JUDITH my Wife send Greeting. Know yee that sd EVAN DAVIS and JUDITH his Wife for divers good causes and especially the sum of Three thousand pounds of Tobb: in cask do hereby acknowledge have granted unto JOSHUA MASON of sd County his heirs all that parcell of land conteyning Two hundred acres to be made up the complement being in Rappa. County on the South side Rappa River and upon the Branches of PISCATAWAY CREEKE and begining at THOMAS WILLIAMSONs old field and runing thence along a line of JOHN COLEVOW and from thence alonge a line formerly belonging to THOMAS PATTYSON, thence up a Swamp called the GLADYE SWAMP, thence to the first mentioned place including the complement of Two hundred acres of land To have and to hold the sd bargained land and premises with all rights woods Mills houses and buildings with all profitts to him sd JOSHUA MASON his heirs paying therefore yearly unto our Dread Sovereign Lord the King his

heirs rents and services as shall become due In Witness whereof I sd EVAN DAVIS and JUDTIH my Wife have sett our hands and fixed our seales this Twenty ninth day of March 1690 and in the second yeare of the Reigne of their Majesties &c.
Sealed and delivered in presence of us

EDWARD ADCOCKE, EVAN Signum T DAVIS
HENRY ADCOCKE JUDITH Signum X DAVIS

Recognitr in Cur Comt Rappa 2 die Aprillis 1690

KNOW ALL MEN by these presents that I EVAN DAVIS am firmly bound unto JOSHUA MASON of same County in sum of Six thousand pounds of good Tobb: and caske as witness my hand and seale this Twenty ninth day of March 1690

The Condition of this obligation is that if EVAN DAVIS his heirs shall at all times warrant and defend ye title of Two hundred acres of land to JOSHUA MASON his heirs forever as by Deed may appear and by him the sd DAVIS and JUDITH his Wife make acknowledgment of ye said Deed in Rappahannock County Court next held for sd County that then the above obligation is void else to stand in full force
Signed sealed and delivered in presence of

EDWD. ADCOCKE, EVAN Signum + DAVIS
HENRY ADCOCKE

pp. 124-125 TO ALL XPIAN PEOPLE to whom these presents shall come I JOHN LACY of County of Rappa send Greeting. Know yee yt. I the sd JOHN LACY for divers good considerations and the sum of One thousand Six hundred pounds of good sweet sented Tobacco and caske have sold unto WILLIAM JEFFERYES of the same County his heirs all that parcell of land by estimation One hundred acres of land being in Rappa. County on the South side of Rappa. River and lying on North West side a branch containing in the sd One hundred acres of land an old feild formerly made by JOHN STANFORD late deced of this County, the sd branch being the So:So: East bounds of his One hundred acres of land as formerly granted to the sd JOHN STANFORD To have and to hold the sd land and premises with rights of hunting waters mills houses and other buildings with all profitts to him sd WILLIAM JEFFERYES his heirs and assigns forever paying yearly unto our Dred Sovereigne Lord ye King all such rents and services as shall become due In Witness whereof JOHN LACY have sett his land and Seal this 29th day of November 1689 and in the first yeare of the Reigne of their Majesties &c.
Signed and sealed in the presence of

HENRY ADCOCKE, JOSHUA Signum + LACY
RICHD. his mark X WARWICK
EDW. ADCOCKE

Recognitr in Cur Comt Rappa 2 die Aprilis 1690

p. 125 Vide Fol. 24). I LEONARD CHAMBERLAINE with the Consent of SUSANNA CHAMBERLANE do assigne all our right of within mentioned Bill of Sale of One hundred acres of land unto WILLIAM JOHNSON his heirs from us our heirs or any other person that may lay clame to and to acknowledge the sd land next Court held for South side of Rappa. County As Witness our hands and seales this sixth day of November 1689 Signed Sealed and Delivered in the presents of us

JAMES BOUGHAN, LEONARD CHAMBERLANE
THOMAS PETTIS SUSANNA CHAMBERLANE

Recognitr in Cur Comt Rappa 2 die Aprilis 1690

pp. 125-128 THIS DEED Indented made the Five and Twentieth day of January in ye yeare of our Lord God according to the Computation of the Church of England One thousand Six hundred Eighty and nine Between QUINTON SHERMAN of Parish of North Farnham in County of Rappa., Plantr., of ye one part and RICHARD DUDLEY ye Younger of ye same Prish and County, Plantr., of ye other part Witnesseth that QUINTON SHAREMAN for ye sum of Two thousand pounds of good sound merchantable Tobb: at and before sealing of these presents in hand paid doth hereby grant unto ye sd RICHARD DUDLEY the Younger a parcell of land being in the Parish and County above menconed beginning at a marked red Oak that parts the land of RICHARD DUDLEY ye Elder and the land above recited to be by these presents sold and runing up the line of one SAMUEL SANFORD adjoining to ye land of MARTIN SHAREMAN, Brother of the above named QUINTON SHAREMAN, thence runing down to a line of new marked trees which was markt by the consent of them the said QUINTON SHAREMAN and RICHD. DUDLEY ye Younger conteyning (blot) acres more or less with all appertiinances belonging being ye moiety of part of one hundred acres of land given to sd QUINTON SHAREMAN by QUINTON SHAREMAN, his Father, by Will as in and by ye sd Will relacon being had will appear To have and to hold the Fifty acres of land with the appertinances unto said RICHARD DUDLEY ye Younger his heirs In Witness whereof the sd above named QUINTON SHAREMAN hath sett his hand and seale

Sealed and Delivered in presents of

RICHARD JASPER RI the mark of QUINTON SHAREMAN
THOMAS DUDLEY, JAMES ELLIS

Recognitr inCur Comt Rappa 2 die Aprilis 1690

KNOW ALL MEN that I QUINTON SHAREMEN of ye Parish of North Farnham and County of Rappa am bound unto RICHD. DUDLEY the Younger of the same Parish and County in sum of Four thousand pounds of every way good sound mercht. tobacco dated this five and twentieth day of January One thousand Six hundred Eightie nine

The Condition of this obligation is if the above bound QUINTON SHAREMEN his heirs in all things do fully perform all covenants specified in one Deed indented between bounden QUINTON SHAREMAN of the one part and the abovesd RICHD. of the other part then this obligation to be void or else abide in full force

Sealed and Delivered in ye presence of

RICHARD the marke of RI JASPER QUINTON the marke of x SHAREMAN
THOMAS the marke of 0 DUDLEY
JAMES ELLIS

KNOW ALL MEN that I QUINTON SHAREMAN of County of Rappa in Parish of Farnham being now (blot) and not able to come to this present Court held for the County of Rappa doe hereby impower my friend, RALPH WHITEING, of TOTASKEY CREEKE in Rappa my lawfull attorney to acknowledge parcell of land by me sold to RICHD. DUDLEY JUNIOR for which land I have received satifaction ye sd land being markt out betwixt us and contayns Fifty acres for which sold unto said RICHARD DUDLEY JUNIOR I have passed bond under hand and seale and what my sd Attorney shall do I do hereby allow of In Witness I have sett my hand & seale this last day of April 1690

Teste PHILLIP HUNNINGS, QUINTON x SHERMAN
RICHARD JASPER his mark RI

p. 128 Mr. COLSTON Sir: This is to request you to record my marke (Vizt) a swallow forke in ye left and a cropt and hole in ye right and shall oblige me to make satisfaction and remain your Servant

THOS: DAVIS

Mr. COLSTON Sir: record the marke of WILL: JEFFERYES JUNIOR crop and hole in ye right eare and a crop and slitt in ye left eare

p. 128 I the Subscriber doe by these presents give one Cow called by name of Primrose being black of colour and cropt off both eares upper keele of the right and under keele of the left to my Son, JOHN BALL, with all her increase forever, as Witness my hand this 2nd day of Aprill 1690

WILLIAM his marke O BALL

p. 129 GRIFFIN ROBERT. I gave yor Daughter, ALICE, a cow calfe which since is increase to a pretty quantity and because I would have her be sure of them I send you these that you may have my Gift put upon the Record to her and heirs forever, with all the increase

yr. Loveing friend Apl: 2nd 1690 MARGARETT & THOMPSON
Witness WILL: TAYLOR

pp. 129-130 TO ALL &c. I FRANCIS LORD HOWARD Barron of Effingham his Majesties Lieut. Governor Genll. of Virginia &c. Whereas &c. Now know yee yt. I sd FRANCIS LORD HOWARD &c. accordingly give unto Mr. JOSEPH GOODRICH, WILLIAM BALL and JOHN PRICE of Rappa County Six hundred Twenty nine acres of land in ye sd County and bounded Begining at a stooping white Oake corner tree belonging to the sd GOODRICH runing North along ye sd line to a corner white Oake now made by THOMAS HARPERs line on the head of a mossey branch, thence West to another corner white Oake, thence South by West along HARPERs line to a corner stooping white Oake of the sd HARPERs being a scrubby tree at ye head of a deep Vally, thence West along another of ye sd HARPERs lines to Collo: HILLs line to a small black Oake corner tree now made, thence West South along Colo. HILLs line to a small black Oake in ye said line, thence South East to a corner white Oake being a scrubby tree by the INDIAN PATH side thence South to West on a levell neare a branch, thence East South East to ye edge of a Hill over a great branch to a corner red Oake now made thence East by North along an old continued line supposed to belong to JOSEPH JONES to a white Oake corner to Mr. JOSEPH GOODRICH, his northwesterly line, thence alonge ye said line North to a great corner white Oake by WILSONS PATH thence North East to the begining place, the said land being due &c. To have and to hold &c. to be held of our Sovereigne Lord the King &c. yeilding and paying &c. Provided &c. Given under my hand and Seale of the Colony this 21st of October 1684

EFFINGHAM

Recordr. NICHO: SPENCER

KNOW ALL MEN by these presents that wee WILLIAM BALL and JOHN PRICE of Rappa: County do assigne and make over all our right of the within mentioned Patent forever unto JOHN CLARKE of County aforesd. his heirs or assigns from ye day of ye date hereof forever as witness our hands the Eleventh day of October 1689

Test RICHARD BOND, WM. his O BALL
WILLIAM CLOVER JOHN his marke ## PRICE

Recognitr in Cur Comt Rappa 2 die Aprilis 1690

pp. 130-131 TO ALL CHRISTIAN PEOPLE to whom these presents shall come wee MATRUM and RUTH WRIGHT of ye County of Rappa send Greeting. Know ye that we said MATROM and RUTH WRIGHT for divers good causes but especially for a fitt and valued Exchange of a certain tract of Twelve hundred acres of land in aforesd County of Rappa obtained and agreed for with Mr. JOHN BARKER of County of NEW KENT as by a certaine obligation under his hand and seale bearing date with these presents will appeare have for ourselves our heirs sold and delivered and the severall Patents of the same do acknowledge have assured and will assigne unto sd Mr. JOHN BAKERof sd County all our right in all that our Plantacon and land in GLOCESTER COUNTY called by ye name of WINTER HARBOR but more especially all the land and Plantacons coneyned in a late Survey made by Coll. LAURENCE SMITH, Surveyor of sd County of GLOCESTER, on the Ninth day of November 1687 and the Patent for the same according to the said survey wee do promise ourselves to make over unto MR. JOHN BAKER his heirs and assigns so soone as he or they shall receive the same from ye Secretaries Office & make thenceforth sd Plantacons and lands wee the sd MATRUM and RUTH WRIGHT by warrant and averr wee have a good and lawfull right being vested in us and the heirs of the body of the sd RUTH as by the last Will and Testament of Mr. ROBERT GRIGGS, Father to the sd RUTH WRIGHT, that now is and further wee the sd MATRUM and RUTH WRIGHT for ourselves our heirs are become bound unto JOHN BAKER his heirs or assigns the sum of Five hundred pounds Sterling that he the sd JOHN BAKER his heirs shall hold all the premises without hindrance of us sd MATRUM and RUTH RIGHT our heirs whereof we hereunto sett our hands and seales this 4th day of December One thousand Six hundred Eighty and nine in the first yeare of the Reigne of our Sovereigne Lord and Lady William and Mary &c.

Signed sealed and delivered in presents of us

ROBERT BIRD, MATRUM WRIGHT
EDMUND TUNSTALL RUTH WRIGHT

Acknow: in Rappa County Court by MOTRAM WRIGHT and Mrs. RUTH WRIGHT personally the 2nd day April 1690. Recorded the 25th day of said month

pp. 131-132 TO ALL TO WHOM these presents shall come I FRANCIS MORISON Esqr. Governor and Capt: Genll. of Virginia &c. Whereas &c. Now know yee that I the sd FRANCIS MORISON &c. accordingly give and grant unto Mr. ROBERT GRIGGS and Mr. EDWARD WYATT Three hundred and seventy acres of land and Marsh being in ye Parish of Kinston and in County of GLOUCESTER bounding upon tract of land of JOHN SMITHs from a markt Pine No. W. and from a markt Gum running E.N.E. runing from GARDEN CREEK upon the BAY S. E. to place where wee first began the sd land being due &c. To have and to hold &c. To be held of our Sovereigne Lord the King &c. yeilding and paying &c. Provided &c. Given at JAMES CITTY under my hand and the Seale of the Colony this 19th of April 1662 and in the Fourteenth year of the Reigne of our Soveraigne Lord King Charles the Second &c.

FRANCIS MORYSON
THO: LUDWELL Sectry.

I EDW. WYATT doe assigne with the consent of my Wife all my right of this Patent of land within mentioned from me my heirs to ROBERT GRIGGS his heirs and assigns forever and doe oblige myselfe that my Wife shall acknowledge her consent in Court with me when it shall be required Witness our hands this 27th day of October One thousand Six hundred and Sixty three

Teste MATH: KEMP, EDWARD WYATT
JOHN his 6 marke WILKINSON JANE WYATT

Acknowledged in Court at GLOCESTER xber 16th 1663

Recordatr p THO: MORRIS Cl Cur Glo:

KNOW ALL MEN by these presents that wee MATRUM and RUTH WRIGHT do hereby assigne unto Mr. JOHN BAKER his heirs & assignes all our right to the within Patent with warranty from ye claime of us our heirs Witness our hands this 4th day of December 1689

Test ROBERT BIRD MATRUM WRIGHT
EDMUND TUNSTALL RUTH WRIGHT
Recordatr Teste WM. COLSTON
Acknow: in Rappa County Court by Mr. MATTRUM WRIGHT and by Mrs. RUTH WRIGHT personally the 2nd day of April 1690 and recorded the 25th day of sd month and year
Teste WM. COLSTON Cl Cur

pp. 132-133 TO ALL TO WHOM these presents shall come I Sr. WILLIAM BERKLEY Knt. Governor and Capt. Genll. of Virginia &c. and Whereas &c. Know yee that I the sd Sr. WILLIAM BERKLEY Kt. &c. accordingly give unto ROBERT GRIGGS Two hundred and fifty acres of land lying in WINTER HARBOR Begining at a markt tree on the BAY side and runing Westerly up the Creek and North West by markt trees dividing this land from another parcell of land belonging to sd GRIGGS, North East to the markt tree of CHARLES SALLACEs and by the sd SALLACEs tree South East of a Creek & down the Creeke where the Creeke divides this line and the land of the sd SALLACEs, South to the markt tree first specified the sd land being formerly granted to WALTER RICHARD by Patent bearing date the first day of June 1654 and by sd WALTER RICHARD sett over to sd ROBERT GRIGGS To have and to hold &c. to be held of our Sovereign Lord the King &c. yeilding and paying &c. Provided &c. Given at JAMES CITTY under our hand and the Seale of the Colony this eighteenth day of March 166(blot) and in the Fifteenth yeare of the Reigne of our Soveraigne Lord King Charles the second &c.
ROBERT GRIGGS Patent for 252 acres of land
Teste FRA: KIRKMAN WILLIAM BERKLEY
Recordatr 1st of April 1665 Teste PHILL. LUDWELL CC. C. Off

KNOW ALL MEN by these presents that wee MATRUM and RUTH WRIGHT do hereby assigne over unto Mr. JOHN BAKER his heirs all our right to the within Patent with warranty from the claime of us our heirs Witness our hands this 4th day of December 1689
Teste ROBERT BIRD,
EDMUND TUNSTALL Recordt. Teste WM. COLSTON Cl Cur

p. 133 TO ALL TO WHOM these presents shall come I FRANCIS MORISON Esqr. Governr. and Capt. Genrll. of Virginia &c. Whereas &c. Know yee that I sd FRANCIS MORYSON Esqr. &c. accordingly give and grant unto WILLIAM SMART Four hundred and fifty acres of land lying in WINTER HARBOR begining at a marked Pine of JOHN SMITHs lane and runing along the sd SMITHs marked trees North West to the markt Pine first specified the said land being formerly granted to one THOMAS TODD by Patent dated the 27th of October 1652 and by assigned to the sd WM. SMART and now removed in his Majesties name by order of the Quarter Court To have and to hold &c. to be held of our Sovereign Lord the King &c. yeilding and paying &c. Provided &c. Given at JAMES CITTY under my hand and ye Seale of ye Colony this 20th of November 1661 and in the Thirtieth yeare of the Reigne of our Sovereigne Lord King Charles ye second
FRANCIS MORRYSON
Recordatr 1st April 1665 THO: LUDWELL Secr:
Acknowledged in Court by Mr. TOD who sold ye land within mentioned unto Mr. ROBERT GRIGGS and hath acknowledged the sale thereof at a Court holden for GLOCESTER February 17th 1661
Teste THO: MORRIS D. C.
KNOW ALL MEN by these presents that we MATRUM and RUTH WRIGHT do hereby assigne over unto Mr. JOHN BAKER his heirs or assigns all our right the within Pattent

with warranty from ye claim of us our heirs Witness our hands this 4th day of December 1689

Teste ROBERT BIRD MATRUM WRIGHT
EDMUND TUNSTALL RUTH WRIGHT

Recorded WM. COLSTON Cl. Cur

Acknowl. in Rappa County Court by Mr. MOTTRUM WRIGHT and Mrs. RUTH WRIGHT his Wife personally the 2nd of April 1690 and recorded the 25th said month and yeare

Teste WM. COLSTON Cl Cur

pp. 133-135 KNOW ALL MEN by these presents that I JAMES ORCHARD and MARY his Wife of ye County of Rappa for a valuable consideration already received by us of THO: BRADLY, Carpenter, of County of Rappa. have sold THO: BRADLY his heirs a certain tract of land being in County of Rappa on North West side of the Main Run of RAPPA CREEKE and bounded begining at a white Oake at the head of a branch in the line that is between ELIAS WILSON and JAMES ORCHARD and runing thence down the sd Branch to another line of sd ORCHARD and thence along the sd line East and South to a red Oake corner tree of sd JAS. ORCHARD standing in the land of JOHN GARTON neer a Pockikery that is corner tree of sd GARTONs, thence along line of the land of sd ORCHARD and THO: NORTON South to a red Oake that is now a corner tree between ELIAS WILSON and JAMES ORCHARD, thence along the sd line West by North to the first menconed white Oake being One hundred acres of land To have and to hold the sd Woodland ground with the appertinances belonging unto sd THO: BRADLY his heirs and further sd JAMES ORCHARD and MARY his Wife do oblige ourselves that sd THO: BRADLY shall forever quietly enjoy sd land without hindrance of us JAMES ORCHARD and MARY my Wife and heirs In Witness whereof we have sett our hands and seals this Twenty sixth day of April in the second yeare of the Reign of our Soveraigne Lord and Lady King Wm. and Queen Mary sixteen hundred and ninety

Signed sealed and Delivered in ye presents of us

ELIAS WILSON, JAMES ORCHARD
JAMES HUGHGALE MARY her M marke ORCHARD

Recognitr in Cur Comt Rappa 7 die May 1690

KNOW ALL MEN by these presents that I MARY ORCHARD, Wife of JAMES ORCHARD, do appoint my loveing friend, DAVID STERN, to be my true and lawfull Attorney to acknowledge my part of a parcell of land sold to THOMAS BRADLEY granted by my sd Husband and what my sd Attorney doth do to be as ample as if I were there in Court myself as Witness my hand and seale this 6th day of May 1690

Signed sealed and delivered in the presents of us

JOHN SEARLE, MARY her M marke ORCHARD
REES EVANS

pp. 135-137 THIS INDENTURE made the Third day of March in year according to the computation of the Church of England One thousand Six hundred eighty and nine between ZACHARIAS NICCOLLS of ye Parish of North Farnham in County of Rappa., Plantr., of one part and HENRY CLARKE of same Parish and County, Plantr., of other part Witnesseth that sd ZACHARIAS NICCOLLS for sum of seven thousand pounds of Tobba: to him paid hath granted unto sd HENRY CLARKE his heirs his peice of Woodland ground being in the Parish and County abovesd nere a Mill there called TOTASKEY MILL upon a branch there called the MILL MAINE BRANCH begining at a markt pokikory standing in a small valley the head of a small branch issuing into the sd MILL MAINE BRANCH thence runing into the woods South and by East to containe a square in length and breadth the full quantity of Two hundred acres with all the appertinances unto the same belonging To have and to hold the Two hundred acres of land above granted unto HENRY CLARKE his heirs and assigns forever and that sd ZACHARIAS NICCOLLS will at all times hereafter upon the request and charge of HENRY CLARKE his heirs further do make lawfull act for more perfect assuring of the lands and premises menconed unto sd HENRY CLARKE his heirs In Witness whereof the above named ZACHARIAH NICCOLLS to this present hath sett his hand and seale

Sealed and Delivered in presents of us

CHRISTOPHER NEALE JUNIOR ZACHARIAH NICKOLS

GEORGE LAMKIN, JAMES ELLIS

Recognitr in Cur Comt Rappa 7 die Maii 1690

pp. 137-138 KNOW ALL MEN by these presents yt. I GEORGE LAMBERT of County of Rappa with the consent of JOYCE my Wife do for Fifteen hundred pounds of Tobacco to me secured grant unto THO: BARTLETT of County aforesd his heirs a certain tract of land conteyning fifty acres more or less being in the Freshes of Rappa. and on the South side of the River being on the North and West side on HEN: LONG and dividing the sd GEORGE LAMBERT by a line of markt trees runing Easterly through a Glade to a red Oake corner tree of THO: THARP, thence down the sd Branch according to its severall courses to a line of THOS: THARPs ye said Land to have and to hold with all profits whatsoever as may collect out of Patent without any lett from me the sd GEO: LAMBERT my heirs or any persons whatsoever under me In confirmacon thereof we have hereunto sett our hands and seals this 9th day of December 1689

GEORGE Signum LAMBERT

Signed Sealed and Delivered in the presents of us

FRAN: SLAUGHTER, SAMLL. WARD

Recognitr in Cur Comt Rappa 7 die Maii 1690

pp. 138-139 KNOW ALL MEN by these presents that I JAMES JACKSON of Parish of Cittinburne in ye County of Rappa, Planter, for a valuable consideracon (vizt) the sum of Fifteen hundred pounds of good Tobacco and caske to me in hand paid by PITHAGORAS POWELL of aforesd Parish and County, Plantr., doe sell unto PITHAGORAS POWELL his heirs a certain tract of land conteyning Seventy and one acres being in Parish and County aforesd and on the North side the River some Nineteen outes back in the woods Begining at a Spanish Oake corner tree of GREENes in line of CLOTHWORKERs and runing along sd CLOTHWORKERs line to a Hickory sapling in a Deep Branch in line of Mr. HARRISON, thence along his line W. to a white Oake corner tree to a Gum upon a hill on a Branch corner tree of Mr. HARRISON, thence over the branch W. to a white Oake corner tree of Mr. GREEN, thence along sd GREENs line S. E. to the first mentioned Spanish Oake To have and to hold the sd Seventy and one acres of land with all the appertinances belonging to him sd PITHAGORAS POWELL his heirs without the lett of me sd JAMES JACKSON my heirs and I do further oblige myself to acknowledge this Deed in the County Court of Rappa within six months and also that I will cause my Wife to do the same either by her self or Lawfull Attorney In Confirmacon I have sett my hand and seale this second day of May 1690

Signed sealed and delivered in presents of us

JAMES HARRISON, JAMES JACKSON

JOHN BALL

Recognitr in Cur Comt Rappa 7 die Maii 1690

KNOW ALL MEN by these presents that I SUSANNA JACKSON, Wife of JAMES JACKSON, do appoint my loving Friend, Mr. JAMES HARRISON, to be my lawfull Attorney for me to acknowledge at the Court of Rappa County my part of a parcell of land sold by my Hus-

band, JAMES JACKSON, to PITHAGORAS POWELL as by Deed may appear As Witness my hand and seale this 6th day of May One thousand six hundred and ninety
Signed Sealed and Delivered in presents of us

SUSANNA her S mark JACKSON

pp. 139-140 THIS DEED INDENTED made this nine and twentieth day of April in year of our Lord according to the computation of the Church of England One thousand Six hundred Eighty and nine Between JOHN LANDMAN of County of WESTMORELAND of one part and WILLIAM HASSELL of the County of Rappa of other part Witnesseth that JOHN LANDMAN for Four thousand pounds of every way good and sound well conditioned Tobacco to him in hand paid hath sold unto WILLIAM HASSELL a parcell of land being in Parish of Farnham in County of Rappa on the North side of a Creek there called TOTASKEY CREEKE at the head of same Creek between two Swamps and binding upon the Poccoson conteyning One hundred acres which sd One hundred acres of land is part of a tract formerly purchased by one WILLIAM LANDMAN, Father of the abovesd JOHN LANDMAN, of one EDWARD LEWIS as by the Deed relation being thereunto had will appeare To have and to hold the hundred acres of land unto WILLIAM HASSELL his heirs and sd JOHN LANDMAN for himselfe his heirs grant with the sd WILLIAM HASSELL his heirs by these presents that sd JOHN LANDMAN and ELIZABETH his Wife on or before the Seventh day of August next ensuing the date hereof in Rappa County before the Justices then and there sitting in Open Court acknowledge this psent Deed and also all their right of Dower thirds or otherwise to the land above menconed In Witness whereof sd JOHN LANDMAN hath sett his hand and Seale the day and year abovesd
Signed sealed and delivered in ye presents of

MILES GOWHAM, JOHN LANDMAN
GEORGE LAMKIN, JAMES ELLIS

Recognitr in Cur Comt Rappa 7 die Maii 1690

KNOW ALL MEN by these presents that I ELIZABETH LANDMAN, Wife of the within named JOHN LANDMAN, do hereby acknowledge my consent to the Deed within and also to release my right and Interest of Dower and thirds of the land within menconed to be sold unto the within sd WILLIAM HASSELL his heirs Witness my hand this Thirtieth day of June 1689

Witness PETER SMITH SENIOR, ELIZABETH + LANDMAN
JAMES ELLIS the marke of

KNOW ALL MEN by these presents that I ELIZABETH LANDMAN, the Wife of JOHN LANDMAN, of ye County of WESTMORELAND do appoint my good friend, JOHN COLE, my lawfull Attorney for me to the next Court to be holden for County of Rappa in open Court before their Maties Justices of the Peace to acknowledge my consent to a Deed of Sale to land sold by my Husband, JOHN LANDMAN, to one WILLIAM HASSELL lying neer TOTASKEY CREEKE in the County abovesd and I doe ratifie to be as firm and stable in the Law as if I myself had been personally present and done the same Witness my hand and seale this Three and twentieth day of Apl. 1690
Signed Sealed and Delivered in the presence of

GEORGE LAMKINS, ELIZABETH + LANDMAN
SAMUEL S RUSKE, JAMES ELLIS her marke

pp. 141-142 KNOW ALL MEN by these presents yt. RICHARD DYSON of County of Rappa. of the Parrish of Sittenburne doe with the consent of CHRISTIAN my Wife and Father VALL ALLEN and MARY his Wife for the valuable consideration of Six thousand pounds of Tobo: at hand received grant unto JAMES BOULWARE of County and

Parish aforesd his heirs Four hundred and fifty acres of land lying in County of Rappa on the South side of the River and upon the branches of POPOMAN RUN beginning at Pokkery near the old line and extending thence nigh the old crooked line West to a small red Oake by a PATH side, thence North crossing the head branch of POPOMAN and to three Maples in the Head of the BUCKEN BRANCH, thence South East to a saplin near two white Oakes, thence South to the first menconed tree the sd Four hundred and fifty one acres of land with all its rights and privilidges To have and to hold from sd DYSON my heirs in as large maner as may be collected out of the Patent without hindrance of me the sd RICHARD DISON my heirs or any persons claiming under me my heirs to the sd JAMES BOULWARE, ye sd JAMES BOULWARE paying ye rights and services from hence forth due of right accustomed and in confirmacon hereof I sd DISON do bind myself to acknowledge the said land to the sd JAMES BOULWARE his heirs in the County Court of Rappa when demanded In Witness whereof we the parties above menconed have sett our hands and seales the 3d December 1689 being part of a tract of land formerly belonging to THOMAS PAGE Patent of 3075 acres

Signed sealed and delivered in ye presence of

FRAN: SLAUGHTER, — RICHARD Signum R DISON
WARWICK Signum W GRAY — CHRISTIAN Signum X DISON
VALENTINE ALLEN
MARY ALLEN

Recognitr in Cur Comt Rappa 7 die May 1690

KNOW ALL MEN by these presents that I RICHARD DYSON of County of Rappa of the Parish of Sittenburne my heirs stand indebted unto JAMES BOULWARE his heirs of the County and Parish aforesd in sum of Twenty thousand pounds of good tobacco in cask to be paid on all demands Sealed with my Seal 3rd day of Decr. 1689

The Condition of this obliglation is that if the above bounden RICHARD DYSON his heirs and all persons whatsoever by or under sd DISON doe suffer sd JAMES BOULWARE his heirs without any molestation quietly to enjoy a parcell of land qt. 451 acres as by a conveyance may appear bearing date ye third day of December 1689 bought of the sd DYSON for a valuable consideracon by sd JAMES BOULWARE this bond to be void otherwise to remain in full force

Signed Sealed and delivered in the presence of

FRAN: SLAUGHTER, — RICHARD Signum R DISON
WARWICK Signum W GRAY — CHRISTIAN Signum + DISON

pp. 142-143 THIS INDENTURE made the Third day of March One thousand Six hundred Eighty and nine and in the second yeare of the Reigne of our Sovereigns Lord and Lady William and Mary &c. Between NATHANIEL CALE of Parish of Farnham & County of Rappa in Virginia of one part and JOHN PHILLIPS of Parish and County aforesd. on the other pt., Witnesseth that sd NATHANLL. CALE for divers goods and chattels (to the value of Five thousand five hundred pounds of tobb: and cask) to him in hand well and truly paid have sold unto sd JOHN PHILLIPS Ihis heirs One hundred acres of land being in Parish and County aforesd and being part of a Patent for Six hundred acres and taking in a part of the Plantacon whereon sd PHILLIPS now lives Beginning at a Stake in a Marsh and runing along the line that parts the sd CALEs land and the sd PHILLIPS his land, South West to MORATTICO CREEKE then up the North side of said Creeke its several courses in a strait line to a white Oake and red Oake corner trees, then North West to a red Oake and chesnut corner tree standing in the foot of a branch of a little Creek that parts the plantation of sd PHILLLIPS and WM. SMITH, then down the Run of the sd Branch untill it meets with the sd Little Creeke and then down the sd little Creeke to the aforesd Stake where it first began & also all profitts and appertinances appertayning To have and to hold unto JOHN PHILLIPS his heirs subject nevertheless the quit rents from henceforth shall grow due In Witness whereof the sd parties have sett their hands and seales

Signed Sealed and Delivered in presence of

EDWIN CONWAY, NATHANIEL CALE

THOMAS the marke of B BRYANT

Recognitr in Cur Comt Rappa 7 die Maii 1690

p. 144 (On margin: The originall so torne that in all parts to (blot)er Read)

TO ALL &c. I Sr. WM. BERKLEY Knt. Capt: Genll. of Virginia &c. Whereas &c. Now know yee &c. do accordingly give and grant unto RICHARD REYLEY four hundred acres of land begining at a marked Oake at the head of a Branch in WINTER HARBOR nere NEW POINT COMFORT runing according to marked trees North East by East to the BAYSIDE South to the mouth of the sd Branch, Westerly up the sd Branch to the first specified tree paying &c. Provided &c. Given under my hand and the Seale of the Colony this 29th day of July 1652

WM. BERKLEY

Wee MOTTRUM and RUTH WRIGHT do hereby assigne over unto JOHN BAKER his heirs all our right and interest to the with in Patent with warranty from the claim of us our heirs Witness our hands this 4th day of 10ber 1689

ROBT. BIRD, EDMD. TUNSTALL

Acknow. in Rappa County Court by MOTTRUM WRIGHT and RUTH WRIGHT in Rappa County Court the 2nd day of Apri. 1690 and recorded the 2d day of June following

Teste WM. COLSTON Cl Cur

pp. 144-145 TO ALL CHRISTIAN PEOPLE to whome these presents shall come Know yee yt. we VALL. ALLEN and MARY my Wife of the Parish of Sittenburne and County of Rappa meerly out of the affection and love we bear and for other good causes give and make over unto my Son, RICHARD DISON and Daughter, CHRISTIAN DISON, their heirs forever Four hundred and Fifty one acres of land according to a Survey for the same made by WILLIAM MOSELEY will appear bearing date the 22nd day of November 1689, ye sd land with all its rights and priviledges being part of a devident of land taken up by my Father, THO. PAGE, as will appear by a Patent bearing date the Third of April 1667, wee firmly and clearly as before exprest unto my Son and Daughter, RICHD. and CHRISTIAN DISON, their heirs from us our heirs and we do bind ourselves to acknowledge this Deed in ye Court of Rappa to our abovesd Son and Daughter to the true performance of each particular mentioned in this Deed we have hereunto sett our hands and seales the 29th of November 1689

Signed Sealed and Delivered in ye presents of us

JAMES BOULWARE, VALLENTINE ALLEN

FRAN: SLAUGHTER MARY ALLEN

Recognitr in Cur Comt Rappa 7 die Maii 1690

pp. 145-149 THIS DEED INDENTED made the Two and Twentieth day of February in yeare of our Lord God according to the computation of the Church of England One thousand six hundred Eighty and nine Between ABRAHAM COOKE of Parish of North Farnham in County of Rappa, Plantr., of one part and JOHN MORGAN of same County and Parish, Blacksmith, of other part Witnesseth that ABRAHAM COOKE for the full sum of Two thousand pounds of every way good sound merchantable to him in hand paid by JOHN MORGAN sd ABRAHAM COOKE doth sell unto JOHN MORGAN his heirs all that my parcell of land being in Parish and County abovesd on the West side of a Creek there called TOTASKEY CREEKE conteyning Fifty acres being the moiety or half of a parcell of land formerly purchased by one WILLIAM CLAYTON deced of one WM. LANDMAN deced as by Deed relation being thereunto had may appear which sd Fifty acres of land to be sold sd ABRAHAM COOKE had of the Deed of WILLIAM CLAYTON, Son of the above named WILLIAM CLAYTON deceased, as by the Deed relation being had and it doth appeare To have and to hold the Fifty acres of land with all the appertinances belonging unto the said JOHN MORGAN his heirs In Witness whereof the above named ABRAHAM COOKE to these presents Deeds indented hath sett his hand and seale

Sealed and Delivered in the presents of

THO: LEWIS, ABRAHAM COOKE
THOMAS the marke of T GLADMAN
JAMES ELLIS

Recognitr in Cur Comt Rappa 7 die Maii 1690

Sealed and Delivered peaceably and quiet possession of the land within menconed to be sold was had and taken by within ABRAHAM COOKE and imediately by him delivered to the within written in the Presents of THOMAS LEWIS, JAMES ELLIS

KNOW ALL MEN by these presents that MARTHA COOKE, Wife of the within named ABRAHAM COOKE, doe hereby give my free consent to the Deed within written and also do relinquish all my right of Dower and thirds in the land within menconed unto the within said JOHN MORGAN his heirs and assigns Witness my hand the day and year fist written

Witness the marke of DEBRAH DB BRAMHAM, MARY MC COOKE
THOMAS LEWIS the marke of

KNOW ALL MEN by these presents that I MARTHA COOKE, the Wife of ABRAHAM COOKE, of County of Rappa., Planterk made my good friend, JOHN COLE, my true Attorney before the Justices of the Peace for County of Rappa to acknowledge my free assent to Deed made between my Husband, ABRAHAM COOKE, of the one part and one JOHN MORGAN of other part and there relinquish all my right of Dower and thirds to the land I do hereby confirm the same as if I myself had been there present Witness my hand and seale this Two and Twentieth day of February in year One thousand Six hundred Eighty and nine Sealed and Delivered in the presents of

DEBO: the marke of DB BRAMHAM, MARY the mark of C COOKE
THOS. LEWIS

KNOW ALL MEN that we ABRAHAM COOKE and WILLIAM CLAYTON both of County of Rappa., Planter, are bound unto JOHN MORGAN of said County and Blacksmith in sum of Five thousand pounds of every way good sound Mercht. tobacco to be paid dated the two and twentieth day of February in year One thousand Six hundred Eighty and nine

The Condicion is such that if they the above bound ABRAHAM COOKE and WILLIAM CLAYTON doe in all things keep the covenants in one Deed indented of conveyance between the above ABRAHAM COOKE of the one part and the above menconed JOHN MORGAN of the other part and also that if the above bounded ABRAHAM COOKE and MARTHA his Wife at some Court holden for the County aforesd within six months next in open Court before their Maties Justices of the peace then sitting acknowledge all her right of Dower and thirds in sd Deed unto JOHN MORGAN his heirs then this present obligation to be void else abide and remain in full force

Sealed and Delivered in the presents of

THOS: LEWIS, ABRAHAM COOKE
JAMES ELLIS, WILLIAM W CLAYTON
THOMAS T GLADMAN the marke of the marke of

p. 149 TO ALL XPIAN PEOPLE to whom these presents shall come Greeting. Know yee that I MARY ALLEN of the Parish of Cittenburne and County of Rappa doe mearely out of the affection and love I have and other good causes make over unto my Eldest Daughter, ELIZABETH BROWNE of same County and Parish, Four hundred Fifty and one acres of land according to a Survey made by Capt. WILLIAM MOSELEY, Surveyor of sd County, as will appear bearing date the 22nd of Novr. 1689, ye sd land with all rights being part of divident of land taken up by my Father, THOMAS PAGE, by Patent bearing date the third day of Apl. One thousand six hundred and sixty seaven I freely and absolutely give the same unto my Daughter, ELIZABETH, her heirs and to acknowledge the Deed of Gift in the County Court of Rappa unto my Daughter as aforesd to the true performance I have hereunto put my hand and seale this 29th day of November 1689

Signed sealed and delivered in the presents of us
FRAN: SLAUGHTER, MARY ALLEN
HUGH CRABB

Recognitr in Cur Comt Rappa 7 die May 1690

p. 150 KNOW ALL MEN by these presents that wee GEORGE LAMBERT and JOYCE LAMBERT of County of Rappa doe for ourselves our heirs sell a certain parcell of land unto HENRY LONG of sd County his heirs, the sd parcell of land conteyning Fifty acres is part of the Devidend of land I the sd GEORGE LAMBERT do now live on being in sd County of Rappa: on the South side of ye River of Rappa. in ye woods neare to BLACKBURNS CREEKE and joining the land I the sd LAMBERT sold to WILLIAM BROWNE and land I sold to THO: BARTLETT and the land of THOMAS KIRK also lying beyond a certain Swamp or Pond called the HUCCKLEBERRY POND it being all the land that I the sd GEORGE LAMBERT claim beyond the sd POND To have and to hold to sd HENRY LONG the sd parcell of land to him his heirs from us the sd GEORGE LAMBERT and JOYCE LAMBERT and our heirs To have hold and enjoy to him of a valuable consideracon to us in hand paid before the ensealing hereof. Witness our hands and seales this Seventeenth day of February 1689

Witness BERNARD GAINES, GEORGE GL LAMBERT
ROBERT JOHNSON the marke of

Recognitr in Cur Comt Rappa 7 die May 1690

p. 150 KNOW ALL MEN by these presents that I EDWARD JEFFERYES doe for a valuable consideracon in hand reced assign over from me my heirs and assigns forever unto JAMES ORCHARD his heirs all my right of a parcell of land bought by MATHEW KELLY of JOSEPH CHISWELL as by a Deed of Sale will appear bearing date ye 19th day of January 1672 and by sd KELLY made over to me, EDWARD JEFFERIES, as by an assignment bearing date the 2nd day of September in the year 1681 will appeare. In Testimony hereof I have sett my hand and seale the 6th day of May 1690

Signed Sealed and Delivered in the presents of us
REES EVANS, EDWARD EJ JEFFERYES
EDWARD THOMAS his marke

Recognitr in Cur Comt Rappa 7 die Maii 1690

p. 151 Mr. COLSTON Sr: This comes to request you to record for WM. DANGERFIELD two Cowes & encrease each ear a cropp two slitts and the middle peice taken out square a slitt under the right eare also for ANNE DANGERFIELD the same marke being a Gelt Staple with a slitt under the left eare two cows and encrease to them and their heirs if one dies without heires to fall to the other JOHN DANGERFIELD

p. 151 KNOW ALL MEN by these presents yt. I THOMAS GLADMAN doe for a considerable consideration to me paid doe assigne and sett over all my right to the land within mentioned to be sold with the appurtenances and also the Deed within written to ABRAHAM COOK his heirs and assigns forever Witness my hand this first day of February in year One thousand six hundred eighty & nine

Witness THOMAS LEWIS, THO: HALLUMNE, JAMES ELLIS — THOMAS the marke of GLADMAN

Recognitr in Cur Comt Rappa 7 die May 1690

KNOW ALL MEN by these presents that I KATHERINE GLADMAN, the Wife of THOMAS GLADMAN, of Rappa., Plantr., have made my good friend JOHN COLE my true and lawfull Attorney for me before their Maties Justices of the peace for the County aforesd in open Court sitting acknowledge my assent of a Deed of Sale of land made between my Husband THOMAS GLADMAN and ABRAHAM COOKE of the aforesd County bearing date the two and twenty of February One thousand six hundred eighty & nine for me to relinquish and release all my right of dower and thirds to sd land Witness my hand and seale this third day of March in year 1689

Sealed and delivered in ye presents of THOMAS LEWIS, RICHARD BRAMHAM — KATHERINE Signum GLADMAN

p. 152 KNOW ALL MEN by these presents yt. I JANE FRISTOE, Widdow in TOTASKEY CREEKE, in County of Rappa doe impower EDWARD JONES of ye sd County in the Parish of Farnham my lawfull Attorney for me to acknowledge unto RICHD. DUDLEY SENIOR at next Court held for the County of Rappa all my right of my thirds of a parcell of land sold by my said Son, QUINTON SHAREMAN, to the sd RICHD. DUDLEY JUNIOR for good consideration of one Ell of fine Holland granting to RICHD. DUDLEY JUNIOR his heirs all my right and title therein In Witness hereof I have sett my hand and seale this third day of February One thousand six hundred eighty and nine

Witness RICHARD DUDLEY, THOMAS ye marke of DUDLEY — JANE Signum FRISTOE

pp. 152-153 June Court 1690

TO ALL CHRISTIAN PEOPLE to whom these presents shall come I JAMES TAYLOR of ye Parish of St. Stevens in County of NEW KENT, Plantr., for divers good causes especially for his clearing planting and tending an acre of ground and the building a house for the Seating and Saving of a Patent of Seven hundred and Forty four acres of land to me granted and one bay Gelding to me in hand paid have for myselfe my heirs sold unto JOHN WAGGONER JUNR. his heirs or assignes forever One hundred acres of land being part of the Pattent relation being had which sd land is being in County of Rappa and Parish of Farnham begining at a marked corner dead Hickory with a small markt red Oake standing by it being a corner tree belonging to me the sd JAMES TAYLOR, JOHN MEADDOW and JOHN EVANS and standing by the side of a PATH adjoining to the land of JOHN MEADDOWs which he bought of EDMUND THACKER South West to a Pine and further along sd MEADDOWs line something more Westerly to a red Oake of ye sd JOHN MEADDOWes, thence South East along a line of markt trees two corner Oakes a red Oake and a Spanish Oake, thence South to a small red Oake sapling standing in a small vally being one of JOHN EVANS line trees parts him ye sd EVANS and TAYLER and thence along sd EVINS line North West to the place where it first began To have and to hold the abovesd One hundred acres of land with all the houseing orchards gardens woods belonging unto JOHN WAGGONER JUNR. his heirs, sd JOHN WAGGONER making and finishing planting and tending the abovesd acre of ground exprest being part of the consideration for ye above one hundred acres of land and also pay unto our Sovereigne Lord and Lady King Will and Queen Mary their heirs and Successors yearly rents as shall become due for the same, further I do oblige myself to acknowledge this my Deed with my Wifes acknowledgment of right of Dower in Rappa Court when it shall be held for South side of Rappa County either by herself or lawfull Attorney when required As Witness my hand and seale this fourth day of June One thousand Six hundred and Ninety

Signed sealed and delivered in presents of us

THO: WHEELER, JAMES TAYLOR
THOMAS PETTIS

Recognitr in Cur Comt Rappa 4 die Junii 1690

pp. 153-157 THIS INDENTURE made the ninth day of April in year of our Lord One thousand six hundred and Ninty and in the second year of the Reigne of our Soveraigne Lord and Lady William and Mary &c. Between Mr. JOHN JONES and MILLICENT his Wife of ye County of Rappa and Colony of Virginia Gent., of the one part and RICHARD EASTERBY of the same County and Collony, Planter, of the other part Witnesseth yt. ye sd Mr. JOHN JONES for and in consideration of one Horse and Three thousand five hundred pounds of Swt. tobacco and caske to him paid doth sell unto RICHARD EASTERBY his heirs all that parcel of land conteyning One hundred sixty and seven more or less being a dividend of land taken up and Patented by sd Mr. JOHN JONES as by the sd Patent bearing date ye 20th of April 1685 may appeare and bounded beginning at a white Oake in ye Forke of a Swamp called GREEN SWAMP and runing So. West to a white Oake, thence same course continued to a Spanish Oake at THOMAS TOZLEYs line, thence No. West to HUDSONS BRANCH along the aforesd TOZLEYs line to two corner trees the one a Locust ye other a red Oake where we meet Mr. WILLIAMSONs line, thence along that line East by North to an old corner Hickory of ye sd WILLIAMSON, thence No. by West to another Hickory on the brow of a Hill, thence East & North to a white Oake of ye sd Mr. WILLIAMSON the same course continued to a Spanish Oake thence to the place it first began including the aforesd quantity of One hundred sixty and seven acres of land more or less Together with all woods and timber standing and being To have and to hold the said Parcell of land and all priviledges unto the sd RICHARD EASTERBY his heirs and Mr. JOHN JONES and MILLICENT his Wife for themselves their heirs grant the sd RICHARD EASTERBY his heirs by force of these presents shall be lawfully seized in the bargained premises In Witness whereof sd JOHN JONES and MILLICENT his wife to these presents hath sett their hands and seales

Signed Sealed and delivered in the presents of

THOMAS his T marke DAVIS, JNO. JONES
GEORGE (Sign) POWELL MILLICENT JONES

Recognitr in Cur Comt Rappa 4 die Junii 1690

KNOW ALL MEN by these presents yt. I JOHN JONES of County of Rappa in ye Colony of Virginia Gent. doe standing firmly bound unto RICHARD EASTERBY of same County and Colony, Plantr., in ye sum of Nine thousand pounds of every way good substantial swt: Tobb: free from all manner of ground leaves trash and seconds with sufficient cask to conteyn the same to be paid convenient to Landing in Rappa County the wch payment I bind myself my heirs Sealed with my Seale this (blot) day of April 1690

The Condicon of the above obligation is such yt. if the above named RICHARD EASTERBY his heirs and every of them shall from henceforth forever peaceably and quietly have and enjoy all that parcell of land containing One hundred Sixty and seven acres in So. side Rappa. County back in the woods taken up and Pattented by ye above bound Mr. JOHN JONES as p Pattent bearing date the 20th of April 1685 may appeare without

the lett of the above bound Mr. JOHN JONES his heirs or any other person claiming title under sd Mr. JOHN JONES his heirs according to the meaning of a Deed of Sale bearing date with these presents then the above obligation to be void and of none effect otherwise to stand in full force As Witness my hand and seal this 9th day of April 1690
Signed Sealed and Delivered in presents of
THOMAS Sign T DAVIS, JNO. JONES
GEORGE Sign POWELL

KNOW ALL MEN by these presents that I MILLICENT JONES, Wife of JOHN JONES, of County of Rappa. do appoint my Friend, EDWARD THOMAS, to appeare for me at the next Court held for County aforesaid there in my name to acknowledge as my voluntary act and deed one Indenture for my right of Dower of One hundred sixty and seven acres of land whereunto I have sett my hand and seale bearing date the 9th of April 1690 unto RICHARD EASTERBY his heirs as by my sd Attorney shall lawfully doe I shall ratifie to be as firme as if I myselfe had been personally present. Witness my hand and seale 1st of June 1690
Signed Sealed and Delivd. in presents of us
GEORGE Signum POWELL, MILLICENT JONES
MARY the marke of M B BARTLETT
Recognitr et Record in Cur Comt Rappa 4 die Junii 1690

p. 157 TO ALL CHRISTIAN PEOPLE to whom these presents shall come I WILLIAM PRISE of ye County of Rappa, Plantr., send Greeting. Know yee that I WILLIAM PRISE as well for ye naturall effection and fatherly love which I bear unto my well beloved Daughter in Law, MARTHA DAVIS, as also for divers causes have hereby given unto MARTHA DAVIS one Mare about six or seven years old and one Cow which are to be delivered when she attains ye age of Twenty and one years or at the time of Marriage or which of them shall happen first and furthermore I sd WILLIAM PRISE do freely give unto sd MARTHA DAVIS one Chest, one iron pott, pott hooks and a Diaper table cloth and six diaper napkins, one large hammock and a pair of Sheets with two pewter dishes and six pewter plates, two brass candlesticks and a pewter flagon and one pewter bason and a small silver spoon to her the sd MARTHA DAVIS forever to enjoy without any matter of claim of sd WILLIAM PRISE or any other person in my name without any thing of value to be payed unto me sd WILLIAM PRISE my heirs and I the sd WILLIAM PRISE all and singular the aforesd Goods and Chattels and promise to the sd MARTHA DAVIS her heirs to the use aforesd doe warrant and forever defend by these presents as Witness my hand and seale this 3rd day of June 1690
Signed Sealed and Delivered in ye presents of us
BERNARD GAINES, WILLIAM ye marke of PRISE
JOHN VICHICE
Recognitr in Cur Comt Rappa 4 die Junii 1690

p. 158 KNOW ALL MEN by these presents that I WM. BOULWARE of County of Rappa. together with ELIZABETH my Wife doe for a good and valuable consideration in hand received for me my heirs and assigns firmly bargain and sell unto TIMO: DAVIS of the sd County his heirs and assigns forever One hundred and fifty acres of land in said County of Rappa on the South side the River being part of a greater tract of land granted by Pattent to THO: PAGE and by him assigned unto me the sd WM. BOULWARE and my Brother, JAMES BOULWARE, the sd One hundred and fifty acres of land to begin on the back line of Mr. MARTIN JOHNSON and runing on the sd JOHNSONs line to the line of Mr. LUCAS, then runing into the woods in the COUNTY ROAD then along the sd ROAD in the land whereon SAMLL. WARD now liveth but if these bounds shall not conteyne the full complemt. of One hundred and fifty acres to go over the ROAD next to the land of SAMLL. WARD for the residue to compleateth it and the sd hundred and fifty acres we do warrant from us our heirs and assigns unto the sd TIMO: DAVIS his heirs and assigns forever for the true performance hereof we hereunto sett our hands and seals this 26th day of February 1688

Sealed and Delviered in the presents of

ROBT. PLEY, WM. BOULWARE
GEO: PLEY, WM. HARPER ELIZABETH BOULWARE

Recognitr in Cur Comt Rappa 4 die Junii 1690

BE IT KNOWNE unto all men by these presents that I ELIZ. BROWNE of County of Rappa have made and appointed my trusty and well beloved friend, JOHN WILLIAMS, of the same County my true and lawfull attorney for me in my name to acknowledge my thirds of parcell of land unto TIMO: DAVIS of sd County, Taner, and what my sd Attorney shall lawfully doe to be as good in the Law as if I had done the same in my own person As Witness my hand and seale this 1st day of April 1689

Sealed and Delviered in presents of

WM. HARPER ELIZ. BOULWARE
DAVID RAINE

Recognitr in Cur Comt Rappa 4 die Junii Ano 1690

p. 159 KNOW ALL MEN by these presents that I SAMLL. GRIFFIN and MARY my Wife of County of Rappa: in Virginia, Ship Wright, for and in consideracon of Fifteen pounds Sterling already in hand received have sold unto JAMES FULLERTON of the aforesd County his heirs Two hundred acres of land being in the aforesaid County it being part of the land formerly belonging to JAMES FULLERTON and by the sd FULLERTONs Will given unto sd MARY GRIFFIN, Daughter of the aforesd FULLERTON, which Two hundred acres of land I the sd SAMLL. GRIFFIN do bind myself my heirs unto the aforesd JAMES FULLERTON JUNR. his heirs in the just sum of One hundred pounds Sterling to warrant the sd land from the claim of all manner of persons that may lay any clame and likewise to acknowledge this Deed in Rappa Court with my Wife when ever required by the aforesd FULLERTON his heirs To the true performance of the same I bind myself my heirs unto the aforesd FULLERTON JUNR. his heirs and assigns As Witness our hands and seales this 4th day of June 1690

Teste JAMES BAUGHAN, SAMLL. his mark S GRIFFIN
RICHARD COVINGTON MARY + GRIFFIN

Recognitr in Cur Comt Rappa 4 die Junii 1690

pp. 159-160 KNOW ALL MEN by these presents that I RALPH NELL with the consent of my Wife, ANN, do by these presents make over all our right of the within menconed Bill of Sale with warranty to HENRY PRICKETT and the sd PRICKETT his heirs forever and to acknowledge the same in Rappa Court when required as Witness our hands this 5th day of February 1689/90

Test THO: GANES, RALPH NELL
ANN Sig A GANES, WM. JOHNSON ANN NELL

Recognitr in Cur Comt Rappa 4 die Junii 1690

p. 160 KNOW ALL MEN by these presents that I RALPH NELL with consent of my Wife, ANN, do assign to HENRY PRIKETT his heirs or assigns with warranty and to acknowledge this same in Rappa Court when required as Witness my hand and seale this 6th day of Febry 1689/90

Teste THO: GANES, ANN Sig A GANES, RALPH NELL
WM. JOHNSON ANN NELL
Recognitr in Cur Comt p NELL and ANNAM uxorem 4 die Junii 1690

pp. 160-161 KNOW ALL MEN by these presents that I RICHARD BERRY of County of Rappa do for a good and valuable consideracon in hand received do for me my heirs firmly sell unto WILLIAM BOULWARE his heirs and assigns forever One hundred and fifty acres of land bounding upon Brother, HENRY BERRY, and upon the land of Mr. JAMES KEY, and on my own land and upon the land of ROBT. PECK To have and to hold the sd land with warranty from me my heirs To have and to hold at all times to him his heirs and to the true performance hereof I have hereunto sett my hand & seal this 6th day of September 1687
Signed Sealed and Delivered in the presents of us
JOSEPH RUTTER, RICHARD his RB mark BERRY
HENRY BERRY, TIMO: DAVIS
Recognitr in Cur Comt Rappa 4 die Junii 1690
KNOW ALL MEN by these presents that I RICHARD BERRY of Rappa. do appoint JOHN WILLIAMS my lawfull Attorney to acknowledge in Rappa County Court One hundred and fifty acres of land unto WM. BOULWARE his heirs and assigns lying on the North side of Rappa. River according to a Deed of Sale made over to him as Witness my hand this 22d day of March 1689/90
RICHARD his RB mark BERRY

p. 161 KNOW ALL MEN by these presents that I THO: COOMER of NEW KENT COUNTY in the Colony of Virginia have granted unto JOHN WAUGH of STAFFORD COUNTY, Clerk, his heirs all and singular tract of land conteyning the full complemt. of Two thousand acres comonly known and called by the name of WHITEHEADs PLANTACON being in the Forest between the North side of Rappa River and POTOMACK CREEK in County of STAFFORD being part of a grand tract of land granted by Patent bearing date (blank) to JOHN & GEORGE MOTT and by them and their assigns made over to me the sd THO: COOMER as by Deeds in Rappa Records recorded will more at large appear To have and to hold to him the said JOHN WAUGH for and during the space of Eleven years to begin at the date of these presents and to continue to be fully accomplished and at the expiracon of the term of Eleven yeares as abovesd the sd WAUGH paying therefore yearly the Chief Rent that shall become due to the Lord of the fee In Witness whereof I have sett my hand and Seal this third day February 1689/90
Signed Sealed and Delivered before us
WILLIAM SEDGWICK, THO: COOMER
WILLIAM SMITH, JOHN his mark 8 TONEY
Recognitr in Cur Comt. Rappa. 4 die Junii 1690

pp. 161-163 KNOW ALL MEN by these presents that I THO: COOMER of NEW KENT COUNTY for a valuable consideracon in hand received for me my heirs do release & forever quitt claime unto JOHN WAUGH of STAFFORD COUNTY in OVERWOTTEN CREEK his heirs being now in full quiett and peacable possession of one tract of land conteyning the full complemt. of Two thousand acres comonly known by the name of WHITEHEADS LAND being in the Forest between the North side of Rappa River and the lands of POTOMACK CREEK in STAFFORD COUNTY being part of a grand Patent of land granted bearing date (blank) to JOHN & GEORGE MOTT and by them and their assigns made over to me sd THO: COOMER as by Deed in Rappa Records recorded will more at large appeare All the right which ever have belonged to me sd THO: COOMER my heirs

which ever did belong to me my heirs Together with all appertinances fencing gardens orchards woods at all times to him sd JOHN WOUGH his heirs and assigns forever reserving only the quit rents which shall accrue due to the Chief Lord of Fee In Witness whereof I have hereunto sett my hand and Seale this 4th day of April 1690
Signed Sealed and Delivered in the presents of us

WM. SODGEWICK THO: COOMER
WM. SMITH, JOHN his mark S TONEY

Recognitr in Cur Comt Rappa 4 die Junii 1690

KNOW ALL MEN by these presents that I JANE COOMER, Wife of THO: COOMER, of Parish of St. Johns in County of NEW KENT Virginia Plantr., do hereby appoint my Friend, LEONARD CHAMBERLANE, of County of Rappa my lawfull Attorney for me to acknowledge my right of Two thousand acres of land being in the Freshes of Rappa County aforesd commonly called Mr. WHITEHEADS LAND being part of a Patent granted to JOHN and GEORGE MOTT and by them conveyed to sd WHITEHEAD and by Mr. WHITEHEAD to the sd THO: COOMER the sd land lying in the Forest of Rappa between that and POTOMACK CREEK as by the Patent thereof bearing date April 4th 1690 granting unto my sd Attorney all my right unto JOHN WOUGH of County of Rappa as if I myself were present at next Court to be held for Rappa County In Witness whereof I have sett my hand and seale June the 2nd 1690

WM. SEDGEWICK JANE COOMER
JOHN GREEN

Recognitr in Cur Comt Rappa 4 die Junii 1690

pp. 163-165 THIS INDENTURE made the 20th day of October 1685 and in the first yeare of the Reigne of our Sovereigne Lord JAMES the Second Between JOHN COLLIVOWE of County of Rappa, Docctr. in Phisick, of one part and CHRISTOPHER CHAUNT of sd County, Plantr., of other part Witnesseth that JOHN COLLIVOWE for sum of Twenty pounds of lawfull money of England to be paid to him sd JOHN COLLIVOWE his heirs by sd XPHER CHAUNT his heirs at days and times in manner and form hereafter menconed for divers other causes hath granted unto XPHER CHAUNT his heirs all that parcell of land conteyning by estimacon One hundred acres being in Rappa aforesd and bounded begining North upon a NECK called HATTERS NECK and East upon the land of THO: LANE, South upon the land of RALPH WHITTON and West upon the land of THO: WILLIAMS and now at the sealing and delivery hereof in Custody of sd JOHN COLLIVOWE Together with due share of all mines and mineralls therein conteyned and also free priviledges of hunting hawking fowling and fishing and also all buildings and fencing To have and to hold ye sd land Together with all appertenances unto sd XPHER CHAUNT his heirs and assigns to their own proper use and paying therefore to him sd COLLIVOWE his heirs the sum of Twenty Sterling money of England to be paid by Bill of Exchange at Twenty days sight provided that if said Bills of Exchange should happen to come in protested and the money not paid that then XPHER CHAUNT his heirs will truly pay unto JOHN COLLIVOWE his heirs the sd sum of Twenty pounds Sterling in Tobacco at the price current to be paid at two severall payments that is the first paymt. to begin upon the Tenth day of December next ensuing the Protest of sd Bills of Exchange, the second payment to begin upon the Tenth day of October next after such first payment at some convenient landing in Rappa and sd JOHN COLLIVOWE for himselfe his heirs grant sd XPHER CHAUNT his heirs the sd land is clear from other guifts or other incumbrances and also will Warrant and defend the sd land against any persons claiming any right therein In Witness the sd parties have set their hands and seals

Sealed and Delivered in the presents of
ANNE mark A SOAPER XPHER his mark C CHAUNT
SAMLL. JONES
Recognitr in Cur Comt Rappa 4 die Junii Ano 1690

p. 165 AN INVENTORY of the Goods sold to XPHER CHAUNT by JOHN COLLIVOWE this 20th day of October 1685
Imprs. One bedstead, one table, one chest, one porridge pot & hooks, two iron hooks, three wedges, one iron pestle, one drawing knife, one carpenters adds, one bill of Fifteen Shillings Recordr. Teste

pp. 165-166 TO ALL PEOPLE to whom these present writings shall come I RICHARD MATHEWS and ELIZABETH my Wife of Cittenburne Parish in County of Rappa send Greeting Know yee that I RICHARD MATHEWS and ELIZABETH as abovesd for Four thousand and five hundred pounds of Tobacco and Caske in hand already reced from RICHARD SHIPWAY SENR. of the same County hath sold unto RICHARD SHIPWAY his heirs one hundred and fifty acres of land part of a tract conteyning Three hundred acres of land as by Patent doth appeare and by the sd HALL conveyed to Mr. SPICER his heirs and I the sd RICHARD MATHEWS intermaried with the Daughter of the sd SPICER, further I the sd RICHARD MATHEWS and ELIZABETH my Wife have granted One hundred and fifty acres of land lying on OCCUPATION CREEK in Cittenburne Parish in Rappa County on South side the Creek begining at a white Oake corner tree on the Creek next to JOHN WILLIAMS so runing for breadth on the Creek side extending itself parallel thereunto North East as by Patent appears, further sd RICHARD MATHEWS and ELIZABETH my Wife do warrant the abovesd One hundred and fifty acres of land unto RICHARD SHIPWAY SENR. his heirs from any person whatsoever, and further I RICHARD MATHEWS and ELIZABETH my Wife to acknowledge the same at the next Court held for Rappa County if required In Witness we have sett our hands and seals this 22nd day of May 1690
Signed Sealed and delivered in the presents of us
HENRY AWBREY, RICHARD mark TZ MATHEWS
GEO: PLEY, ANN KING ELIZ. ɸ MATHEWS
Recognitr in Cur Comt Rappa 4 die Junii 1690
KNOW ALL MEN by these presents that I ELIZABETH MATHEWS do appoint Mr. HENRY AWBREY my true and lawfull attorney in my behalf to acknowledge a peice of land my Husband sold to RICHARD SHIPWAY and I the sd ELIZABETH do ratifie and confirm what my sd Attorney shall do in the premises as if I were there personally present Witness my hand and seal this 24th May 1690

(no signatures)

pp. 166-169 THIS INDENTURE made the 16th day of June 1690 Between Capt. JOHN PURVIS of the Citty of LONDON, Marriner, of one part and JOHN OCKLEY of the Parish of South Farnham in Rappa County in Virginia, Plantr., of other part. Whereas THO: MADISON of Rappa County under his hand and seal bearing date the 28th day of August 1674 for the consideracon therein menconed did sell unto sd JOHN PURVIS a tract of land containing One thousand forty and eight acres being in sd County of Rappa at the head of MORATTICO CREEK and was the Plantacon whereon the sd THO: MADISON then dwelt being the remaining part of a greater Tract of land to him granted by Patent bearing date the fifth day of April 1660 in which Deed is conteyned a Proviso that if sd THOMAS MADISON his heirs shall pay unto JOHN PURVIS his heirs the full quantity of Five thousand Seven hundred pounds of good and well condiconed tobacco

and caske on the Tenth of 10ber next ensuing as by the sd Deed acknowledged and recorded in Rappa County Court, But sd THO: MADDISON not making payment of the sd Five thousand Seven hundred pounds of Tobb: according to the tenure of the Deed the sd land and premises reconvey unto sd JOHN PURVIS his heirs, and sd JOHN PURVIS thereupon brought his suit in Rappa Court for the legall records of the sd land and on the first day of March 1675 obteyned judgment of the sd Court for immediate possession of sd land and premises and sd JOHN PURVIS in pursuance of sd Judgment was on the 19th day of March 1675 by the Sheriff of sd County possessed with all the land and premises as by said Judgment Now This Indenture Witnesseth that JOHN PURVIS for Eight Thousand pounds of principall sweet sented Tobb: and cask hath granted to JOHN OCKLEY his heirs all the before menconed land and premises with the appertinances and all houses buildings thereupon standing erected and all gardens orchards woods and all the right of the same To have and to hold unto sd JOHN OCKLEY his heirs fully and compleatly without the hindrance of JOHN PURVIS or any other person under him and JOHN PURVIS doth hereby authorize Mr. PAUL WOODBRIDGE to enter into & upon the before bargained land to deliver unto sd JOHN OCKLEY to the use and behoof of him his heirs and assigns forever In Witness whereof the sd parties have sett their hands and seals
Signed sealed and delivered in the presents of us
THOS: GLASCOCK, JOHN PURVIS
ALEXR. NEWMAN, ROBERT CARTER

Memoran: That according to the power within made unto the within PAUL WOODBRIDGE in his own proper person did enter into the within granted land and the full possession livery and seizen thereof did deliver by turff and twigg unto the within named JOHN OCKLEY his heirs In Testimony whereof sd PAUL WOODBRIDGE hath hereunto sett his hand and seal this 19th day of June 1690
Livery and Seizin delivered and this Testimony PAUL WOOD BRIDGE
signed and sealed in presence of us
ALEXR. NEWMAN, THO: GLASCOCK
JOHN mark 王 THOMAS Jax, tenant
GEORGE GLASCOCK, THOMAS GLASCOCK JUNR.
Recognitr in Cur Comt Rappa 2 die July 1690

KNOW ALL MEN by these presents that I JOHN PURVIS of Citty of LONDON do make Mr. WM. COLSTON my true and lawfull Attorney for me to acknowledge before the Justices of the Peace of Rappa County sitting in Court one Indenture of Bargain & Sale bearing date with these presents between me the sd JOHN PURVIS of one part and JNO. OCKLEY of Parish of South Farnham in Rappa County, Plantr., of other part In Witness whereof I the sd JOHN PURVIS have sett my hand and seal this 16th June 1690
Signed Sealed and Delivered in the presents of us
ALEXR. NEWMAN JOHN PURVIS
THO: GLASCOCK
Probatr p sacramt. NEWMAN and GLASCOCK in Cur Comt Rappa 2 die July 1690

pp. 169-170 THIS INDENTURE made the 17th day of June in year 1690 according to the computation of the Church of England and in the second yeare of the Reigne of our Sovereigne Lord and Lady King William and Queen Mary &c. Between JAMES ORCHARD of County of Rappa. of one part and GEORGE LUCKE of County of WESTMORELAND Gent. of other part Witnesseth that JAMES ORCHARD for divers good causes and for a valuable consideration in hand already received have granted unto the sd LUKE his heirs from me the sd ORCHARD with warranty all my right of that land I the sd ORCHARD doth lay claim to of that Thirty seven acres with the Reservacon of that my Draft of Three thousand thirty and seven acres Surveyed by Capt. WM. MOSELEY bearing date the 28th of Febry. 1688, begining at a small Pine where formerly stood a white Oak corner to Capt. JOHN WEIRE and extending thence along the sd WEIREs line N. E. to the Hiccory that stands by sd branch side that was marked for the Triangle of a Stake, thence up the sd Branch to a Chesnut by the branch side, thence crossing a small ridge to a Gum at the head of MARTINS SPRING BRANCH, thence down sd branch to meet with the sd WEIREs line, this abovesd land being granted to JOHN MARTIN by Patent bearing date the 16th of June 1663 and by sd MARTIN sold and made over to the sd ORCHARD the Third day of December 1688 Now Know yee that I sd JAMES ORCHARD for the divers good and weighty causes and valuable consideration reced do grant the thirty seven acres of land within menconed for me my heirs he or they peaceably enjoying the same without the lett of me my heirs In Witness sett my hand and seale the day and yeare above menconed

Signed Sealed and Delivered in the presents of us

OWEN Mar: I⁊ PRICE — JAMES ORCHARD

THO: RICHARDSON

Recognitr in Cur Comt Rappa 2 die July 1690

pp. 170-171 TO ALL XPIAN PEOPLE to whom these presents shall come I JOSEPH BECKLEY of Parish of Sittenburne in County of Rappa., Carpenter, Know yee that I sd JOSEPH BECKLEY for good causes and especially for the consideration of Three thousand pounds of Tobb: and one Cow and Pigs in hand the receipt I do acknowledge to have received from CHARLES KELL of aforesd Parish and County have sold unto the sd CHARLES KELL his heirs One hundred acres of land lying in the aforesd Parish and County bounded upon WM. JETTs and SAMLL. BOWERs line and the Deviding line betwixt him and me is the head of MATTOX BRANCH so called the Corner of a Branch is a great white Oake; To have and to hold the sd One hundred acres of land and all the premises to be granted with their appertinances unto CHARLES KELL his heirs In Witness whereof I have sett my hand and seal the 2d day of April 1690 and in the 2nd yeare of the reigne of our Sovereigne Lord King William and Queen Mary

Signed Sealed and delivered in the presents of us

JOHN RENNALLS, — JOSEPH BECKLEY

RICHD. RIVINGTON

Recognitr in Cur Compt Rappa 2 die July 1690

p. 171 KNOW ALL MEN by these presents that I HENRY LEWIS of County of Rappa, Plantr., have sold all my right and interest of a track of land of Ninty six acres which I bought of ANGELL JACOBUS & FRAN: GOORE with their Deed of Sale and all things therein conteyned unto BENJA: TUCKER him his heirs and from me my heirs forever Witness my hand and seal this 1st day of July 1690

Signed Sealed and delivered in the presents of

XPHR. ASCOUGH, — HEN: Mar: ++ LEWIS

MORRIS mark M HAMBLETT

Recognitr in Cur Comt Rappa 2 die July 1690

pp. 171-172 KNOW ALL MEN by these presents that wee THO: GOST of County of Rappa and MARGARETT GOST do for a valuable consideracon of Two thousand pounds of Tobb: to us in hand payd from JOHN NICHOLLS of the sd County do hereby sell unto sd NICOLLS his heirs one devident of land conteyning Two hundred and Eighty acres being in County of WESTMORELAND bounded N. W. with two tracts of land belonging to Mr. FRANCIS WRIGHT begining at a marked red Oak belonging to sd WRIGHT and extending N. W. to a black Oake then N. by W. to a white Oake standing on the West side of a small branch at the head whence N. E. down the sd branch to a white Oake by the sd branch side, then S. E. to a corner marked of 1200 acres belonging to the sd WRIGHT, finally up the sd WRIGHTs line to the first station To have and to hold the said land with all privilidges whatsoever belonging and wee the sd THOMAS and MARGARETT GOST hereby covenant that the premises are free from claim by us our heirs to him the sd NICOLLS his heirs forever Witness our hands and seals this 13th of March 1689/90

Teste GEO: GREEN, THOMAS T GOST
ROBERT VINCENT MARGARETT a GOST

Recognitr in Cur Comt Rappa 2 die 7ber 1690

MARGARETT GOST came voluntarily and in person acknowledged the above Deed in Rappa County Court on the 2d day of 7ber 1690

pp. 172-173 TO ALL XPIAN PEOPLE to whom these present writings shall come I JOHN NICOLLS of Rappa County in the Colony of Virginia, Plantr., send Greeting this 15th day of April in yeare of our Lord One thousand Six hundred and ninty and in the second yeare of the Reigne of our Sovereigne Lord King Wm. Now Witnesseth that I sd JOHN NICHOLLS for sum of Two thousand six hundred pounds of Tobb: in hand paid by THO: HUGHES of the aforesd County and Colony, Cooper, do by these presence grant unto sd THOMAS HUGH his heirs one tract of land conteyning Two hundred and Eighty acres in the County of WESTMORELAND bounded North and West with tracts of land belonging to Mr FRAN: WRIGHT being butted and bounded begining at a marked red Oak belonging to sd WRIGHT and extending West to a black Oak N. by West to a white Oake then N. N. E. to a white Oak standing on the West side of a small branch at the head, then E. down sd branch to a white Oake by the sd branch side Southerly to a corner marked of 1200 acres of land belonging to the sd WRIGHT, finally up the sd WRIGHTs line to the first station Together with all houses gardens pastures woods and appertinances belonging unto the use and behoof of him the sd THOMAS HUGHES his heirs he the sd THO: HUGHES his heirs paying the yearly fee rent due for the same payable unto our Sovereign Lord the King In Witness I have hereunto sett my hand and affixed my seal

Signed Sealed and delivered in the presents of us
WM. M WHELER, JOHN NICHOLLS
JOHN RULLINGS

Recognitr in Cur Comt Rappa 2 die Junii 1690

pp. 173-174 TO ALL &c. Whereas &c. Now Know yee that I the sd WM. BERKLEY Governor &c. give and grant unto ROBERT KING Two hundred and fifty acres of land scituate and being in County of NORTHUMBERLAND being bounded Easterly and Southerly by branch of WICCACOMAC RIVER which divideth this land from land of JAMES POPE Northerly by an other branch which runeth out of the aforesd branch and West by North by a line of marked trees wch cuteth MATCHOTRICK HORSE PATH at acute angles and endeth at the head of a vally coming up from the branches of MORATTICO CREEK and is lined by marked trees to the head of the Southermost branch of this Devident by a line of ninty poles runing Easterly the sd land being due to sd KING by Transporting of Five persons into this Colony &c. To have and to hold &c. yeilding and paying &c. Provided &c. dated the 11th of Febry (blot)

Vera Copia Test W. EDWARDS Cur Cour

WHEREAS the land menconed in the within Patent was in dispute in the Genll. Court at JAMES CITTY in 8ber Between DENNIS McCARTY and Mr. EDWARD SAUNDERS of NORTHUMBERLAND COUNTY and the sd Court then and there dismissing the action with

opinion neither the sd CARTY nor SAUNDERS had any right to the sd Land the sd CARTY prevailed with me the Subscriber to petcon for sd land for the sd CARTYs use and at the proper cost accordingly I did Now Know all men by these presents that I JOHN ALLAWAY the Subscriber above menconed have for a valuable consideracon of Four thousand pounds of Tobb: and caske to me paid bargane and sold sd land to sd DENNIS MACARTY his heirs with warranty from me my heirs forever To have and to hold the sd premises without hindrance hereby quitting claim to the sd land or any part thereof or any interest thereunto notwithstanding the grant to me given by the Genll. Court hereby confessing it to be the proper right of sd CARTY being petconed for at his own proper cost and charges and for his use & behoof in Testimony of the truth of which I have hereunto sett my hand and seal the second day of July 1690 and do further promise to make him his heirs any further assurance of it when thereunto required
Signed Sealed and Delivered in the presents of

THO: PARKER — JOHN his mark IA ALLOWAY
GEO: TAYLER
Recognitr in Cur Comt Rappa 2 die July 1690

pp. 174-176 IN OBEDIENCE to an order of the Worshipfull Court of Rappa County bearing date the second day of April 1690 all of the Jury have enquired and adjudged the land of Mr. RALPH WARINER now in SAMLL: THACKER be first survayed and have accordingly seen the Survay there perfected by Capt. WM. MOSLEY as to the best of our Judgment as by Capt. MOSLEYs Plat and report may appear both which Patents bearing date according to the Expression of the sd order As Witness our hands and seales this Twenty ninth day of April 1690

THOMAS PARKER	ANTHO: Sig. A NORTH
JOHN DANGERFIELD	JOHN WELLS
ROBERT BROOK	JOHN I HINES
RICHARD STOAKES	JOHN BUGHAN
THO: MUNDAY	JOHN WAGINER
WILLIAM BENDRY	ROBERT 8br MILLS

Recordr. Test WM. COLSTON Cl Cur

IN OBEDIENCE to an order of Rappa County Court bearing date the 3rd day of April 1690 hve in presents of an able Jury surveyed two Patents for land is expressed the sd order and bearing the same date the Patent granted to RALPH WARINER being the first surveyed by sd Jurys order as will appear by their virdict and runing for the same beginning at a red Oake upon a bank by RALPHS CREEK and thence down sd Creek to an Hickory neere a branch that runeth into the woods is S. Easterly wanting 38 perches of the sd distance given in the sd Patent (it meeting then with EXUMs line) and thence along the sd line of EXAM Easterly (being bounded by that line of trees to a small white Oake we marked the other mentioned in the Patent not to be found the sd tree standing by the North of a Creek called the MILL CREEK thence parrallel to the first 147 per: and lastly Westerly by an old line of marked trees to the first Station leaving part of an old Dwelling house wch Mr. KEALING formerly lived in and including but 223 in abovesd bounds Now the reasons of the course is difering from the Patent the Cut dg. in the first & 2nd 45 pr: in the second in the first it is the natural bounds of the Creek that being our cases to walk on and in the second being bounded with the line of WM. EXAM wch gives us the course above menconed and then consequently we must run parrallel to the two first courses by the Rules of the Patent otherwise to Run the two last courses and distances given in the Patent (for want of our measure in the first line) would include 86 acres more than now it doth, which yr. Worship may see by the pricked line but the Jury thought first I should run the same distance at the head as at the force and distance being as in to an old line which was undoubtedly the old Devision line of those two Patents Wee run a parrallel to the second which line butted upon the first station but the sd line being crooked our straight course left it without us in the midle of our distance as your Worships may see by the Tree set down in the Platt the diffrance being small the Jury notwithstanding thought fitt to make the old line trees they being of so long standing so much for the first Patent: for the second Patent we began at the abovesd red Oake the begining tree of the sd Patent and extended by the sd old line of trees Easterly to the extend thereof and further to make the complemt. of the mile given in the Patent the sd distance ending in the Marsh by the Creeke, it not being the due course given in the Patent, the other Patent being first surveyed, and for the reasons above menconed, thence wee run N. W. according to the Patent not being obstructed by any elder grant runing through a great old field to a stake in a corn field formerly Mr. ROB: PARKERs now in the possession of Mr. ROBERT PLEY, thence parralel to the two first including 346 acres in the sd bounds, this being all the Report can be offered from

Your Worships Humble Servant to comand WM. MOSLEY Survr: R. C.

pp. Aug. Court 1690
176- THIS INDENTURE made in the year of our Lord God 1690 and in the second year of
178 the Reigne of their Majties by the Grace of God King & Queen &c. between WM.
COVINGTON SENR. of County of Rappa., Plantr., of one part and PHILIP PARR of said County, Plantr. of other part; Witnesseth that WM. COVINGTON SENR. in consideracon of Three thousand Five hundred pounds of Swt. Tobb: and Caske and Twenty Shillings Sterling to him paid the sd WM. COVINGTON SENR. doth grant to him sd PHILIP PARR his heirs Three hundred acres of land formerly known to belong to RICHARD GLOVER his land being in Rappa County on South side PISCATAWAY CREEK called GLOVERS NECK bounding upon EVAN DAVIS his land and GEO: BROOKES his land and JOHN WEBSTER land To have and to hold sd tract of Three hundred acres of land with all houses fences cleared grounds woods to him sd PHILIP PARR his heirs forever and also all mines mineralls therein conteyned Together with all free liberty ingress egress and release to and from sd land paying the quitrents that shall become due In Witness whereof the parties have sett their hands and seales

Signed Sealed and delivered in the presents of

ROBT. COLEMAN, WM. COVINGTON

FRAN: BROWNE, SAMLL. PAVEY Mar: /—

Recognitr in Cur Comt Rappa 6 die April 1690

pp. KNOW ALL MEN by these presents that I THO: PETTUS in County of Rappa in Vir-
178- ginia, Planter, for divers good causes but more especially for One thousand
179 pounds of sweet sented Tobb: and caske already received have sold unto JOHN
BAKER Gent. of GLOCESTER COUNTY in Virginia, Plantr., his heirs One hundred acres of land being in the aforesd County of Rappa it being part of a tract of land formerly belonging to Mr. THO: BUTTON of aforesd County and by sd BUTTONs last Will & Testament bequeathed to me sd THO: PETTUS as by the Will may appeare which said One hundred acres of land I sd THO: PETTUS do warrant unto sd BAKER his heirs from me my heirs In Witness whereof I have fixed my hand and Seale this Sixth day of August One thousand Six hundred and ninty

Signed Sealed and delivered in the presents of us

GERARD LOUTHER, THOMAS PETTUS

AUGU. WINGFIELD

Recognitr in Cur Comt Rappa 6 die Augt 1690

pp. 179-181 THIS INDENTURE made the first day of April in year 1690 and in the second year of the Reign of their Maties. Between JOHN LACY of County of Rappa., Plantr., of one part and ROBERT DEPUTIE of the same County, Cergeon, of other part, Witnesseth that sd JOHN LACY for Three thousand pounds of Tobb. and cask to him paid have granted to sd ROBERT DEPUTIE and his heirs forever all that parcell of land Two hundred acres formerly known to be JOHN STANFORDs land lying and being in Rappa County on the South side of Rappa River joyning upon the land of THO: CROW his land and Mr. DANIEL DOBYNS land and a branch that devideth his land and a parcell of land sold by the sd JOHN LACY unto WM. JEFFERIES, the two parcells sold being by Patent three hundred this being Two hundred thereof To have and to hold sd tract of Two hundred acres of land with all houses fences woods to him sd ROBERT DEPUTIE his heirs forever and also his due share of all mines mineralls therein together with free liberty of ingress egress and regress from sd land paying the quitrents that become due for the sd land the said JOHN LACY for himself that said ROBERT DEPUTIE his heirs may quietly hold before menconed for his own proper use and further the sd JOHN LACY do grant to warrant and defend the land from JOHN LACY his heirs and all other persons that shall have or pretend to have any right therein In Witness whereof the parties to these presents have sett their hands and seals

ROBERT DEPUTIE JOHN Sig. X LACY

Signed Sealed and Delivered in the presents of us

EDWARD ADCOCK,
ALEXANDR. HENDERSON, ELIZ. ADCOCK

Recognitr in Cur Comt Rappa 6 die Augt. 1690

KNOW ALL MEN by these presents that I JOHN LACY of County of Rappa confess myself to stand jutly indebted unto ROBERT DEPUTIE in the sum of Six thousand pounds of good sweet tobacco in caske the which payment I bind me my heirs as Witness my hand and seale this first day of April 1690

The condicon of this obligacon is such that if the above bound JOHN LACY his heirs shall truly perform all the covenants in one Deed of Indenture bearing date with these presents and made between JOHN LACY of one part and ROBERT DEPUTIE of other part and also if JOHN LACY by himself his lawfull attorney without fraud or further delay at the next Court held for the South side of Rappa. County make acknowledgemt. of this Indenture with Bond and other writtings assigned unto sd ROBERT DEPUTIE then the obligation is of non effect else to remain in force

Signed Sealed and delivered in the presents of us

EDWD. ADCOCK, JOHN X LACY
ALEXR. HENDERSON,

pp. 181-184 THIS INDENTURE made the 28th day of July 1690 and in the second year of the Reign of our Sovereigne Lord and Lady Wm. and Mary &c. Between HENRY BRADLEY of Parish of White Chappell in County of LANCASTER, Plantr., of one part and JAMES BALL, Son of Capt. WM. BALL, of the Parish and County aforesd of other part Witnesseth that sd HENRY BRADLEY for love and true respect he ths sd HENRY BRADLEY bears unto sd JAMES BALL as also other good causes have granted and confirmed unto JAMES BALL his heirs all that Divident of land whereon sd BRADLy now lives being Two hundred acres of land part of a Patent of Four hundred acres granted to JOHN PHILLIPS the 13th day of July 1655 and afterwards became the right of Mr. MOORE FANTLEROY, who assigned it to VINCENT STANFORD as by Assignmt. may appear and by sd STANFORD assigned unto WM. BLUNKARD assignment dated the 15th of Jany. 1657 and afterwards sold unto ROBERT POLLARD deced, and since by ROBERT POLLARD's Son and heire to sd ROBERT POLLARD deced, the sd Two hundred acres of land sold unto

the sd HENRY BRADLY as by Deed bearing date the 7th day of June 1682 may fully appear the sd Two hundred acres of land bounded begining at a marked red Oake nere WHITE CHAPPLE CHURCH on the brow of a Hill, thence W. by N. by W. by marked trees and stakes drove down in the old field where the sd POLLARD deced formerly lived to a corner red Oake standing at the uper end of sd old field in a vally or little within the woods by PATH side, thence N. E. to a corner red Oake standing by the side of a PATH at the head of a vally on PATH leads from the sd POLLARDs old field unto the Plantation formerly belonging to JOHN HARTOP and HENRY PUTMAN from the sd red Oake down the vally by marked trees, thence down part of the vally the severall courses to a marked corner Ash tree standing in sd Swamp which parts this land from a land sold by ROBERT POLLARD deced unto JOHN HARTOP and since belonging to WILLIAM BOND all deced, thence S. along a line of marked trees to the place it began and also all profitts and appertenances belonging unto sd Two hundred acres of land as all the rights which sd HENRY BRADLEY now hath except and serve unto himself for and during his naturall life all the sd Two hundred acres of land and all and singular the premises thereunto belonging and sd JAMES BALL shall not possess the sd land or any part thereof until the day of the death of sd HENRY BRADLY and sd HENRY BRADLY further reserve that if at his death he should leave a Widow, then his sd Widow shall enjoy the one third part of the land during her naturall life; To have and to hold all the premises and appertinances unto sd JAMES BALL his heirs (except as before excepted) subject to the quit rents which shall grow due and sd HENRY BRADLY doth order that sd land and premises shall fall unto JAMES BALL before he arrives to age of Sixteen that then sd Capt. WILLIAM BALL look to and oversee the same until JAMES BALL arrives unto the age of Sixteen years and then to surrender the same to his said Son, JAMES BALL, his heirs &c. In Witness whereof the parties have set their hands and seals
Signed Sealed and delivered in the presents of
EDWIN CONWAY, HENRY BRADLY
WILLIAM BALL JUNR.
Recognitr in Cur Comt Rappa 6 die Augt. 1690
Sept. Court 1690 (marked out)
KNOW ALL MEN by these presents that I HENRY BRADLY of Parish of White Chappell in County of LANCASTER, Plantr., do make Mr. COLSTON of County of Rappa. and Parish of Farnham, Gent., my lawfull Attorney for me to acknowledge a certain Deed of Guift for two hundred acres of land scituate in LANCASTER COUNTY by sd BRADLY given to JAS. BALL the Son of Capt. WILLIAM BALL, I give unto my sd Attorney full power to make or do the same in any Court of Record within the Dominion of Virginia which acknowledgement I sd HENRY BRADLY do hereby ratifie and do declare it to be as valid as I myself could have made or performed had I been personally present. In Witness whereof I sd HENRY BRADLY have sett my hand and seal this 26th of July 1690
Signed Sealed and delivered in the presents of
EDWIN CONWAY, HENRY BRADLY
WM. BALL JUNR.
Proved by the Oaths of CONWAY & BALL in Rappa County Court 6 day of Augt 1690

pp. Sept. Court 1690
184- THIS INDENTURE made the 29th day of August 1690 Between JOHN PATRIDGE and
185 FRANCES his Wife of one part and JOSEPH DAVIS and KATHERINE his Wife of the other part Witnesseth that JOHN PATRIDGE and FRAN: his Wife for Three thousand pounds of Tobb: in Cask already pd. and satisfied have sold unto the aforesd JOSEPH DAVIS and KATHERINE his Wife their heirs all and singular that neat parcell of land being in Rappa County the Parish of North Farnham and near FARNHAM CHURCH being

part of a parcell of land whereon I now live being bounded and seperated from the residue of sd land by a mane great branch issuing out of RICHARDSON CREEK and on one side bounding upon and alongst the sd Branch and outwards as far every way as it can extend itself untill stopt with other Elder Deeds or Patents the sd Parcell of land conteyning Fifty acres with all woods waters belonging granted to JOSEPH DAVIS and KATHERINE his Wife their heirs forever quietly to enjoy and possess without the hindrance of all persons In Wittness whereof we have set our hands and seals
Signed Sealed and Delivered in presence of us

SAMLL. SANFORD, JOHN PATRIDGE
MARTIN HAMMOND, FRAN: Sig. F PATRIDGE
JOH: mark Ƶ HAMMOND

Recognitr in Cur Com Rappa 3 die 7bris 1690

pp. 186-187 THIS INDENTURE made the 23rd day of August 1690 in the second year of the Reign of our Sovereigne Lord and Lady King William and Queen Mary &c. Between WILLIAM JENNINGS of Parish of Sittenburn and County of Rappa., Plantr., of one part and MARTIN FISHER of aforesd Parish and County of other part Witnesseth that WM. JENNINGS hath granted unto MARTIN FISHER all that the Plantacon whereon sd WM. JENNINGS now liveth conteyning One hundred and fifty acres together with all houses buildings and all appertinances more fully expressed being in the Parish and County aforesd and adjacent to JOHN JENNINGS, Brother of sd WM., being the moyety or one half part of a tract of land conteyning Three hundred acres given to sd JOHN & WM. by the last Will and Testament of JOHN JENNINGS, the Father, in joynt tenancy and since by a line of division run through sd land and Deed of Particon thereon made divided between them out of which sd Plantation of sd WILLIAM is only excepted as if aforesd Fifty acres thereof being allready sold to HENRY GARING of Parish and County aforesd and to be layed out for him at the upper end of sd Plantacon of sd WM. JENNINGS into the woods by a line run across from the deviding line of aforesd JOHN & WILLIAM to the outside line of sd WILLIAM and so to the extend of the bounds of the land into the woods to compleat the sd Fifty acres which sd Plantacon with the appertinances the aforesd Fifty acres only as aforesd excepted is given in exchange for the Plantation whereon the aforesd MARTIN FISHER now liveth in the Parish and County aforesd. consisting of all the cleared ground with all the houses buildings fences and other appertinances belonging with as much more adjoining land of the sd Mr. MARTINs begining on JOHN BUTLERs line as will include the sd cleared ground make up the complement of Two hundred acres To have and to hold the Plantation conteyning One hundred & fifty acres Except as before excepted with all its appertinances to sd MARTIN FISHER his heirs and sd WM. JENNINGS for himself doth promise with sd MARTIN FISHER his heirs the Plantation with the appertinances granted unto sd MARTIN in exchange is free from all manner of incumbrances and sd MARTIN FISHER hath likewise on his part granted unto WM. JENNINGS the above mentioned Plantation whereon he sd MARTIN now liveth with all the premises and appertinances already above declared and expressed and being as aforesd To have and to hold the Plantacon consisting as aforesd of all the cleared ground with all houses buildings fences thereunto belonging with as much more land of sd MARTAINs begining on JOHN BUTLERs line as will with the aforesd cleared ground make the complement of Two hundred acres as above expressed to the sd WM. his heirs for and in exchange for the Plantation whereon sd WILLIAM now liveth conteyning One hundred and fifty acres with such exceptions as abovesd In Witness the parties to these presents have sett their hands and seals

Signed Sealed and Delivered in the presents of
ARTHUR SPICER, WILLIAM JENNINGS
AUGUST: WINGFIELD
Recognitr in Cur Comt Rappa 3 die 8brs 1690

pp. 187-189 THIS INDENTURE made the three and twentieth day of Augt. 1690 Between WM. JENNINGS of Parish of Sittenburne and County of Rappa., Plantr., of one part and MARTIN FISHER of aforesd Parish and County of other part Witnesseth that WM. JENNINGS hath given unto MARTIN FISHER all that plantation whereon sd WILLIAM JENNINGS now liveth conteyning One hundred and fifty acres together with all houses buildings and every their appertinances Except fifty acres thereon in the presents more fully expressed being in Prish and County aforesd adjoining to JOHN JENNINGS, Brother of sd WILLIAM, being the moyety of one half part of a tract of land conteyning Three hundred acres given to sd JOHN and WILLIAM by the last Will and Testament of JOHN JENNINGS, their Father, in joint tenancy and since by them by line of Division run through the sd land absolutely devided between them out of which Plantation of sd WM. is only excepted as aforesd Fifty acres thereof being already sold to HENRY GARING of the sd Parish and County and to be layed out for him at the upper end of the Plantation of said WILLIAM JENNINGS which sd Plantation with the appertinances the aforesd Fifty acres of land only excepted given in Exchange for the Plantation whereon the aforesd MARTIN FISHER now liveth To have and to hold said Plantation with all its appts. unto MARTIN FISHER his heirs given and granted to sd WM. JENNINGS in Exchange free from all incumbrances In Witness whereof the parties have sett their hands and seales
Signed and delivered in the presents of
ARTHUR SPICER, MARTIN Sig. ℭ FISHER
AUGUST: WINGFIELD
Recognitr in Cur Court Rappa 3 die 7bers 1690

p. 189 MR. COLSTON Record this marke as followeth Two crops and slitt in the right eare on South side of River in the freshes it being the proper marke of CHARLES MORGAN. Recordr. Teste WM. COLSTON C. C. C.

p. 189 KNOW ALL MEN by these presents that I JOHN MARTIN for divers good causes hereunto moving do give unto ROBERT COLE a Cow Calfe being marked with a crop and a slitt in the right eare and a crop and two slitts under the left eare for the true performance hereof I have set my hand this 3rd day of 7ber 1690
Teste GEO: ANNEKING JOHN + MARTIN

p. 190 KNOW ALL MEN who it may concerne that wee ROBERT COLEMAN and LEONARD CHAMBERLANE of County of Rappa holding in Joint Tenancy a Divident of land by us purchased of ROBERT PAYNE of aforesd County which sd land is situate on South side of Rappa River and on both sides of a Creek known by name of HOSKINS CREEK we sd COLEMAN and CHAMBERLANE do for ourselves our heirs by these presents declare that sd land be forever herafter the division and bounds of each of our claimes and that sd COLEMAN and CHAMBERLANE keep their Plantation that are now seated on with the land on each side the Creek without the molestation of either of them or either of their heirs or assigns forever In Testimony whereof sd parties have sett their hands and seales the 1st day of 8ber 1690

Signed Sealed and Delivered in the presents of

THO: EDMONDSON, ROBERT COLEMAN
JAMES BOUGHAN LEONARD CHAMBERLANE

Acknowledged by ROBERT COLEMAN and LEONARD CHAMBERLANE each to other interchangably the first day of 8ber Ano 1690 before Mr. HENRY AWBREY and Mr. SAMLL. PEACHEY two of their Majesties Justices of the peace for Rappa County and recorded the 4th day of the sd month

pp. 190-192 TO ALL XPIAN PEOPLE to whom these presents writtings shall come Know yee that WILLIAM JENNINGS of County of Rappa and Colony of Virginia, Plantr., send Greeting this 29th day of September in year 1690 Now Know yee that sd WM. JENNINGS in consideracon of Three thousand pounds of Tobb: and caske in hand paid have granted unto HENRY GARING his heirs and assigns forever one tract of land being in Rappa County on North side of the river in Colony aforesd by estimacon Fifty acres more or less runing North East at the upper end of sd JENNINGS line and so right across his land begining at a red Oak at the uper side of sd JENNINGS line and so marked right across unto a marked Hickory and so ending at the lower side Begining upon the line of THO: ELWINs Childrens land and MARTIN FISHERs at the upper end with all its rights together with all woods and mineralls and quaryes whatsoever water and other comodities belonging To have and to hold unto HENRY GORING his heirs and assigns forever without the molestation of WILLIAM JENNINGS or MARY his Wife or their heirs In Witness whereof sd WILLIAM JENNINGS or MARY his Wife have hereunto sett their hands and seals

Sealed and Delivered in presents of us

JOSHUA DAVIS, WILLIAM JENNINGS
HEN: COLESTREAME MARY M JENNINGS

Recognitr in Cur Comt Rappa 1 die 8ber 1690

p. 192 Vide folio 77). KNOW ALL MEN by these presents that I GEORGE SUGGETT of County of Rappa hath granted PETER RICHARDSON of MIDLESEX his heirs and assigns my full whole interest of one assignment of Two hundred acres of land therein specified with warranty and by these presents do oblige me my heirs in the penalty of Five thousand pounds of Current sweet sented Tobb: and caske to be payed unto PETER RICHARDSON or his order upon the non payment of same. Witness my hand and seal this 28th dy of August 1689

Teste JOHN DIKE, GEO: W. SUGGETT
RICHARD LACKLAND

pp. 192-193 THIS INDENTURE made the 4th day of 7ber in year 1690 and in the second yeare of our Sovereigne Lord and Lady William and Mary &c. Between ANTHO: NORTH of County of Rappa of one part and JOHN WAGGONER of other part Witnesseth that ANTHO: NORTH released to farm lett unto JOHN WAGGONER a certain parcell of land being on North side of Rappa in Parish of South Farnham begining at a marked white Oake standing in the side of a branch bounding upon an antient line of marked trees belonging to Mr. RICHARD WHITE and so long the branch to a marked Hickory and a marked Sapling W. or thence standing upon the North side of ye KINGS HIGH ROAD from thence along ye sd ROAD W. or thereabouts to a marked red Oake and from thence South by a line of marked trees to a pare tree standing in the line of sd RICHARD WHITE and from thence along the line of the sd WHITE East to the begining white Oak the sd JOHN WAGONER to have and to hold sd tract of land with woods housing orchards fences water and all other the appertinances belonging without the molestation of ANTHONY

NORTH his heirs or from any other person for the full terme of Ninety and nine years from the date of these presents and until the sd end be fully finished To have and to hold the demised premises during the whole terme as aforesd he paying yearly upon the feast of St. Michael the archangell an year of Indian Corne if demanded In Witness of all the agreements the parties have set their hands and seales the date above written
Signed Sealed and delviered in the presents of
THO: HUCLESCOTT, ANTHO: Sig. A NORTH
MARY HUCLESCOTT JOHN WAGONER
Recognitr in Cur Com Rappa 1 die 8ber 1690

pp. 193-194 KNOW ALL MEN by these presents that I WILLIAM BOWLER of County of Rappa and Parish of Cittenburne for sum of Four thousand foure hundred pounds of Tobb: and cask secured to be paid to me by DAVID JAMISON of sd County and Parish have with the consent of ELIZABETH my Wife granted unto DAVID JAMISON his heirs Two hundred and fifty acres of land formerly taken up by THO: PAGE in the freshes and on the South side of Rappa River as by Patent bearing date 1666/7 and begining at a Hickory neere the ROAD thence runing up a line of marked trees according to the course of the Patent to a great branch of POWOMAN which divides my Brothers land from mine being part of the same tract and so including all my part of the sd land between the abovesd Branch and the ROAD the sd Two hundred and fifty acres of land with all rights from me the said BOULWARE my heirs to sd DAVID JAMISON his heirs in as large manner as may be collected out of the Patent without the hindrance or interruption of sd WM. BOULWARE my heirs or any persons claiming under me my heirs &c. the sd JAMISON paying the rights and services from henceforth to accrue and of right accustomed In Witness whereof wee have hereunto sett our hands and seals the (blot) of August 1690
Signed Sealed and Delivered in the presents of us
FRAN: SLAUGHTER, WILLIAM BOULWARE
JAMES BOULWARE ELIZABETH BOULWARE
Recognitr in Cur Comt Rappa 1 die 8ber 1690
KNOW ALL MEN by these presents that I ELIZABETH BOULWARE do hereby appoint my well beloved friend, ROBERT PLEY, my lawfull Attorney for me in my name to acknowledge a parcell of land menconed in a conveyance made unto DAVID JAMISON bearing date the 25th day of Augt. 1690 unto him the sd JAMISON and do hereby ratifie what he my sd Attorney shall doe thereunto according to Law as my hand and seal this 19th 7ber 1690
Signes Sealed and Delivered in the presents of us
ELIZ: HENSELEY, ELIZA. BOULWARE
SAMLL. COX

pp. 194-196 THIS INDENTURE made this 2st day of 8ber ano dom 1690 and in the second year of the Reigne of our Sovereign Lord and Lady Wm. and Mary &c. between EDWIN THACKER of Parish of Christ Church in County of MIDLESEX, Surveyour, of one part and JAMES TAYLOR of Parish of St. Stephens in NEW KENT COUNTY Gent. of other part Witnesseth that EDWIN THACKER for a full and valuable consideraction already reced have sold unto JAS. TAYLOR and his heirs Two hundred acres of land part of Sixteen hundred Sixty and three acres granted unto EDWIN THACKER by Patent dated the 20th day of April 1687, scituate in Rappa County on the North side of Rappa River and bounded begining to be measured at a corner red Oake of sd TAYLORs land and runing thence South West by WAGGONERs line to a Hickory and Pine on a Brow of a valley, thence North West to another line of WAGGONERs to a Stake between two marked red Oakes on a Hill on West side a branch, thence SouthWest to JAMES BOUGHANs line to a Hickory and red Oak, thence by his line of marked trees East to the land of the above-sd Mr. JAMES TAYLER, thence by his land North West to the place it began being bounded round with lines of marked trees and also all profitts and appertinances unto sd Two hundred acres of land as all the right to which the sd EDWIN THACKER have to the same To have and to hold unto JAMES TAYLER without the lett of sd EDWIN THACKER In Witness to all the above premises the sd EDWIN THACKER hath set his hand and seal the day and year first above mentioned

Signed Sealed and Delivered in the presents of us

RICHD. JOHNSON, EDWIN THACKER

JONATHAN FISHER

Recognitr in Cur Comt Rappa 1 die 8ber 1690

KNOW ALL MEN by these presents that I MARY TAYLOR Wife of JAMES TAYLOR of Parish of St. Stephens in County of NEW KENT do by these presents appoint my loving Bro: THO: WHEELER, my true and lawfull Attorney for me to acknowledge unto JOHN WAGONER in Rappa Court all my right of Dower I have to one hundred acres of land according to a Deed under the hand & seal of my sd Husband bearing date the 4th of this Instant June holding firme what my said Attorney shall do as if I myself were personally present as Witness my hand and seal this 1st day of June 1690

Signed sealed and delivered in the presents of us

THOMAS Sig. W WHITE, MARY TAYLOR

JONATHAN FISHER

Recognitr in Cur Com Rappa 1 die 8ber 1690

pp. 196-198 THIS INDENTURE made the first day of 8ber One thousand Six hundred and Eighty and nine and in the second yeare of the Reigne of our Sovereign Lord and Lady Wm. & Mary &c. Between EDWIN THACKER of Parish of Christ Church in County of MIDLESEX of one part and ANDREW WAGONER and JAMES WAGONER of the Parish of South Farnham in County of Rappa of other part Witnesseth that EDWIN THACKER for the full quantitie of Two thousand five hundred and twenty pounds of sweet sented Tobb to me in hand paid by these presents have sold unto ANDREW WAGONER and JAMES WAGONER their heirs Two hundred acres of land in Rappa County on the South side of Rappa River being part of Fifteen hundred & sixty three acres granted unto EDWIN THACKER by Patent dated the 20th day of Apl. 1687 begining at three Oake saplins in JOHN MEADORs line of marked tees on a Hill on East side a branch and thence alonge sd line West by North by the land of Mr. HENRY AWBREY to two corner trees, thence by his line South by West to a corner white Oake of sd AWBURYs on a levell, thence South East by a marked line to a corner Hickory and Pine on the brow of a vally, thence North East to One hundred and five acres of land belonging to sd MEADOR by a red Oake and thence North by East along sd land to the place it began being bounded in with lines of marked trees and also all profitts belonging to sd Two hundred acres of land and all the rights which sd EDWIN THACKER had to the same To have and to hold the sd Two hundred acres of land with all the premises unto ANDREW WAGONER and JAMES WAGONER their heirs and assigns forever In Witness thereof sd EDWIN THACKER hath sett his hand and seal

Signed Sealed and Delivered in the presents of us

THO: HUCLECOTT, EDWIN THACKER

JOHN MEADOR

Recognitr in Cur Comt Rappa 1 die 8ber 1690

pp. 198-199 TO ALL XPIAN PEOPLE to whom these presents shall come Know yee that wee CHARLES WALKER and JOHN SOTHERNE of Parish of Farnham in County of Rappa for good causes but more especially for the sum of Four thousand pounds of sweet sented Tobb: and caske to us payd or secured to be payd by JONATHAN FISHER in Parish of St. Stephens and County of NEW KENT do by these presents sell unto JONATHAN FISHER his heirs all our right to Three hundred acres of land being in County of Rappa in Parish of Farnham and on Branches of PISCATAWAY SWAMP at a corner red Oake standing on a Hill by a branch, runing thence N.E. parting this land from the land of WM. BALL and JOHN RICE to a corner Oake, thence W. to a corner white Oake by a PATH, thence W. to a Pine and a white Oake, thence South to a red Oake by a Hickory, thence S.E. to the place where it first began wch sd land being part of a Devident of Five thousand One hundred acres granted to Mr. HENRY AWBREY by Patent bearing date the 19th day of March 1677 and by JOHN FRY purchased of sd AWBREY, Majr. GEORGE MORRIS and BENGA. GOODRICH and by us sd CHARLES WALKER and JOHN SOTHERNE purchased of sd JOHN FRY by bargaine and sale bearing date the first day of July 1686 relation being had will appeare To have and to hold the above sd three hundred acres of land with every part thereof with all woods belonging Further the sd CHARLES WALKER and JOHN SOUTHERNE doe declare that we have full power to make sale of the same Further we do warrant the above land from clame of any persons whatsoever for the true performance of the abovesd premises wee bind ourselves our heirs in the penall sum of Eight thousand pounds of good sound sweet sented Tobb: and caske to be paid unto JONATHAN FISHER his heirs In Witness whereof wee have sett our hands and seals this 28th day of June 1690

Signed Sealed and Delivered in the presents of

JAMES TAYLOR, CHARLES WALKER
ROBT: Sig. R POWELL JOHN SOUTHERNE

Recognitr in Cur Com Rappa 1 die 8ber 1690

p. 199 JOHN ANTONs marke a crop and underkeel in the left eare and a crop and slitt in the right

The mark of FRAN: ELMOREs croped on both eares and two Flower de luces

pp. 199-200 Vide Folio 77). KNOW ALL MEN by these presents that we GEORGE SUGGETT of County of Rappa., Planter, and ELIZABETH SUGGETT my Wife have for a valuable consideracon sold unto PETER RICHARDSON of County of MIDLESEX, Plantr., his heirs the full right of Two hundred acres of land according to the meaning of sd Assignment and Patent and also we the sd GEO: SUGGETT and my Wife, ELIZABETH, our heirs do agree with PETER RICHARDSON his heirs that sd land is free from all former gifts grants or other incumbrances and lastly we sd GEORGE and ELIZABETH SUGGETT warrant the sd Assignment and land specified its appertenances to sd PETER RICHARDSON his heirs from us our heirs and any other persons that shall clame any right therein. As Witness our hands and seales this 28th day of Augt. 1689

Signed Sealed and Delivered in presents of

JOHN DYKE, GEORGE Sig. W SUGGITT
RICHARD LACKLAND ELIZA: + SUGGITT

Recognitr in Cur Comt Rappa 1 die 8ber 1690

pp. 200-201 TO ALL XPIAN PEOPLE to whom these presents shall come we WILLIAM <u>HENDSON</u> of County of Rappa and REBECCA my Wife send Greeting in the Lord everlasting Know yee that we the sd WILLIAM <u>HODSON</u> and REBECCA my Wife for divers good considerations and especially for One horse and the sum of One thousand pounds of Tobb: have sold unto THO: DAY of sd County his heirs One hundred acres of land being part of a parcell of land conteyning Three hundred fifty six acres being in Rappa County on South side of Rappa River and bounded begining at a corner white Oake by a branch and runing thence to DAVIS his land alonge his line W:, thence E: over certain branches to land of EVAN DAVIS S:E: dividing the land from the land of THO: PRICKETT to the first mentioned Branch W. by E. to the place it first began as by a Patent bearing date the 24th of May 1666; To have and to hold sd bargained land being the Plantation part with all rights of hunting hawking fishing & fowling woods waters Mill building with all other appertenances whatsoever thereunto belonging to him sd THO: DAY his heirs paying unto our Sovereign Lord the King such rents as shall be due and sd WM. HUDSON & REBECCA his Wife for themselves promise to warrant and defend sd land from the claim of any person unto sd THOMAS DAY his heirs In Witness whereof sd WM. HENSON have sett my hand and seal this Twenty fifth day of January 1687/8

Signed Sealed land Delivered in the presents of us

DANLL. DOBYNS, WILLIAM Sig. W HUDSON

JAN. LAUNY

Recognitr in Cur Comt Rappa 4 die 10bris 1689

To the Worshipfull Bench held for Rappa County on the South side I REBECCA HUDSON do make my Husband, WM. HUDSON, my lawfull Attorney to acknowledge unto THO: DAY one hundred acres of land being her right according as the conveyance specifieth as Witness my hand and seal this 4th day of 10ber 1689

In the presents of

RICHARD BROOKE, REBECCA R HUDSON

REBECCA BROOKE,

pp. 201-203 THIS INDENTURE made the Three and twentieth day of August 1690 and in the second yeare of the Reign of our Sovereigne Lord and Lady King and Queen of England &c. Between JOHN JENNINGS of Parish of Sittenburn in County of Rappa, Plantr., of one part and WM. JENNINGS of sd Parish of Scittenburne County of Rappa of other part. Whereas JOHN JENNINGS late of Sittenburne of County of Rappa deced, Father of them the sd JOHN and WILLIAM JENNINGS, parties to these presents being in his life time seized in his demise as of ee and in a certain tract of land conteyning Three hundred acres and being so seized the premises and every of their appertenances the sd JOHN JENNINGS, the Father, did by his last Will and Testament bearing date the 11th day of February Ano Dom 1669 give and bequeath the before menconed devident of land with the appertinances unto his Sons, JOHN JENNINGS and WILLIAM JENNINGS, being fully minded and agreed that sd land with the appertinances shall be divided & that a just proportion thereof may be made between them the said JOHN JENNINGS & WILLIAM may have in certainty his own part and dispose thereof as to him or either of them deem most convenient and they with unanimous assent have by a line of Division run between them of the tract of Three hundred acres of land by Capt. WM. MOSLEY bearing date the first day of March 1688 as by sd Platt may more fully appeare made full division & particon of the aforesaid Devident of land as aforesaid and this Indenture Witnesseth that the two Brothers, JOHN JENNINGS and WILLIAM JENNINGS , are fully satisfied and agreed with the sd Division so made and for ratification of sd Partition and for voyding all contentions which might hereafter chance to arise touching the same it is granted and agreed between the sd parties by these presents that the sd partition so made shall be deemed and taken to be as good effectuall in the Law as any devision or particon might have been made in any manner whatsoever howsoever and sd JOHN JENNINGS and WILLIAM JENNINGS parties to these presents do grant each other that he the sd JOHN JENNINGS and he the sd WILLIAM JENNINGS their heirs and assigns forever hereafter enjoy from each other and their heirs devided in severally and not in Joynture each his full moyety of all and singular the sd lands so to them the sd JOHN and WILLIAM given by their sd Father, JOHN JENNINGS, and as afore-sd in full recompence and satisfaction thereof In Witness whereof the parties have sett their hands and seals

Signed Sealed and delivered in the presence of
ARTHUR SPICER, WM. JENNINGS
AUGUT: WINGFIELD
Recognitr in Cur Comt Rappa 5 die 9ber 1690

pp. 203-205 THIS INDENTURE made the Three and Twentieth day of August Ano Dom 1690 between JOHN JENNINGS of the one part and WILLIAM JENNINGS of the other part (Repeats the foregoing Indenture between JOHN and WILLIAM JENNINGS)

In Witness whereof the parties to these presents have interchangably sett their hands and seals

Signed Sealed and delivered in the presents of
ARTHUR SPICER, JOHN JENNINGS
AUGUT: WINGFIELD
Recognitr in Cur Comt. Rappa 5 die 9ber 1690

pp. 205-206 TO ALL XPIAN PEOPLE to whom these presents shall come that I JOHN COLLIVOWE of County Rappa in Virginia send Greeting And Now know yee that I JOHN COLLIVOWE for several considerations in hand already received or secured to be paid do hereby sell unto JOHN EYLES of Farnham Parish in County of Rappa and unto his heirs all that parcell of land containing One hundred acres more or less being in sd County of Rappa joyning on land of THOS. WILLIAMSON and bounded West from THO: WILLIAMSON, South from RALPH WHITTEN, North from a Neck called WATERS NECK East from JOHN HARFORDs which land was formerly in possession of WILLIAM COOKE and XPHER CHAUNT who right have invested in me sd JOHN COLLIVOWE by purchase firmly to be acknowlegded in Open Court To have and to hold with all houses fences orchards and all other appertinances thereunto belonging with all priviledges unto him sd JOHN EYLE or unto his heirs he paying unto our Sovereigne Lord the King his heirs and Successors all such rents and services as shall become due for the same In Witness whereof I sd JOHN COLLIVOWE have sett my hand and seale the first day of April in yeare of our Lord Sixteen hundred and Ninty

Teste ROBT Sig. R WELLS, JOHN COLLIVOWE
JOHN ELLIOTT
Rec Comt Rappa 5 die 9ber 1690

pp. 206-207 KNOW ALL MEN by these presents that I JOHN WILTON of County of Rappa. of the Parish of Sittenburne for and in consideration of the sum of (blot) thousand pounds of Tobb. to me secured by HIGH CRABB sell unto sd HIGH CRABB his heirs or assigns One hundred acres of land computation be it more or less being part of a Patent granted to RICHARD COLEMAN begining at the end of a Pare tree ditch that butts against COLEMANS CREEK thence extending alongst the sd Creek Ditch W. to a small red Oak by a Pocoson thence along the Pocoson and up the River its severall courses being brought in a streight line in a small red Oake on the River bank thence into the woods South upon the line of the sd WATSON which devides him and RICHARD WEST to a marked Gum by the sd line in a branch thence down the sd branch by a line of trees to COLEMANS CREEK thence down the Creek according to it severall courses to its first

menconed station the sd One hundred acres of land with the priviledges of the Marsh thereunto belonging and all other rights To have and to hold from me the sd WATSON my heirs or assigns in as large manner as may be collected out of the Patent without the lett of me the said JOHN WATSON my heirs or any person claiming thereof under me the sd HIGH CRABB paying the rights and services from henceforth to grow due In Witness whereof I have hereunto set my hand and seale this 3d day of 9ber 1690
Signed Sealed and Delivered in the presents of us

FRAN: SLOUGHTER, JOHN Sig. *F* WATSON
MARGARETT SLOUGHTER

Recognitr in Cur Comt Rappa 5 die 9ber 1690

pp. 207-209 KNOW ALL MEN by these presents that I JOHN PROSSER of Parish of St. Marys in County of Rappa, Plantr., for a valuable consideracon to me in hand payed by WILLIAM SMYTH and THO: HILLARD both of Parish and County aforesd, Planters, hath granted unto sd WM. SMYTH and THO: HILLARD their heirs that parcell of land lying between Mr. JOHN BUCKNERs land and the land of Mr. JOHN HASLEWOOD formerly JOHN PAYNEs & extends begining at a Stake by a Hickory at the head of a branch of MUZENSEEN RUN thence South East to the Main Run of GOLDEN VALE CREEK thence down the sd Run to a Hickory thence up a branch to a marked white Oake in the line of JOHN HASLEWOODs by estimation fifty acres more or less being in Parish of St. Marys and County of Rappa. on South side thereof being part of a Patent of sd PROSSERs bearing date the 21st of 8ber 1684 To have and to hold sd land with all rights to sd SMYTH & HILLARD their heirs & assigns forever in as full measure as may be collected out of the sd Patent and JOHN PROSSER for himself his heirs doth grant that he will at all time forever hereafter keep indemnified sd SMYTH and HILLARD their heirs from all persons claiming under him and that sd PROSSER and ELIZABETH his Wife shall make acknowledgment in the County Court of their act and deed In Witness whereof I have by these presents sett my hand & seal this 30th of 10ber 1689
Signed sealed and delivered in the presents of us

JOHN CATLETT, JOHN PROSSER
WM. CATLETT

Recognitr in Cur Comt Rappa 5 die 9ber 1689

TO ALL TO WHOM it may concerne I ELIZABETH PROSSER of County of Rappa do hereby authorized Mr. JOHN BATTLE my lawfull Attorney for me to make and acknowledge in Court of Rappa all my right to a parcell of land in a Deed of Sale signed Sealed and delivered by my lawfull Husband, JOHN PROSSER, and bearing date the thirtieth day of 10ber 1689 hereby ratifying whatsoever my sd Attoeney shall lawfully do about the premises to be as good as if I myself were personally present, Further I do herein and by these presents to be voluntarily & freely of my own accord without the threat or compulsion of my sd Husband In Witness whereof I hereunto sett my hand this fourth day of 9ber 1690

Witness thereunto ROBT. WRIGHT, ELIZA. as Sig *P* PROSSER
REES EVANS

Recordatr. Test WM. COLSTON Cl Cur

TO ALL TO WHOM it may concern I THO: HILIARD of Rappa County do hereby impower my friend, WM. SMYTH, my true and lawfull Attorney to take acknowledgement of a parcell of land bought from JOHN PROSSER as by Deed of Sale appears to WM. SMITH and myself confirming what my sd Attorney shall do in the premises to be as good in the Law as if I myself were personally present Witness my hand this 4th day of 9ber 1690

Witness hereunto REES EVANS THOS: HILLIARD
ROBT. WRIGHT

pp. 209-210 THIS INDENTURE made the 4th day of Octr. 1690 Between HENRY AWBREY of Rappa. County Gent. of one part and RICHARD AWBREY, only Son and heire apparent of the sd HENRY of other part Witnesseth that HENRY AWBREY as well for the great love and effection which he hath and beareth unto the sd RICHD. AWBREY and towards the present maintainance and settlement & pferment in the World of him sd RICHD. as also for the sum of five Shillings Sterling money to him the sd HENRY in hand before the sealing and delivery hereof by the sd RICHARD well and truely paid and for other good causes hath sold and fully give unto RICHARD AWBREY Five hundred acres of land being part of a Tract of One thouand and fifty acres of land being on South side of Rappa River in sd County and granted to sd HENRY by Patent dated the 9th day of April 1664 all which Five hundred acres of land is adjoining to the land now of JOHN MEADOUR and is to run its severall courses expressed in the sd Patent and to include all the Plantation houses orchards and fences therein as it is now seated planted or tended and all houses orchards buildings whatsoever thereupon standing and all yards gardens pastures inclosures to the Five hundred acres of land belonging and all woods timber trees thereupon standing or growing and all ways waters profitts privilidges belonging and all the right & demand of sd HENRY AWBREY to the premises and all Deeds Charters writings touching the premises or any part thereof To have and to hold unto RICHARD AWBREY his heirs and assigns from day of date hereof the yearly rents which from henceforth grow due and right to be pd. to Chief Lord or Lords of the fee of the premises only excepted, Provided always & upon condition that if the sd RICHD. AWBREY shall happen to die or depart this life unmarried intestate and without issue of his body lawfully begotten that then this present grant & sale shall cease & be utterly void anything in these presents conteyned to the contrary thereof notwithstanding. In Witness whereof the sd parties have set their hands and seals
Signed Sealed and delivered in the presents of us

RALPH RYMER, HENRY AWBREY
HEN: SEAGER

This Instrumt. of Writing was acknowledged before us this 4th day of Octor: 1690
JOHN STONE GEO: TAYLOR
Recordtr. in Cur Comt. Rappa 12 die 9ber 1690

p. 210 THIS INDENTURE made the Eight day of October 1690 and in the second yeare of the Reign of our Sovereigne Lord & Lady William & Mary &c. Between Mrs. EASTER TOMLIN of Parish of Farnham in County of Rappa, Widow, of one part and MATHEW BURROU(blot) of the Parish of Christ Church in County of LANCASTER of other part Witnesseth that EASTER TOMLIN for (all marked out, not in the Original book)

pp. 211-212 TO ALL PEOPLE to whom these present writtings shall come I HENRY AWBREY of Rappa County Gent. send Greeting. Know yee that I HENRY AWBREY as well for the naturall love & effection which I bear unto my only Son, RICHARD AWBREY, and towards his present meyntaynance & Prfermt. as also for sum of Five shillings Sterling money to me in hand paid have granted unto RICHARD AWBREY four Negroes that is to say Jupiter, Sambo and his Wife, Betty, all which are now remaining and being on my plantation commonly called my Quarter scituate neere and adjoining to the Run of HOSKINS CREEK in Farnham Parish in sd County and one other all working Negroe which I intend to put on the sd Plantation and Twenty five head of old Cattle and all the Stock of hoggs now running and belonging unto the sd Plantation and for the consideration aforesd I do grant unto RICHD. AWBREY Fifty pounds Sterling in money or Ten thousand pounds of good sound merchantable sweet sented Tobb: & cask to be laid out to the best advantage in good and convenient house hold stuff &

implemts. of house hold fitt & necessary for him To have and to hold all the sd unto the sd RICCHARD AWBREY his heirs and assigns from the date of these presents to his own use forever under the proviso hereafter menconed and will warrant Provided always that if sd RICHARD AWBREY shall hapen to depart this life unmarried intestate and without lawfull issue of his body (living me the sd HENRY) that then the present grant shall revert unto me the sd HENRY my Exrs. & assigns anything in these presents to the Contrary In Witness said AWBREY have sett my hand and seal dated the 4th day of Octr 1690

Signed Sealed and delivered in the presents of us

RALPH RYMER, HENRY AWBREY

HEN: SEGAR

This Instrument of Writing was acknowledged before us the 4th of 8ber 1690

JOHN STONE GEO: TAYLOR

Recordatr. Cur Com Rappa 12 die 9ber 1690

pp. THIS INDENTURE made the Eight day of October 1690 and in the second yeare of
212- the Reign of our Sovereign Lord and Lady William & Mary &c. Between Mrs.
214 EASTER TOMLIN of Parish of Farnham in County of Rappa., Widow, of one part
and MATHEW BURROWS of the Parish of Christ Church in County of LANCASTER of other part Witnesseth the sd EASTER TOMLIN for sum of Ten thousand five hundred pounds of Tobb: in cask to her in hand paid fully sell & confirm unto MATTHEW BURROWS his heirs Three hundred acres of land scituate in Parish of Sittenburne in Rappa County being part of a Patent of Two thousand acres of land formerly granted to WALTER GRANGER as lapsed for Colnll. FLEET and by the sd GRANGER sold unto Colo: WALKER Father of the sd EASTER TOMLIN and her Sister, SARAH, and devided between them the sd Three hundred acres of land begining at an Oake on the upper side of RAPPA CREEK standing on a point by the sd Creeke being a corner tree of the sd Devision & runing thence along the deviding line now in the possession of MOTTRUM WRIGHT to an other corner tree in the back line, thence runing North East along the back line so far that a line runing West down sd Creeke may include the quantity of Three hundred acres and also all the profitts belonging unto sd land as all the right which sd EASTER TOMLIN now hath to the same To have and to hold unto sd MATTHEW BURROWS his heirs from henceforth forever subject Nevertheless unto the quit rents from henceforth grow due to be paid for the land to their Majesties In Witness whereof the parties have set their hands and Seales

Signed sealed and delivered in the presence of

EDWIN CONWAY, EASTER TOMLIN

WM. BALL

Recognitr in Cur Comt Rappa 19 die 9br 1690

p. KNOW ALL MEN that I the within named EASTER TOMLIN for Three hundred and
214 seventy pounds of good Tobb: in hand reced of MATTHEW BURROWS have
granted unto MATTHEW BURROW his heirs Twenty acres of land joying unto the Three hundred acres menconed within this Deed all which I the sd EASTER TOMLIN grant unto MATTHEW BURROWS his heirs with as full Warranty as is expressed in the sd Deed altogether being Three hundred & Twenty acres of land bounded Begining at a white Oake corner tree standing on a point on the Westward side of RAPPA CREEK being the upper corner tree of Mr. MOTTRUM WRIGHT land and runing alonge his line West to another corner white Oak of sd WRIGHTs, then North East to a Spanish Oake by the sd Creek thence down the sd Creek its severall courses to the begining including the Three hundred & twenty acres In Witness whereof I sd EASTER TOMLIN hereunto sett

my hand and seal this 18th day of November 1690
Signed Sealed and delivered in the presents of
EDWIN CONWAY, EASTER TOMLIN
WM. BALL
Recognitr in Cur Comt Rappa 19 die 9ber 1690

p. 214 WALTER ANDERSON this day owned the marke of the Cow belonging to his Daughter, SARAH ANDERSON, to be a crop in the left eare and an half spade & underkeel in the right eare & desired that the same might be recorded
Teste WM. COLSTON Cl Cur

pp. 214-215 KNOW ALL MEN by these presents that we BENJAMIN TACKER and my Wife, ELIZABETH THACKER of Rappa County have sold and made over all our right to a tract of land of Ninty six acres which was formerly purchased of ANGELL JONES and FRAN: GOURE and with their Deed of Sale all things therein conteyned unto HENRY LEWIS his heirs or assigns and from us our heirs In Witness hereof we have sett our hands & seals the 8th day of January Ano 1690
Signed Sealed & delivered in presents of us
RALPH RYMER, BENJA. THACKER
CHRISTR. ASCOUGH ELIZA. Sig + THACKER
Recognitr in Cur Comt Rappa 8 die Jany 1690
KNOW ALL MEN by these presents that I ELIZABETH TUCKER, Wife of BENJA. TUCKER, do hereby impower my very good friend, WM. HARWOOD, to be my true and lawfull Attorney for me in my behalf to acknowledge this next County Court of Rappa all my right of my thirds of a track of land of Ninty six acres unto HENRY LEWIS his heirs from me my heirs forever in as full force as if I the sd ELIZABETH TUCKER were personally present Witness my hand and seal the 8th day of Jany 1690.
ELIZA. Sig + TUCKER

pp. 215-216 THIS INDENTURE made the 24th day of 9ber 1690 Between WM. TOMLIN of Parish of North Farnham in County of Rappa. Gent. and ANN his Wife of the one part and SAMLL. BAYLEY & FRAN: GORE of Parish and County aforesd. also Gent. of other part Witnesseth that WM. TOMLIN & ANN his Wife for the setting & establishing the lands and premises herein expressed for the uses and purposes in these presents menconed have granted transferred and confirmed unto SAMLL. BAYLY and FRAN: GOURE all that Plantation or tract of land conteyning Four hundred and fifty acres being part of a Devident of Eighteen hundred acres of land formerly taken up and Patented by JAMES WILLIAMSON being neere Rappa. River, Together with all houses profits and priviledges to the sd Four hundred and fifty acres apperteyning late in the occupacon of CHARLES DAVIS and by him in his last Will and Testament given and bequeathed to sd ANN her heirs and assigns To have and to hold the sd Foure hundred and fifty acres of land hereby granted with all appertinances thereunto belonging in as full and ample manner as is expressed in the original Patent or as they sd WM. TOMLIN and ANN his Wife might enjoy the same to the uses herein expressed that is to say to and for the uses and purposes of sd WM. TOMLIN and ANN his Wife for and during their naturall lives and the longest liver of them and after their decease to the use and behoof of sd WM. TOMLIN his heirs and assigns forever and no other use or purpose whatsoever And sd WM. TOMLIN and ANN his Wife do for themselves their heirs promise that sd SAMLL. BAYLEY and FRAN: GORE and their heirs shall be seized in the land and premises with their appertinances hereby granted in good indefeazabel Estate of Inheritance for the uses and purposes afore declared and to no other purpose whatso-

ever In Witness whereof the parties have set their hands and seales
Sealed and delivered in the presents of

GERARD GREENWOOD, WM. TOMLIN
ANN Mar: 7 BEAR The Mark of sd ANN

The day & year within written livery and seissen were made of the premises by the within named WM. TOMLIN and ANN his Wife unto the ffeoffees in Trust within specified for the uses within written by Turffe and Twigge

GERARD GREENWOOD JANE Mar: TB BENGEE
ANN Mar: 7 BEARE, JOHN TAVERNER

Recordatr Cur Comt Rappa 22d day Jany 1690

pp. 216-217 KNOW ALL MEN by these presents that we the Subscribers having taken up a parcil of land lying on South side of PISCATAWAY POCOSON between the land of THO: HARPER and JOHN IMGRAMs land being in Quantitie One hundred acres as appeare by a Patent bearing date the 16th day of April 1683 in joint tenancy between us have impremised of some of the neighbourhood make a Devision between us that is to say beginning at a marked white Oake corner tree which is the South side menconed in the sd Patent and runing thence Sotherly along a line of marked trees to a Swamp and so the severall courses up sd Swamp to a marked Pine standing in the Fork of the Swamp and so runing Southerly by a line of marked trees to a corner white Oake standing at the head of the aforesd land which I sd JOHN PRICE do own myself satisfied with that side of land joyning to THO: HARPERs and I WM. BALL do own myselfe satisfied with the other side to which we have agreed to be a equall division for us and our heirs As Witness our hands and seales this second day of December 1690
Signed sealed and delivered in the presents of us

JAMES BOUGHAN JOHN Sig HH PRICE
JAMES FULLERTON WM. Sig. D BALL

p. 217 KNOW ALL MEN by these presents that I WM. CATLETT of County of Rappa Parish of Sittenburne for and in consideracon of the sum of Five thousand pounds of Tobb: and cask secured to be paid to me by JOHN SMYTH of County and Parish aforesd. have granted unto JOHN SMYTH his heirs One hundred acres of land lying in County of Rappa on South side the River commonly called by the name of THICKETT taking its breadth on the River from the THICKETT SWAMP adjacent to ROBT. PAYNE extending back in the woods for its length the sd hundred acres of land with all its rights and priviledges To have and to hold from me sd WM. CATLETT my heirs and assigns in as large manner as may be collected out of the Patent without the hindrance of me sd WM. CATLETT my heirs or assigns In Witness whereof I have sett my hand and seal this 18th of 9ber 1690
Signed Sealed & delivered in the presents of us

BERNARD GANES, WM. CATLETT
RALPH ROWZEE

Recognitr. in Cur Comt. Rappa 4 die January 1690

p. 218 TO ALL TO WHOM these presents may concern I ROBERT CADE of Parish of Farnham in County of Rappa send Greeting in our Lord God everlasting. Now know yee that I ROBT. CADE for divers good causes grant unto WM. FREEMAN of County & Parish aforesd all my right which I have to part of a Devident of land being in the Parish aforesd being part and parcell of the land which I now live on by estimacon One hundred acres more or less and bounded beginning at a corner white Oake standing nigh a branch side arme of the Midle Branch called the BRIDGE BRANCH and so runing up the said Branch to a corner red Oake standing by or nigh the head of sd branch and thence by a line of marked trees Easterly to corner red Oake standing by a branch side called CRUMPLES QUARTER BRANCH and thence Southerly by a line of marked trees to a red Oak standing nigh the line of JOSEPH GOODRICH and thence Easterly along the sd GOODRICH line to a corner white Oake standing by a branch side, and thence Westerly to a corner white Oake of FRAN: BROWNE standing on a Hill side and so with the line of sd BROWNE to a corner Elm standing by a branch side called the MIDLE BRANCH and thence down the sd branch to the place first began To have and to hold the bargained land and premises unto WM. FREEMAN his heirs forever with all rights belonging with Warranty from me the sd ROBT. CADE my heirs or any persons whatsoever laying any claim under me or any other persons whatsoever. In Witness whereof I have sett my hand and seal this fourth of February 1690

Signed Sealed and delivered in the presents of us

JAS. BOUGHAN, ROBT. R CADE

JOHN BURNETT, FRAN: BROWNE LETTICIA Sig. L CADE

Acknowld. in Rappa County Court by ROBT. CADE and LETICIA his Wife this 4th day of February and recorded 28th day

pp. 218-220 THIS INDENTURE made the 19th day of 8ber 1689 in the first year of the Reigne of Lord King William Between JOHN HARPER of Parish of Sittenburne and County of Rappa of the one partie and ROBERT RICHARDSON of the Parish of St. Stephens and County of NEW KENT, Planter, of the other part Witnesseth that JOHN HARPER for sum of Two thousand pounds of Tobacco to him in hand paid and secured to be paid and for divers other causes hath granted unto ROBT. RICHARDSON his heirs a certain parcell of land being in the Parish of and County of Rappa conteyning One hundred acres beginning at the uppermost corner tree of ROBT. CADE and from thence up the MANE SWAMP to the corner tree of HENRY BOUGHAN for breadth to conteyn the complement of the aforesaid One hundred acres of land Together with all ways and appertinances to the same belonging and all the right the sd HARPER now hath To have and to hold the sd bargained tract of land and bargained premises with their appertenances unto ROBERT RICHARDSON his heirs and that sd JOHN HARPER will warrant and forever defend the sd ROBERT RICHARDSON his heirs in the quiet enjoyment against all persons claiming under him and lastly that JOHN HARPER and LIDIA his Wife herself or lawfull Attorney shall make acknowledge of these presents and her right of Dower in Court next held for Rappa County In Witness I sd HARPER to this presents his hand and seal hath putt

Sealed and Delivered in the presents of us

JOHN GORDON, JOHN HARPER

WM. LEE

Recognitr in Cur Com Rappa 4 die Febry 1690

pp. 220-221 KNOW ALL MEN by these presents that I THOS: BURGESS of County of NEW KENT do for divers good causes but especially for the sum of Eight thousand pounds of Tobb: in cask in hand to me paid do sett over from me my heirs forever all that parcell of land menconed in the recited Deed (blot) HEAD formerly bought of Mr. JOHN FRY late of the aforesd County deced unto JOHN OLIVAR and JANE his Wife and their heirs forever and do oblige myself my heirs to acknowledge the same in County Court of Rappa when thereunto required by sd OLIVAR to the truth of which I sett my hand and affixed my seal this 22nd day of 9ber 1690. I do further oblige myself my heirs in the penall lsum of Sixteen thousand pounds of Tobb: and caske that I will acknowledge this at the next Court held for Rappa is required

Signed sealed and delivered in the presents of us

PHILIP GRITH, THOMAS BURGESS
JOHN CHAMLER, JOHN ʘ MINTON ELIZ. E B BURGESS

Recognitr in Cur Comt Rappa 4 die Febry 1690

KNOW ALL MEN by these presents that I ELIZABETH BURGESS do by these presents appoint my well beloved friend, ROBERT BURCH, to be my true and lawfull Attorney for me to acknowledge my part of Dowry or thirds of Six hundred acres of land lying in Rappa County which my Husband, THO: BURGESS, bought of Mr. JOHN FRY and by my Husband assigned over to JOHN OLIVAR as by Assignmt. under the seal of JOHN FRY to my Husband will appeare bearing date the 22nd day of 9ber 1690 in the County Court of Rappa which shall be held for sd County next after date hereof and what my said Attorney shall do in the premises I shall oblige me to ratifie as lawfully as if I myself were personally present as Witness my hand & Seal this 30th day of Jany. 1690/1

Signed & Sealed in presents of

ROGER MALORY JUNR., ELIZ: E B BURGESS
HEN: Sig. + SAUNDERS

Recognitr in Cur Comt Rappa 4 die Febry. 1690

KNOW ALL MEN by these presents that THO: BURGESS of Parish of St. Johns in NEW KENT COUNTY my heirs & assigns do assigne over all my right of this bond from me my heirs unto JOHN OLIVAR his heirs to the true intent & meaning of the within menconed Bond Witness my hand

Teste THO: MERIDEN, THOMAS Signum B BURGESS
JOHN WOOD

Recordr. Cur Comt Rappa 18 die February 1690

pp. 221-222 KNOW ALL MEN by these presents that I JOSEPH MOORE and MARY my Wife do assigne over unto HENRY BAKER his heirs and assigns all our right & title of the within menconed Bill of Sale the contents being three hundred and fifty acres of land As Witness my hands and seals this 14th of 9ber 1690

Signed Sealed and delivered in the presents of

LEWIS WATSON, JOSEPH Sig I MOORE
JANE I C COLE, MATTHEW COLE MARY ΠΓ MOORE

KNOW ALL MEN by these presents that I JOSEPH MOORE of Abington Parish in County of GLOCESTER do hereby appoint Mr. LEONARD CHAMBERLANE of Rappa County to be my true and lawfull Attorney to acknowledge in Rappa County Court unto HENRY BAKER of GLOCESTER COUNTY a Deed of three fifty acres of land scituate lying and being in sd County of Rappa. and what my said Attorney shall legally act & do thereby confirm as Witness my hand this 3rd day of 10ber 1690

Test: PHILL: PENDLETON, JOSEPH I MOORE
PHILL: PARR

Recordatr Cur Comt. Rappa 28th die xber 1690

KNOW ALL MEN by these presents that I MARY MOORE the Wife of JOSEPH MOORE of Abington Parish in GLOCESTER for divers good causes me theretunto moving have appointed my beloved friend Mr. ROBERT COLEMAN of Rappa. County my true and lawfull Attorney for me to acknowledge in Rappa Court when requested my part and Dower of land lying in Rappa County unto HENRY BAKER or his certain attorney or his heirs confirming what my sd Attorney shall do in the premises abovesd as if I was personally present In Witness my hand and seal this Twenty second day of (blot) 1690

Signed Sealed & delivered in the presents of

JANE I COLE, MARY ΠΓ MOORE
MATHEW CALE

pp. 222-223 KNOW ALL MEN by these presents that I NICHOLAS LANGFORD & KATHERINE my Wife do for a consideration in hand reced make over unto THOMAS WATKINS his heirs all our right and interest in the within Bill of Sale from us and our heirs or any person that shall lay any claime with warranty as Witness my hand and seal Novr. the 3rd 1690.

Signed sealed & delivered in the presents of

NATHLL. LANDERS, NICHO. Sig. VL LANGFORD
JOSEPH Sig. I MOORE,
MARGARETT M WATKINS

Recognitr in Cur Comt Rappa 24 die Feby. 1690

KNOW ALL MEN by these presents that I NICHOLAS LANGFORD of Abington Parish in County of GLOCESTER do appoint Mr. LEONARD CHAMBERLANE of Rappa County to be my true and lawfull Attorney to acknowledge for me and in my behalf in Rappa County Court a Deed from me and my heirs unto Mr. THO: WATKINS of said County of Rappa. and to his heirs of Three hundred and fifty acres of land being in County of Rappa being the equall half part of a tract of seven hundred acres of land and what my sd Attorney shall do I hereby confirm as Witness my hand and seal this 3rd of Decr. 1690

Teste PHILLIP PENDLETON, NICHO. Sig. VL LANGFORD
PHILL: PARR

Recordatr. Cur Comt Rappa 28 die Febry. 1690

KNOW ALL MEN by these presents that I KATHERINE LANGFORD, Wife of NICHO. LANGFORD, for divers good causes do make and appont Mr. ROBERT COLEMAN my lawfull Attorney to acknoweldge in my name in Rappa my part and dowry of land lying in County aforesd. and do by these presents give full power to my sd Attorney to act and do in all respects as fully as if I was personally present ratifying what my sd Attorney shall do as Witness my hand & seal this 10th day of 9ber 1690

Sealed and Delivered in presents of

JOSEPH MOORE, CATHERINE LANGFORD
MATTHEW COLE

Mr. COLEMAN when acknowledged demand Twenty shillings for ye friend and Servant
CATHERINE LANGFORD

pp. 223-225 THIS INDENTURE made the third day of March 1690 and in the third year of the Reigne of our Sovereigne Lord & Lady William and Mary &c. Between THOMAS FRESHWATER of Rappa in the Dominion of Virginia of one part and WILLIAM DAVIS of Parish and County aforesd., Plantr., on the other part Wittnesseth that JOHN FRESHWATER for the full sum of Twenty thousand pounds of Tobb: and merchantable in good order paid by sd WILLIAM DAVIS have given and sold unto WILLIAM DAVIS his heirs and assigns One thousand acres of land and lying and being in the FOREST between POTOMACK & RAPPA RIVERs part in Rappa. County and part in WESTMORELAND COUNTY being part of a Patent given to RICHD. WEBLEY, ROBT. DAVIS and THOMAS FRESHWATER fallen to sd THOMAS who survived the sd WEBLY and DAVIS so that the right of sd Patent being Seven thousand two hundred Seventy & one acres dated the 24th day of Augst. 1664 did vest in & fall to the sd FRESHWATER in Survivorship the sd One thousand acres of land begining at a red Oake tree of another parcell of land sold out of the Patent to Colo. JOHN HULL deced which goes by the name RICH NECK which sd tree stands by the side of the MAR(blot) SWAMP of the Westward branch of TOTASKEY by the place upon the PATH that goes from the sd RICH NECK Plantation to POTOMACK cutts across the sd MARSHEY SWAMP runing thence by an old line of trees and crossing an old field SW to a Stake, then East to a Hickory in the North line of the sd Patent then N. along sd line to a Stake then W. to a marked red Oake then West to a Stake in the line of Mr. WM. SHOARES then S. W. along the line of sd SHOARES to a Stake by a Hickory corner tree W. along another line of sd SHORES to a Stake by a Hickory tree then N. along another of sd SHOARES to a red Oake sd line then S. W. to a red Oake corner tree standing by the side of the MARSHEY SWAMP on the Westward branch of TOTASKEY then up the water courses the sd Swamp with its severall courses to the begining corner tree and also all houses orchards gardings and enclosures together with all profitts unto sd One thousand acres of land as also all the rights To have and to hold sd One thousand acres of land and all the premises and every rights unto the sd WM. DAVIS his heirs and assigns forever subject nevertheless to the quitrents which shall grow due In Witness whereof the parties to these presents Indentures have set their hands & seals

Signed sealed and Delivered in the presence of us

EDWIN CONWAY, THOS. mark of F FRESHWATER
GEO: GLASSCOCK,
NATHLL. NT THRIFT

Recognitr in Cur Comt Rappa 4 die Martii 1690

pp. 223-228 THIS INDENTURE made the 19th day of November 1690 Between HUGH HARRIS of the one part and JAMES TRAPLEY of Parish and County aforesd of the other part Witnesseth that I HUGH HARRIS for a good consideration to me pd. by JAMES TRAPLEY have given unto sd JAMES TRAPLEY his heirs forever Four acres of land more or less begining at a red Oake being a corner tree belonging to sd HUGH HARRIS and joining upon the land of WM. GIRBTON and running from the said corner E.N.E. to the pitch of the Hill and from thence down the midle of the valley to the Mane Branch so up the Mane run to the sd TRAPLEYs line this land adjoining to sd TRAPLEYs. land To have and to hold sd Foure acres of land to him his heirs forever with all profitts belonging I do also oblige to keep harmless from all former grants and incumbrances made by sd HUGH HARRIS his heirs and the sd HARRIS doth for himself grant with JAMES TRAPLEY his heirs that sd HARRIS his heirs at all times save harmless and keep indemnified sd tract of land to sd JAMES TRAPLEY his heirs against all persons whatsoever In Witness whereof to all and singular the premises conteyned I have hereunto sett my hand & seall

Sealed & Delivered in presents of us

JOHN TRAPLEY, HUGH ++ HARRIS
MARY M TRAPLEY

Recognitr in Cur Comt Rappa 4 die Martii 1690

KNOW ALL MEN by these presents that I HUGH HARRIS of Prish. of Farnham in County of Rappa stand indebted unto JAMES TRAPLEY of sd County the sum of Two thousand pounds of good merchantable Tobb: and cask and I bind myselfe firmly by these presents Sealed with my seal this 20th die of 9ber 1690

Whereas by Indenture under my hand and seal bearing date the 19th day of 9ber being the present month made between me the above bound HUGH HARRIS and JAMES TRAPLEY I the sd HUGH HARRIS for a valuable consideracon sold unto him the sd TRAPLEY foure acres of land in County of Rappa recited Indenture relation being had may appeare Now the Condicion of this obligation is that if the above JAMES TRAPLEY his heirs shall and may at all times forever hereafter possess and enjoy the aforesd land without the molestation of any persons whatsoever that may claime any title to sd Foure acres of land and to acknowledge the same in the County Court of Rappa when required that this obligation to be void otherwise to remain in full force

Signed Sealed in the presents of us
JOHN TRAPLEY HUGH mark of ++ HARRIS
MARY Mark /X\ TRAPLEY
Recognitr in Cur Comt Rappa 4 die March 1690

pp. 228-229 KNOW ALL MEN by these presents that JAMES and ANN DABNEY of the County of County of Rappa in Virginia for a valuable consideration of One thousand five hundred pounds of Tobb: and Caske in hand paid from FRANCIS JAMES of the County abovesd do hereby sell unto FRANCIS JAMES his heirs Seventy five acres of wood land being in County of Rappa and on the North side of the River it being the Quarter part of Three hundred acres formerly taken up by PHILLIP SHEARWOOD late of the County deced, and now in possession of sd JAMES DANBY in right of his Wife the aforesd land bounding on the land of FRAN: TRIPLETT, JOHN ARRINGTON, WM. JETT and DAVID ROSSEN To have and to hold sd land with all hereditaments and priviledges appertaining to him said FRAN: JAMES his heirs and assigns and we also the sd JAMES and ANN DAUBNEY do hereby promise that the premises are free & cleare & shall always be more free and cleare by us the sd JAMES and ANN DAUBNEY our heirs to him sd FRAN: JAMES his heirs warranting the same to him against all persons whatsoever As Witness our hands and seals this 28th day of April 1690
Signed Sealed and Delivered in the presents of us
WM. UNDERWOOD, JAMES DABNEY
JOHN Mark I O COMBE ANN mark /\ DABNEY
Recognitr in Cur Comt Rappa 4th die Martii 1690

p. 229 KNOW ALL MEN by these presents that we JAMES & ANN DABNEY of County of Rappa in Virginia do for the valuable consideration of Three thousand pounds of Tobb: and cask in hand paid do sell and make over unto FRANCIS STERNE of County abovesd from us our heirs forever Fifty acres of woodland being in County of Rappa on North side the River it being the quarter part of Two hundred acres formerly bought of PHILLIP SHARWOOD late of this County deced and adjoining to the land of FRAN: JAMES and on the corner side thereof the aforesd land To have and to hold with all priviledges and hereditaments belonging to him the said FRANCIS STERNE his heirs or assigns forever and also wee the sd JAMES and ANN DAUBNEY do hereby promise the premises are free & cleare and shall always be made free & cleare by us sd JAMES & ANN DAUBNEY their heirs by warranty the same As Witness our hands and Seals the 26th of April 1690
Signed Sealed and Delivered in the prsents of us
WM. UNDERWOOD JAMES DABNEY
JOHN I C COMBE ANN /\ DABNEY
Recognitr in Cur comt Rappa p DABNEY & Uxerem 4 die Martii 1690

pp. 229-230 KNOW ALL MEN by these presents that I JOHN WATERS of County of Rappa in Virginia, Plantr., for divers causes more especially for One thousand pounds of swt. sented Tobb: & caske have by these prests. sold unto JOHN WEBSTER his heirs and assigns two parcells of land being in the aforesd County and bounded upon EVAN DAVIS, JOHN COLLIVOWE and sd JOHN WEBSTER being by compecacon twelve acres of land and the other parcell of land being in aforesd County bounding upon JOHN LAVAG and so to RILSMANS BEAVER being a point or two of land by computation Eight acres of land which land I the abovesd JOHN WATERS do by these presents warrant the aforesd land to the aforesd JOHN WEBSTER his heirs or assigns from the right & interest of me my heirs and from the claim of all persons that shall lay any interest to any parcell of the two aforesd parcells of land and likewise do oblige myself to acknowledge the aforesd sale in open Court when thereunto called. In Witness where I have sett my hand and seal this 1st day of April 1691 and before signed sealed & delivered I do oblige myself my heirs to give the aforesd WEBSTER or his heirs any assurances of the aforesd land if this shall not be thought good and sufficient by the aforesd WEBSTER and heirs & their Councell learned in the Law shall advise As Witness my hand & seal

Signed Sealed and Delivered in the presents of us

DAVID LOYDE, JOHN WATERS

RICHD. DAVIS

Recognitr in Cur Comt. Rappa 1 die Aprilis 1691

pp. 230-231 BEE IT KNOWN unto all men by these presents that I MARY DYKE, Widow, late Wife of JOHN DYKE deced, have right & full power to dispose of Two hundred acres of land be it more or less lying and adjoining Mr. THO: HARWARs Plantacon being my part or proportion of the tract of land belonging to JOHN SHARPE my Naturall Brother for divers good causes do grant & acknowledge all my right of the sd parcell of land with all profits & appertinances thereunto belonging unto THO: TALBOTT my oldest Son & heir & his heirs forever And that it may be lawfull for the sd THO: TALBOTT to make such conveyance as by his Councell learned in the Law shall direct and I sd MARY DIKE, Widow, doth oblige myselfe or any attorney lawfully authorized to acknowledge the within menconed premises in any Court of Judicature as also this to be my full & voluntary perfect Deed of Guift In Witness whereof I have here unto sett my hand and seal this Thirtieth day of March 1691

Signed Sealed and delivered in the presents of

RICHD. LACKLAND, MARY signum + DIKE

Recognitr in Cur Comt Rappa 1 die Aprilis 1691

pp. 231-232 KNOW ALL MEN by these presents that I WILLIAM HUDSON of County of Rappa do ow and stand firmly bound and indebted unto ABRAHAM DEPREE as Guardian and for the use of SARAH, the Daughter & heire of RICHD. SMYTH of the aforesd County deced, her heirs in the sum of Four thousand pounds of good sound merchantable Tobb: sweet sented with sufficient caske to contain the same to be pd. convenient to landing in Rappa County on all demands which payment I bind myself my heirs by these presents Sealed with my seal dated this 3rd day of June 1691

The Condition of the above obligation is that if the above named SARAH SMYTH, the Daughter and heire of the above named RICHD. SMYTH deced, and ABRAHAM DEPREE as Guardian for the use of the sd SARAH untill she arrive at full age by law her heirs or assignes at all times hereafter quietly have and enjoy One hundred acres of land it being part of a tract of land purchased by sd RICHARD SMITH deced of HENRY WOODNOTT quantitie One hundred and seventy acres according to the meaning of a Deed of Sale sealed by sd HENRY WOODNOTT unto sd RICHARD SMYTH deceased bearing date the 3rd day of April 1683 with appertinances without the lett of the abovesd WM. HUDSON or REBECCA his Wife or either of them their heirs that then the above obligation to be void and of non effect otherwise to remain in full force and virtue as Witness my hand and seale the day and year abovesd

WM. mark W HUDSON

Signed Sealed & delivered in presents of us

PHILL. PAR

WILLIAM YOUNG

Recognitr in Cur Comt. Rappa 3 die Junii Ano 1691

p. 232 KNOW ALL MEN that I JOSEPH GOODRICH of JAMES CITTY COUNTY do by these presents sell unto JOHN POWELL of County of Rappa One hundred acres of land being part of a devident taken up by JOHN PRICE and WILLIAM BALL and the sd JOS: GOODRICH binding on JOHN HARPER & LIGHTFOOT and the sd GOODRICH do by these presents warrant the sale of the sd land from him his heirs unto JOHN POWELL & his heirs or assigns In Witness hereof I sett my hand this Third day of March 1690
Signed and Delivered in presents of
JOHN CLARKE JOSEPH GOODRICH
JOHN LEMAN
Recognitr in Cur Comt Rappa 3 die Junii 1691
KNOW ALL MEN that I JOSEPH GOODRICH do by these presents appoint in my name my Friend, Mr. JONATHAN FISHER, to acknowledge abovesd Conveyance unto JOHN POWELL which shall be in as full and ample as if I were personally present myself In Witness hereof I have sett my hand this 31st day of March 1691
Sealed & Delivered in presents of
JOHN LEMAN, JOSEPH GOODRICH
JOHN CLARKE
Recordatr. Cur Comt 10th die Junii 1691

pp. 232-233 KNOW ALL MEN by these presents that I JOHN WATSON of County of Rappa of the Parish of Sittenburne do for a valuable consideracon in hand reced give sell & confirm for me my heirs unto HUGH CRABBE of County & Parish aforesd his heirs or assigns Two hundred Twenty one acres of land bequeathed to me sd WATSON by my Father lying in County of Rappa on South side of the River and bounded Beginning at the (blank) of a peach tree ditch that cuts against COLEMANS CREEK thence extending alonge the sd Ditch North to a small red Oak to a Mill Pococon thence by the Pocoson and up the River its severall courses being brought into a straight line to a small red Oake on the River bank, thence into the woods a mile to two red Oakes and a Spanish Oake on COLEMANS CREEK, thence down the sd Creek its severall courses to the first menconed Station being part of a Patent granted to RICHARD COLEMAN for Six hundred acres the sd Two hundred Twenty one acres of land with all its rights and priviledges To have and to hold from me sd JOHN WATSON my heirs to him sd HUGH CRABBE his heirs or assigns in as ample manner as may be collected out of the Patent without the lett of me sd JOHN WATSON my heirs or assigns or any persons claiming from or under me my heirs In Witness whereof I have hereunto sett my hand and seal this 3rd day of Jany. 1690
Signed Sealed and Delivered in the presents of us
BERNARD GAINES, JOHN Mar: 王 WATSON
JOHN BRAY
Recognitr in Cur Comt Rappa 3 die Junii 1691

pp. 233-234 TO ALL XPIAN PEOPLE to whom these presents shall come I EVAN DAVIS and Wife of County of Rappa & South Farnham Parish send Greeting. Know yee that I EVAN DAVIS and Wife for forteen hundred pounds of Tobb: do give unto JAMES ACRES of same County and Parish his heirs One hundred acres of land being on the South side of Rappa River and in the aforesd Parish and County and formerly being land of EVAN DAVIS SENR. as the conveyance upon record appears and by Patent from JAMES CITTY the sd JAMES ACRES to have and to hold sd land forever and to be layed out of a parcell of land formerly being EVAN DAVIS SENR. Warranty unto sd JAMES ACRES his heirs and assigns forever & from any persons whatsoever In Witness my hand and Seale this Sixteenth day of 10ber in year 1690

Signed Sealed & delivered in presence of us
DAVID MEREDITH EVAN TTT DAVIS
ARTHUR A HODGES, JUDITH Sig + DAVIS
Recognitr in Cur Comt Rappa 3 die Junii 1691
KNOW ALL MEN by these presents that I JUDITH DAVIS do constitute & ordain my well beloved Friend, GEO: TURNER, to be my lawfull Attorney in my place to acknowledge the Thirds of a hundred acres of land in my stead and place and what my Attorney shall do in my behalf shall stand in full force and virtue as if I myself were there present In Witness whereof I have sett my hand and seal this second day of June 1691
Teste SAMLL. PARREY JUDITH Mar: + DAVIS
ANN hir S mark PRICE
Recordr. Cur Com Rappa 10 die Junii 1691

pp. 234-236 THIS INDENTURE made the 19th day of May 1691 and in the Third year of the Reigne of our Sovereign Lord & Lady William and Mary &c. Between THOMAS COOPER of the Parish of South Farnham in County of Rappa, Plantr., and ANN his Wife of one part and GEORGE TURNER of Parish and County aforesd of other part Witnesseth that THO: COOPER and ANN his Wife for ye full (sum) of Three thousand and five hundred pounds of good and merchantable swt. sented Tobb: to them or one of them in hand well paid by the sd GEO: TURNER by these presents have granted unto the sd GEO: TURNER his heirs Two hundred acres of land being in sd Parish and County being part of seven hundred and fifty acres formerly granted to Majr. GEORGE MORRIS by Patent dated the 16th day of April 1683 and by sd MORRIS conveyed to sd THOS. COOPER and bounded begining of ye sd Patent and runing thence S. by sd PERRYs line of marked trees crossing the maine branch of PERRYS CREEK to the land of ARTHUR HODGES to a white Oake on a Hill, thence by his line South to a red Oake, thence W. to the land of BENJA. MATHEWS to a red Oake in his line and thence East by sd MATHEWS line to the first specified station and also all profitts belonging to sd Two hundred acres of land with all the right which the sd THOS: COOPER or ANN his Wife or either of them have to the same To have and to hold unto sd GEO: TURNER his heirs & assigns forever subject nevertheless to the quit rents which from henceforth shall grow due unto their Majesties their heirs and Successors and sd THO: COOPER and ANN his Wife shall not only in due forme of Law and with time hereby limited acknowledge this presēnt Deed before their Worshipfull their Majesties Justices of peace at the Court held for said County at the costs and charges in the Law of sd GEORGE TURNER his heirs and will within the space of seven years from the date hereof acknowledge further or other Deed for the better conveying the premises as by sd Councell shall require In Witness the parties above have sett their hands and seals
Signed Sealed and Delivered in the presents of us
EDWIN THACKER, JOHN his mark I HINDES, THO: Sig. T COOPER
GILS: his mark X YOUNGE ANN Sig. + COOPER
Recognitr pr COOPER Cur Comt Rappa 3 day June 1691

pp. 236-238 TO ALL XPIAN PEOPLE Know yee that I ZACHARIAS NICCHOLLS of Parish of Farnham in County of Rappa and with the consent of MARY my Wife and we both one consent and in consideration of Three thousand pounds of Tobb: and caske to me in hand paid it being from the hand of JOHN GETHIN of the sd County and do release him from the sd Tobb: have sold unto JOHN GETHIN his heirs or assigns One hundred acres of land being in County aforesd and upon the branch of TOTASKEY CREEK & begining tree of WM. DEYEs land and run So. W. to two small Oakes the corner of Mr. JAMES TRAPLEYs land and then along the sd TRAPLEYs land No. W. to a red Oake

corner tree of sd TRAPLEYs, thence N.E. to a bush by a red Oake, then S.E. to a red Oake in sd DEYs line, thence along sd DEYs line to the place where it first began the sd land being part of a tract of land taken up and Patented by HENRY CORBYN Esqr. and by him sold to my Father, GEO: NICHOLLS, and my God Father, MATHEW WILSON, both deceased & given to me by my God Father in his last Wil & Testament as may at large appeare by severall instruments of writing upon record the sd GITHIN to have and to hold sd One hundred acres of land to him his heirs or assigns forever with all rights all comodities belonging to the sd GETHIN his heirs paying the rents and services of right accustomed then I the said ZACHARIA NICHOLLS do for me my heirs neither have nor shall make any other title of the sd land to any other person and that I am lawfully seized of perfect Estate of fee simple and do oblige myself tha the sd JOHN GETHIN his heirs shall at all times forever hold and enjoy the sd land without the incumbrance of me the sd NICHOLLS my heirs or any other persons In Witness to all and singular the articles herein contained I have hereunto sett my hand & seal this last of April 1691
Signed & Sealed in the presents of us

WM. SOUTHERN, ZACH: NICHOLLS
PENEL. EVERTON MARY NICHOLLS

Recognitr pr NICHOLLS Cur Comt Rappa 3 die Junii 1691

KNOW ALL MEN by these presents that I ZACHARIAH NICHOLLS of Parish of Farnham do stand bound unto JOHN GETHIN of Parish and County aforesd the sum of Six thousand pounds of Tobb. with sufficient caske to conteyne the same due to be paid convenient to me on demand the which payment I bind myself my heirs unto sd JOHN GETHIN his heirs signed with my hand and sealed with my seal this 30th day of April 1691

The Condition of this obligation is that the above bound ZACH: NICHOLLS hath sold unto JOHN GETHIN One hundred acres of land as by Instrument of Writing bearing date with these presents may fully appeare Now so it is if sd NICHOLLS doth truely keep all the covinants conteyned this obligation to be of none effect otherwise to stand in full force and so to continue the terme of seven years after the acknowledgement of the same in the County Court abovesd. In Witness I have put my hand and seal the day and year written

WM. SOUTHERNE, ZACH: NICHOLLS
THOS. GLASCOCK

Recordr. Cur Comt Rappa 10 die Junii 1691

pp. 238-241 THIS INDENTURE made the 4th day of May 1691 and in the yeare of the Reigne of our Sovereigne Lord and Lady William & Mary &c. Between ZACHARIAH NICHOLLS of Parish of Farnham in County of Rappa & MARY his Wife of one part and WILLIAM DEY of the Parish of Christ Church in County of LANCASTER, Carpenter, of other part Witnesseth that ZACHARIAH NICHOLLS & MARY his Wife for sum of seven thousand pounds of good sweet merchantable Tobb: & Cask to conteyn the same in hand paid do hereby grant unto sd WM. DAY his heirs & assigns Two hundred acres of land being part of a Patent formerly granted unto HENRY CORBYN Esqr. and by sd CORBYN sold & assigned unto MATHEW WILCOCKS and Mr. GEO: NICHOLLS, Father of the sd ZACHARIAH NICHOLLS, situate in Rappa County in the FOREST on the head branch of TOTASKEY CREEK and so begining at a red Oake corner tree of HUGH his land and runing thence North to a corner white Oak and Hickory, then South East to a white Oak corner tree, then South to a red Oake corner tree in the sd HARRIS his line neere his Plantacon, thence North West alonge the sd HARRIS his line to the first menconed red Oake the place it first began with all profitts & appertenances belonging to sd Two hundred acres of land as all the rights which said ZACHARIAH NICHOLLS and MARY his Wife now have or may claime to the sd land by vertue of Patent grant gift or assignmt. or

other To have and to hold sd Two hundred acres of land and all & singular premises unto sd WM. DEY his heirs from henceforth and forever subject nevertheless unto the quit rents which henceforth shall be due to be pd. unto their Majesties and that sd WM. DEY may his heirs and assigns peacably possess the same without the trouble of the said ZACHARIAH NICHOLLS and MARY his Wife or their heirs or any other persons whatsoever In Witness whereof the parties have sett their hands and Seals
Signed Sealed & delivered in presents of us

WILLIAM BARBER, ZACHARIAH NICHOLLS
EDWARD JONES MARY her M mark NICHOLLS

Recognitr p ZACHARIAH NICHOLLS & uxorem MARIAM in cur comt Rappa 9 die Junii 1691

KNOW ALL MEN by these presents that I ZACHARIAH NICHOLLS of Parish of Farnham in County of Rappa. Plantr., do acknowledge myself indebted unto WM. DEY of the Parish of Christ Church in County of LANCASTER, Carpenter, the full sum of Fourteen thousand pounds of every way good merchantable Tobb. and caske to contain the same to which payment I bind myself this 4th day of May 1691

The Condition of this obligation is that if the above bound ZACHA. NICHOLLS his heirs in all things truly keep all the agreements which ought to be kept conteyned in Deed of Sale for Two hundred acres of land in County of Rappa abovesd and bearing even date with these presents between ZACHARIAH NICHOLLS of one part and WM. DEY of the other part then this obligation to be void otherwise to remain in full force
Signed Sealed and Delivered in the presents of

WILLIAM BARBER, ZACHARIAH NICHOLLS
EDWD. JONES

Recognitr in Cur Comt Rappa 23 die Junii 1691

pp. 241-243 THIS INDENTURE made the first day of May 1691 & in the yeare of the Reigne of our Sovereigne Lord and Lady William and Mary &c. Between JOHN HEWLETT JUNR. of Parish of Foure Fields in County of NORTHUMBERLAND Gent. & MARY his Wife of the one part and THO: GLASCOCK of Parish of Farnham in County of Rappa. Gent. and ANN his Wife of the other part Witnesseth Whereas Mr. GEORGE NICHOLLS late of County of Rappa deceased did by a Deed of Gift give unto the sd MARY & ANN (his Two Daughters) and their heirs forever One thousand acres of land situate at or neere the head of TOTASKEY CREEKE in Rappa. County which he purchased and bought of HENRY CORBYN Esqr. Now This Indenture Witnesseth that sd JOHN HEWLETT & MARY his Wife and sd THO: GLASCOCK and ANN his Wife have mutually agreed in a partition and seperacon of sd One thousand acres of land between them in pursuance whereof have granted unto THO: GLASCOCK & ANN his Wife their heirs and assigns Five hundred acres of the sd land lying Westermost seperated and devided from the other by a line of marked trees (for that purpose) runing from a red Oake corner tree on a levell East to two small Oakes standing by the MILL SWAMP neere or towards the head thereof being in or neere the line that parts this One thousand acres of land from the residue which the sd NICHOLLS bought of the sd CORBIN which sd line of marked trees runs (as neere as may be) thought the midle of the sd One thousand acres of land and also all profitts and appertinances to the sd Westermost Five hundred acres of land belonging as also all the right which the sd JOHN HEWLETT and MARY his Wife may lawfully claime To have and to hold the sd land being the Westermost of the One thousand acres of land divided unto the sd THO: GLASCOCK and ANN his Wife their heirs and assigns forever; Five hundred acres being the Eastermost of the sd Thousand acres of land seperated and devided from the other by the sd line runing from the sd red Oake to the two small Oakes aforesd and all profitts and appertinances belonging to sd THOS: GLAS-

COCK and ANN his Wife have or may lawfully claime to have and to hold said Five hundred acres of land divided as aforesd and all and singular the other the premises with the right unto sd JOHN HEWLETT & MARY his Wife their heirs and assigns from henceforth & forever and sd JOHN HEWLETT and MARY his Wife their heirs do covinant with sd THOS. GLASCOCK & ANN his Wife their heirs will at any time hereafter acknowledge these presents in due forme of Law for the more sure conveying the sd land In Witness whereof the parties have sett their hands & seals

Signed sealed and delivered in the presence of

WM. SOUTHERNE, THO: GLASCOCK
JAMES COLLIN ANN GLASCOCK
MARY Mar: X COLVERT

Recognitr in Cur Court Rappa 3 die Junii 1691

KNOW ALL MEN by these presents that I ANN GLASCOCK do appoint Mr. EDWARD JONES my lawfull Attorney to acknowledge in open Court held for the County aforesd my free will & consent to a Deed of Devision of land made between MARY HEWLETT and myself which land was given by my Father and now divided by a Survey ratifying and confirming what my sd Attorney shall do in as full manner as if I myself were present Witness my hand this 5th day of May 1691

WILLIAM SOUTHERNE ANN GLASCOCK
JAMES OVERTON

Recordr. in Cur Comt. Rappa 23 die Junii 1691

pp. 243-245 THIS INDENTURE made the first day of May 1691 in the Third yeare of the Reigne of our Sovereigne Lord & Lady William & Mary &c. Between ZACHARIAH NICHOLLS and MARY his Wife of County of Rappa in the Dominion of Virginia of the one part and THOMAS GLASCOCK of County aforesd of other part Witnesseth that ZACHARIAH NICHOLLS & MARY his Wife for the full sum of Fourteen thousand pounds of good sound & merchantable Tobacco & cask to contain the same to them paid by sd THO: GLASCOCK they the sd ZACHARIAH NICHOLLS and MARY his Wife do sell unto sd THO: GLASCOCK his heirs all that Plantacon situate by TOTASKEY MILL in County aforesd that did formerly belong unto Mr. GEO: NICHOLLS, Father of the said ZACHARIAH NICHOLLS and Mr. MATHEW WILCOCKS both deceased which Plantation with a considerable quantity of land the sd GEORGE NICHOLLS and the sd Mr. MATHEW WILCOCKS purchased of HENRY CORBYN Esqr. all the sd Plantation with much of the sd land as lyes & bounds on & between Mr. DANIEL SWILLEVANTs land and the land of HENRY CLARKE & land of Mr. JAMES TRAPLEY and WILLIAM GUBTONs land bounded on the Westward Northward & Eastward with their lands and on the Southward with the water course of the MANE SWAMP or pococon above the sd Mill runing into TOTASKEY CREEK down from the sd GUBTON unto sd SWILLEVANTs land being by estimacon Four hundred acres (only excepted & reserved and it is hereby excepted One hundred acres of land with the sd (blot) that is to say joining on the land of the sd GUBTON and on sd water courses of the MANE SWAMP of TOTASKEY which sd one hundred acres of land the sd ZACHARIAH NICHOLLS and MARY his Wife by these prsents. in consideration of the dear affections unto their Kinswoman, ANN GLASCOCK, Daughter of sd THOMAS GLASCOCK, grant & confirm the sd one hundred acres of land and all its appertinances unto ANN GLASCOCK to her and her heirs Also all houses orchards gardens together with all profits belonging unto the sd four hundred acres of land only excepted as is before excepted Also all the right title & interest which ZACHARIAH NICHOLLS & MARY his Wife have or may clame of the same hereby granted land and premises by virtue of Patent grant will guift or otherwise To have and to hold the sd Foure hundred acres of land within the sd bounds together with the premises unto sd THO: GLASCOCK his heirs and assigns from hence-

forth and forever Except as before Excepted subject nevertheless to the quit rents which shall grow due unto their Sovereigne Majties their heirs and Successors In Witness whereof the parties have set their hands and seals
Signed Sealed and Delivered in the presence of

WM. SOUTHERNE, ZACHARIAH NICHOLLS
JAMES COLLIN MARY Mar: M NICHOLLS
MARY Mar: + CALVERT,
JEAN GLASCOCK

Recognitr pr ZACH NICHOLLS et Uxorem MARRIAM in Cur Comt Rappa 3 die Junii 1691

pp. 246-247 THIS INDENTURE made the first day of May and yeare 1691 and in the Third yeare of the Reigne of our Sovereigne Lord and Lady William and Mary &c. Between THO: GLASCOCK of Parish of Farnham in County of Rappa., Gent., and ANN his Wife of one part and JOHN HEWLETT JUNR. of the Parish of Faire Fields in County of NORTHUMBERLAND Gent. and MARY his Wife of the other part Whereas GEO: NICHOLLS late of County of Rappa by a Deed of Guift did give unto sd ANN & MARY his two Daughters and their heirs forever One thousand acres of land neere unto the head of TOTASKEY CREEK in Rappa County which he bought of HENRY CORBYN Esqr. Now this Indenture witnesseth that sd THOMAS GLASCOCK and ANN his Wife and the sd JOHN HEWLETT JUNR. and MARY his Wife have mutually agreed on a particon of the sd One thousand acres between them the sd THOS. GLASCOCK and ANN his Wife in pursuance whereof have granted unto JOHN HEWLETT and MARY his Wife their heirs Five hundred acres of the sd land lying Eastermost seperated from the other by a line of marked trees for that purpose runing from a Red Oake corner tree on a levell South East to a small Oake standing by the MILL SWAMP neere the line that parts One thousand acres from the residue which sd GEORGE NICHOLLS bought of sd CORBYN which sd line of marked trees runs (as neere as may be) through the midle of the sd One thousand acres of land granted as aforesd and also all profitts to the sd Eastermost Five hundred acres of land belonging as also all the right which the sd THO: GLASLCOCK & ANN his Wife have to the same To have and to hold sd five hundred acres of land being the Eastermost of the said One thousand acres of land devided and all the premises belonging unto sd JOHN HEWLETT and MARY his Wife their heirs and assigns forever, Whereupon sd JOHN HEWLETT and MARY his Wife have granted and confirmed unto sd THOS: GLASCOCK & ANN his Wife their heirs Five hundred acres of land being the Westermost of the sd One thousand acres & devided from the other by the sd line runing from the sd Red Oake East to the two small Oakes aforesd and all other appertinances to the Westermost Five hundred acres of land belonging as abovesd

X X X X X X X X X X X

(The foregoing Deed was not completed. The following Deed does not begin at the beginning. Maybe when the material was copied, a page was missing and the material not available.)

X X X X X X X X X X X

pp. 247-248 at a small Hickory in the land line that devided between the sd CLARKE & XPHER PRIDHAM which said Hickory is the Corner tree of the line that parts & devides between the sd JACOBUS and Mr. FRAN: GOURE and runs thence along sd PRIDHAM line North East to a great white Oake neere the HICKORY THICKETT then along an other old line North East to a small Hickory South West to a red Oak in the line that devides betwixt the sd JACOBUS and GOURE then along the same line South West to the place it began To have and to hold the sd land forever with all its rights as fowling hunting hawking and all woods in as large and ample manner as is expressed by

Majesties order for holding of land in this Dominion and to be safely possed with the same free from claim by from or under me the sd ANGELL JACOBUS & my Wife our heirs or assigns and likewise any other person whatsoever, Furthermore we the sd ANGELL JACOBUS and ELIZABETH my Wife do oblige ourselves to acknowledge the same in Court when soever the sd JOHN KELT he his heirs or assigns shall desire the same In confirmacon hereof we the sd ANGELL JACOBUS and ELIZABETH my Wife doth sett our hands and seals this sixth day of May 1691

Test XPHER ASCOUGH, ANGELL JACOBUS
TIMO. Mar: £ DARLEY
Recognitr in Cur Comt Rappa 1 die July 1691

pp. 248-249 TO ALL XPIAN PEOPLE to whom these presents shall come THOMAS COOPER SENR. of South Farnham Parish in County of Rappa sendeth Greeting &c. Now know yee that the sd THOMAS COOPER for a sufficient valuable consideracon in hand reced or secured to be pd. have given unto GILES YOUNGE of sd Parish & County and his heirs and assigns the full & compleat quantity of One hundred acres of land out of a Devident of two hundred & twenty acres of land I purchased of DANLL. BROWN by a firm Deed of Sale bearing date the 24th of Septr. 1690 which sd One hundred acres of land shall begin at a Poplar corner tree and extend itself binding upon the land of JOSEPH SMITH and so to continue with equal extentions of bounds untill the full complemt. of One hundred acres be bounded out upon and equall parralell as neere as possible may be and to be entering together, To have and to hold the sd One hundred acres of land and every part thereof so taken out of Two hundred and twenty acres together with all its rights appertaining unto sd GILES YOUNGE and to his heirs & assigns which shall be bounded to his or their full satisfaction & content, he they or any of them paying unto our Sovereign Lord and Lady King Wm. & Mary or Successors all such rents as shall become due for the same and further I the sd THOMAS COOPER do hereby oblige me my heirs that he the sd GILES YOUNGE his heirs shall forever hereafter quietly have and enjoy the sd one hundred acres of land lying in the abovesd Parish and every part thereof taken out of the aforesd recited Two hundred and twenty acres without the trouble or disturbance of me the sd THOMAS COOPER or any persons whatsoever and will warrant the present sale from any persons and will acknowledge to be my free act & deed in the County Court of Rappa when required, And I ANN COOPER the lawfull Wife of the sd THOMAS COOPER, do hereby relinquish all my right and interest in the sd One hundred acres of land and every part thereof and will acknowledge the same when required In Witness whereof we have sett our hands and seals this 20th day of July 1691

Signed Sealed & delivered in the Presents of us
JNO. RICHARDS THOMAS COOPER
PHILL. PENDLETON, WM. WOOD ANN Sig. × COOPER
Recognitr in Cur Comt Rappa 5 die Augusti 1691

pp. 249-250 TO ALL XPIAN PEOPLE to whom these presents shall come I THOMAS COOPER SENR. of South Farnham Parish in the County of Rappa in Virginia send Greeting &c. Now Know yee that I the sd THOMAS COOPER for a sufficiently valuble consideracon reced or secured to be paid have sold from mE my heirs unto WM. MORRIS of sd Parish and County the full quantity of Two hundred and twenty acres of land being part of the home Devident of land by me purchased of Majr. GEORGE MORRIS deced as by a Deed of Sale under the hands of the sd MORRIS relacon being had will appear bearing date the 20th of February 1683/4 which sd Two hundred and Twenty acres of land being part of the Home Devident is to begin at two red Oakes being corner trees to the same adjoining upon the land of sd COOPERs home devident untill it comes to the land I the sd COOPER procured of DANIEL BROWN thereon binding and extending to the land of Mr. THO: EDMUNDSON so that it compleates the aforemenconed complemt. of Two hundred and Twenty acres which is to ly entirely together as neere as possible may bee to the full satisfaction of the sd MORRIS his heirs and assigns To have and to hold the sd Two hundred and twenty acres of land bounded as aforesd with all its rights & conveyances thereunto belonging unto him the sd WM. MORRIS and his heirs and assigns forever hee or they paying unto our Sovereigne Lord and Lady King William & Queen Mary or to their Successors all such rents as shall become due In Witness whereof we have sett our hands and seals this 21st day of July One thousand Six hundred and Ninety one

Signed Sealed and Delivered in presents of us

JNO. RICHARDS, THO: Sig: COOPER
PHILL. PENDLETON, WM. WOOD ANN Sig. λ COOPER

Recognitr in Cur Comt Rappa 5th August 1691

p. 251 KNOW ALL MEN by these presents that I RALPH WHITTEN and ELIZABETH WHITTEN of County of Rappa for divers good causes and valuable consideracon in hand received have sold unto THO: JOHNSON and HENRY JOHNSON of same County One hundred acres of land of the same Devident whereon I the sd RALPH & ELIZABETH WHITTEN do now live lying on the DRAGON SWAMP with rights and priviledges according to my Patent with all profitts and appertinances there unto belonging without lett or molestation of us RALPH & ELIZABETH or any other persons which shall have any Estate by from or under me and to deliver the sd land and to acknowledge sd Hundred acres of land unto sd THO: & HENRY JOHNSON their heirs and assigns forever in the next Court which will be the next Augt. in the year 1691 In Witness hereof we have joyntly & severly sett our hands & seals this 21st day of June 1691

Test TOBIAS ✓ LEVERETH RALPH WHITTEN
JNO. COLLIVOWE ELIZABETH WHITTEN

Recognitr in Cur Comt Rappa 5 die Augst. 1691

pp. 251-252 ARTICLES OF AGREEMENT made and concluded on by & between JONATHAN GRILLS of Rappa County on the one part & GILES YOUNGE of County of NEW KENT on the other part as followeth, First the sd JONATHAN GRILLS for the reasons & consideracons hereafter expressed do hereby consent and agree to take to live with me the sd GILES YOUNGE upon my Dwelling Plantation being in Farnham Parish in County of Rappa upon or neere PISCATAWAY CREEK from the day of the date hereof for and during the whole terme or our Naturall lives and the life of my Wife, ANN GRILLS in consideracon whereof its mutually agreed by and between me the sd JONATHAN GRILLS & me the sd GILES YOUNGE that all and all manner of Estate both real and personall of what nature or quantity soever shall be deemed and taken and is hereby fully concluded and consented to be deemed and taken that is to say that is now or at any time hereafter to belong to us two aforenamed to be a joint and equall interest & have a Copartner ship in during the whole terme of our respective naturall (blank) from this present day and all the produce of our two respective labours to each other in equally propocon untill it shall please God to make seperacon by Death which if it shall happen that I the sd GILES YOUNGE should die first of us two aforenamed that then and all whatsoever I shall be worth or posed with all shall imediately descend & come unto the sd JONATHAN GRILLS and his heirs of or the survivour of them & their heirs & to them forever and if sd JONATHAN GRILLS and my Wife should die before the sd YOUNGE that then he the sd YOUNGE shall inheritt and enjoy every part and parcell of Estate reall and personall that then belongs to us or either of us & to our heirs unless wee should leave any children begotten on our bodies and then such to have an equall part with him and it is further agreed that (if by any disturbance arising between us two aforenamed either of us shall take occasion to be seperate himself and go away during the terme aforesd then such person or us so differeing and dissenting shall on request have delivered unto them any equall part of the whole estate real & personnall and for the more performance of all & everything and matter herein contained the sd persons aforenamed do hereby enter into the penalty forfeiture of Five thousand pounds of good Tobb: and cask each other to one another severally to be paid by him that shall make the first breach of any part of the same upon demand to the party so damnified. In Witness whereof we hereunto sett our hands and seales this nineteenth day of December One thousand six hundred and Eighty nine

Signed sealed and delivered in the presents of us

JOHN SMITH, JONATHAN GRILLS
PHILL. PENDLETON, GILES ± YOUNGE
OLIVER sig. 9 RICHARDS, ANN GRILLS mark
THO: HUSLICOTT, WM. M MORRISS

Recognitr in Cur Comt Rappa (blot) die Augusti 1691

pp. 252-254 THIS INDENTURE made the 5th day of Augst. 1691 and in the Third year of our Sovereigne Lord and Lady Wm. and Mary over England, Scotland, France, Ireland, Virginia Between JOHN HARPER of County of Rappa in the Colony of Virginia, Plantr., of one part and JOHN PRICE of the same County & Colony, Plantr., of other part, Witnesseth that JOHN HARPER for a valuable consideracon already received have granted unto the sd JOHN PRICE his heirs and assigns forever all his Right and demand of a certain parcell of land conteyning Two hundred acres of land more or less being part of a greater tract of land granted by Patent to THO: HARPER late of the aforesd County and Colony deced, and by him given to sd JOHN HARPER the sd land being in the aforesd County of Rappa on the South side of the PISCATOUN POCOSON and bounded begining at a corner marked Gum of the sd HARPERs thence down the Fork of the sd Swamp thence up the BRIDGE SWAMP to the North of sd PRICES SPRING BRANCH thence up the sd Spring Branch to sd HARPERs line To have & to hold the sd land together with all woods water and appertinances belonging unto the sd JOHN PRICE his heirs and assigns subject nevertheless to the quit rents that from henceforth grow due for the same to our Sovereigne Lord and Lady the King & Queen their heirs & Successors and the sd JOHN HARPER his heirs & assigns for the sd valuable consideracon will warrant and defend unto the sd JOHN PRICE his heirs and assigns forever In Witness whereof the sd JOHN HARPER have hereunto sett his hand and seale

Teste: THO: HUSLESCOTT JOHN HARPER
WM. Sig: XV MORRIS

Recognitr in Cur Comt Rappa 5 die Augt. 1691

KNOW ALL MEN by these presents that I LIDIA HARPER by these presents freely and voluntarily ratify and confirm what my within menconed Husband hath acted and done and relinquish all my right and interest and dower in the premises and have hereunto sett my hand & seal this fifth day of Augt. 1691

Test: THO: HUSLESCOTT, LIDIA HARPER
WM. Sig: XV MORRIS

Recordr. Test WM. COLSTON Cl Cur

pp. 254-255 TO ALL XPIAN PEOPLE to whom these presents shall come Know yee that I DANIEL SWILLIVANT of County of Rappa do for me my heirs in consideracon of one Negro man delivered to my content for One hundred acres of land and an obligation for Six thousand pounds of Tobb: p. hundred to be paid year after year for as many hundred acres as is conteyned within the following devident of land & delivered unto JOHN TRAPLEY & do for these presents sell and make over unto JOHN TRAPLEY his heirs one parcell of land being on the head of TOTASKEY CREEK in the County aforesd and lying as following adjoyning the land sold p me to Mr. NEWTON and from yt. all the land outwards that is within the bounds of the Patent which was granted to my Father, DENNIS SWILLIVANT deceased, and is according to an obligation under my hand bearing date the 3rd day of March last past and from that day the sd TRAPLEY to have & to hold the sd tract of land with all rights conteyned to him his heirs and furthermore by reason of the bounds and Nomber of acres yet cannot be known for want of a survey I the sd SWILLIVANT do by these presents oblige myself my heirs to procure a Surveyor and lay out the sd land at my cost & charges and with the first convenience or at reasonable requet of sd TRAPLEY and the courses of the sd land and nomber of acres are so known then to give to the sd TRAPLEY such Deed or Deeds according to Law for the securitie of the sd land as shall be thought convenient by the sd TRAPLEY his Attorney In Witness to all & singular herein conteyned I have hereunto sett my hand & seal the first day of September Ano Dom: 1691

Signes Sealed in the presents of us

WM. BARBER, DANIELL SWILLIVANT

EDW. JONES

Recognitr in Cur Comt Rappa 2 die 7ber 1691

p. 255 THIS INDENTURE made the 7th day of February in year of our Lord 1689/90 Between PAUL WOODBRIDGE of Farnham in County of Rappa. Gent., of one part and WILLIAM HANKS of Farnham aforesd, Carpenter, of other part, Witnesseth that PAUL WOODBRIDGE for the consideracon of Foure thousand pounds of arenoco Tobb: in hand paid by Bill by sd WILLIAM HANKS hath granted unto WM. HANKS and his heirs forever One hundred acres of land more or less lying on North side of a branch comonly called or known by the name of INDIAN TOWN BRANCH bounded begining at a marked Pockhickory standing on the branch, thence alonge the PATH which is called the SCHOOL PATH extending to the corner tree of the land of EDWARD JEFFERIES, thence to a white Oak standing on a branch of MORATTICO CREEK, from thence to the line of ROBERT PALMER and so alonge the line of sd PALMER till it come to a certain white Oake thence alonge a new line through the land of sd PAUL WOODBRIDGE to a Chesnut and from thence to the place where it first began To have and to hold the sd land with its boundaries and with warranty from me the sd PAUL WOODBRIDGE my heirs to the sd WILLIAM HANKS and his heirs forever In Witness whereof I have sett my hand and Seal

Teste WILLIAM WOODBRIDGE, PAUL WOODBRIDGE

THOMAS WILSON, EDWD. JEFFRIES

This Day WM. WOODBRIDGE, his Father PAULE WOODBRIDGE being deceased, did acknowledge this within Deed to WILLIAM HANKS in the County Court of Rappa the 2d of September ano 1691 and was recorded the 21st of the sd month and yeare

Teste WM. COLSTON Cl Cur

p. 256 TO ALL XPIAN PEOPLE &c. I DANIEL SWILLIVANT of Rappa County send Greeting this 20th of March 1691. Now know yee that I sd DANLL. SWILLIVANT for Foure hundred pounds of Tobb. paid by JOHN NEWTON of WESTMORELAND COUNTY in

the Colony of Virginia by these presents sold unto sd JOHN NEWTON his heirs one acre of land by estimacon be the same more or less being part of a Devident of land granted to my Father, DENNIS SWILLIVANT, by Patent bearing date the 2nd of Feby 1663, part thereof being by my sd Father bequeathed by his last Will dated December 1673, the other part thereof descending to me by the death of my Brother, DENNIS SWILLIVANT, as by the sd Will doth at large appeare and sd land lying in Farnham Parish in the County of Rappa and being the Hill end or part of land that adjoineth on the end of TOTASKEY MILL DAM runing up between the MILL PATH that is the sd NEWTONs bounds of a greater tract formerly bought of sd SWILLIVANT and their Mill Pond or Swamp the other side of the Hill end of land and devided from the remainder of sd SWILLIVANTs land by a line of five marked trees cross the sd point from the sd MILL PATH to the sd Swamp or Mill Pond being as aforesd one acre To have and to hold unto JOHN NEWTON his heirs and assigns forever As Witness my hand and seal
Signed sealed and delivered in the presents of us
WM. BARBER SENR., DANIEL SWILLIVANT
WM. BARBER JUNR.
Recognitr in Cur Comt rappa 2 die 7ber 1691

p. 257 I JAMES ORCHARD of Parish of Sittenburne & County of Rappa send Greeting &c. Know yee that I the sd JAMES ORCHARD for the consideracon of One thousand pounds of Tobb: & cask to me paid I have sold unto ELIAS WILSON JUNR., Forty seven acres of land being in the Forest of Rappa. and purchased by me of a Patent belonging to Mr. WM. LANE and begining upon the line of Mr. ELIAS WILSON SENR. & extending from the sd line of Mr. ELIAS WILSON South to a Stake by a red Oake neere the sd WILSONs Plantation from thence North East to a Stake in COLEMANs line, thence alonge the sd line North to the line that was formerly ELIAS WILSON SENR. it being a red Oake corner tree in the sd COLEMANs line, it being also the corner tree of THO: BRADLEY, thence along the sd BRADLEYs line West by North to the first menconed begining upon the sd WILSONs line To have and enjoy the aforesd Forty seven acres of land unto the aforesd ELIAS WILSON JR. his heirs forever with all rights belonging without the hindrance of me sd JAMES ORCHARD my heirs or persons claiming any right In Witness thereof I have hereunto sett my hand and seale this 26th day of August 1691
Signed Sealed and Delivered in presents of us
ELIZ: BOOTH, JAMES ORCHARD
PETER & CONSALVE
Recognitr in Cur Comt Rappa 2 die 7ber 1691

pp. 257-259 THIS INDENTURE made the 3rd day of March ano Dom 1690 and in the Third yeare of the Reigne of our Sovereigne Lord and Lady William and Mary &c. Between JOHN PRICE of Parish of Farnham in County of Rappa in the Dominion of Virginia and EASTER his Wife of the one part & PETER EVANS of the Parish of Sittenburne of the County aforesd on the other part, Witnesseth that JOHN PRICE and EASTER his Wife for the full sum of Nine thousand pounds of good sound and merchantable Tobb: in good caske to them well and truely pd. do hereby sell unto the sd EVANS his heirs Two hundred and forty acres of land situate and being in Sittenburne Parish in Rappa County being part of a Patent of Two thousand acres of land granted to Lieut. Colo. HENRY FLEET dated 25th day of August ano dom 1657 and by him lapsed and granted to WALTER GRANGER by Patent dated the 25th of March 1661, and by the sd GRANGER sold to Col. JOHN WALKER by Assignmt. of the sd GRANGERs dated 20th day of

May 1662, and One thousand of the Two thousand given by Will of the sd Colo. JOHN WALKER unto the sd EASTER the now Wife of the sd JOHN PRICE, the sd Two hundred & forty acres of land being part of the sd One thousand acres of land so given unto the sd EASTER as aforesd, the sd Two hundred and forty acres of land hereby granted is bounded Begining at a small Spanish Oake standing on the West side of RAPPA CREEK being a corner tree of land belonging to the land of MATHEW BURROWS & runing along the sd BURROWs line West to a Stake in the back line of the sd 2000 acres of land, thence alonge the sd back line North East Stake or post in the sd line, thence South East crossing a Pocoson by the sd Creek to the sd Creek, then down sd Creek its severall courses to the begining and also all houses orchards gardens and inclosures together with all pro=fitts and appertinants belonging To have and to hold the sd Two hundred and forty acres of land and all the premises unto PETER EVANS their heirs and assigns from henceforth & forever subject nevertheless unto the quitrents henceforth shall grow due In Witness whereof the parties have sett their hands and seals
Signed sealed and delivered in the presents of us

RICHD. WHITE, JOHN PRICE
ISAAC his mark ɵ HOWARD EASTER PRICE

Acknowledged in Rappa County Court by Mr. JOHN PRICE and EASTER his Wife personally the sd day of 7ber 1691 and recorded the 22nd of the sd month
Teste WM. COLSTON Cl Cur

pp. 259-262 THIS DEED INDENTED made the first day of May in year of our Lord 1691 Between WM. CLEATON of Parish of North Farnham in the County of Rappa., Planter, of the one part and JOHN MORGAN of the same Parish and County, Blacksmith, of the other part Witnesseth that WM. CLEATON for the full sum of Foure thousand Five hundred pounds of Tobb: to him paid sold unto JOHN MORGAN his heirs and assigns forever that my parcell of land being in ye Parish and County abovesd lying on the West side of TOTASKEY CREEK conteyning Fifty acres being the land formerly purchased by WM. CLAYTON deced of one WM. LANDMAN deced as by Deed thereof made appear and the privilidges & appertinances unto the same belonging the quitrents hence forward growing due to the Chief Lord excepted as also my Mothers thirds likewise Excepted To have & to hold the sd Fifty acres of land to be hereby granted with all the appertinances thereunto belonging unto the sd JOHN MORGAN his heirs and assigns forever and the sd WM. CLAYTON for himself his heirs doth promis that the sd WM. CLAYTON at the time of the delivery of these presents stands lawfully seized in his fee of & in the sd land and also that he the sd JOHN MORGAN his heirs shall at all times have the sd land and premises freely and kept harmless from all other gifts sales whatsoever joynter only excepted and from all other titles In Witness whereof the sd WM. CLAYTON hath sett his hand and seale
Sealed and Delivered in the presents of

ROGER JONES, WILLIAM Signum WC CLAYTON
GILB. FORMBY, JOB: J HAMOND

Recognitr in Cur Comt Rappa 2 die 7ber 1691

KNOW ALL MEN by these presents that I WILLIAM CLEATON of County of Rappa., Plant., am bound unto JOHN MORGAN of same County, Blacksmith, in just sum of Five thousand pounds of good merchantable Tobb: to be paid I bind myself my heirs Sealed with my seale and dated this first day of May 1692

The Condicon is such that if the above bound WM. CLEATON his heirs shall truely keep all the condicons contained in one Deed of Conveyance made between the above bound WM. CLEATON & the above named JOHN MORGAN in all things according to purport of the sd Deed and also that sd WM. CLEATON shall remove from his Plantacon menconed in the sd Deed and give peacable and full possession to sd JOHN MORGAN or assigns at or before the last day of October next ensuing date hereof and sd CLEATON and MARY his Wife at some Court in County abovesd within six months after date hereof before their Majesties Justices of the peace then sitting acknowledge the sd Deed and sd MARY remise her right of Dower & third to the land then this obligation to be void or else abide in full force

Signed sealed and delivered in the presents of

ROGER JONES, WILLIAM W6 CLEATON

JOB ⨍ HAMMOND, GILBT: FORMBY

KNOW ALL MEN by these presents that I MARY CLEATON, Wife of WILLIAM CLEATON of Rappa., Plantr., have authorized my good friend, GILB. FORMBY, in my place before their Majesties Justices of the peace for the County of Rappa to acknowledge my free assent to a Deed of Conveyance between my Husband, WILLIAM CLEATON, of the one part and JOHN MORGAN of the other part bearing date with these presents to relinquish all right of Dower and Thirds in the land As Witness my hand and seale this First day of May 1691

ROGER JONES MARY Sig. # CLEATON

JOB: ⨍ HAMMON

p. 263 MR. COLSTON. Please to record a Cow about sevin years old marked as followeth two crops and two holds on each eare and under keele on the left eare with all her encrease being a Guift from my Wife to TABITHA ROBERTS, Daughter of GRIFFIN ROBERTS, October the Seventh 1691

Sir your Servant THO: HARWAR

P. 263 MR. COLSTON Sir: I would desire you to record a Mare of three years old for my Daughter, KATHERINE SMYTH, branced with JWC on both shoulders it being the Guift of HENRY GALLOP to my Daughter, and a Heifer of two yeares old being crop on both ears and 2 slitts on under side of each ear, it being the Gift of THO: HILLER wch. sd GALLOP and HILLER have attested the same here underneath pray lett it be don and make me your Debtor for the same who am your friend to serve you

WM. SMYTH

Apl. the 30th 1691

Test THO: PARKER, HENRY # GALLOP,

THO: mark T HILLOP Recordr. Test WM. COLSTON Cl Cur

p. 263 RICHD. HUTCHINGS his mark a crop and upper keel on the right eare and on the left eare a hole & slitt out

pp. 263-264 KNOW ALL MEN by these presents that I DANLL. PHATRES of County of Rappa Plantr., for a valuable consideracon to me in hand paid by SAMLL. COATS of the aforesd County, School Master, do grant unto them the sd SAMLL. COATS all my right of a parcell of land conteying Three hundred acres more or less which was formerly taken up by STEPHEN BENBRIDGE lying and being in the Parish of South Farnham in Rappa County and bounded as followeth Begining at a corner white Oake of the North West side of PISCATAWAY PATH and from thence to a corner Pine bounding upon the land that was formerly old THOMAS WILLIAMS and from thence to a corner Gum joyning upon ABELL TATHUMs land and from thence to a white Oake joyning upon

JAMES NEWBALLs land To have and to hold the sd parcell of land to him the sd SAMLL. COATS his heirs forever with all profitts belonging with all woods and waters in as perfect manner as it was granted by the Right Honble. Govr. engageing myselfe my heirs that the sd SAMLL. COATS his heirs shall hold and enjoy every part of the aforesd tract of land without molestation of any person whatsoever that shall lay claim under me In Testimony of the same I hereunto putt my hand and seal this 2d day of October in the year One thousand Six hundred Ninety and one
Signed sealed and delivered in the presents of
JOHN COLLIVOWE, DANLL. PHATRES
LEON: WILLIAMSON
Recognitr in Cur Com Rapa 7 die 8br 1691

pp. 264-265 KNOW ALL MEN by these presents that I JOHNANNA HUDSON of CHARLES CITTY COUNTY in the Province of MARYLAND for sum of Forty pounds Sterling to me in hand paid by Mr. RICHARD BOOKER of GLOCESTER whereof I JOHANNA HUDSON do acknowledge I do make over unto the sd RICHARD BOOKER his heirs this within menconed Bill of Sale or Deed together with all my right and further I the sd JOHANNA HUDSON doe warrant the sale of the within menconed land from me my heirs forever In Witness whereof I have sett my hand and seale this 28th day of August One thousand six hundred and ninety one
Signed sealed and delivered in the presence of
MARY M DUCKSBERRY, JOHANNA her mark I HUDSON
CORNLS. BUTHELL, DAVID COGWELL,
ROWLAND PERION
Recognitr in Cur Comt Rappa 7 die 8ber 1691
KNOW ALL MEN by these presents that I JONATHAN HUDSON of CHARLES CITTY County in the Province of MARYLAND do appoint my loving friend Mr. WM. PEIRCE of Rappa County in Virginia to be my true and lawfull Attorney to acknowledge a Bill of Sale I have assigned over unto RICHARD BROOK of GLOCESTER County bearing date with these presents Ratifying what my sd Attorney does in the premises as if I were personally myself present as Witness my hand and seale this 28th of August 1691
Test ROW: PIRSON JONATHAN Marke I HUDSON
DAVID COGWELL

pp. 265-266 KNOW ALL MEN by these presents that wee RICHD. MATHEWS and ELIZABETH MATHEWS of County of Rappa do for themselves our heirs for the valuable consideracon of Forty Shillings to us in hand paid by JOHN ALEXANDER of the same County make over from us our heirs unto sd JOHN ALEXANDER his heirs & assigns all that Platt of ground being an ISLAND or Peninsula adjoining to & fronting of our land that we now live on and enjoy and extending between the Marshes by a Tongue or point of land unto the Main Creek of OCCUPACE that is to say that ISLAND and only that ISLAND with the skirts of sunken ground marshes and creeks thereunto adjoining and belonging secured from the Maine and rest of our devident of land To him the sd JOHN ALEXANDER his heirs and assigns To have and to hold the sd ISLAND and appertinances with all woods ways from us our heirs in fee simple forever it being that ISLAND whereon groweth a GREAT PINE TREE Witness our hands and seales this 3rd day of Augt. 1691
Signed Sealed and Delivered in the presents of
THO: PARKER, RICHD. MATHEWS
JOHN SORRELL, RICHD. DAVIS ELIZ. Sig. H MATHEWS
Recognitr in Cur Comt Rappa 7 die 8ber 1691

KNOW ALL MEN by these presents that we RICHARD MATHEWS and ELIZABETH MATHEWS of County of Rappa have made our beloved friend, THO: PARKER, of sd County to be our lawfull Attorney for us to acknowledge unto JOHN ALEXANDER of sd County of Rappa at next Court held for the sd County a certain parcell of land being an ISLAND and belonging to our Devident of land we now live on which we the sd RICHARD MATHEWS and ELIZABETH MATHEWS sold unto sd JOHN ALEXANDER by conveyance and whatever our sd Attorney act and do wee do ratifie as if we ourselves were then and there personally present. In Witness whereof we have put our hands and seals this 6th day of 8ber 1691

Teste JNO: PARKER, RICHD. Sig. Λ MATHEWS
ANN PARKER ELIZA ++ MATHEWS

pp. 266-267 TO ALL XPIAN PEOPLE to whom these presents shall come I WILLIAM DUNNE of County of Rappa., Plantr., send Greeting. Know yee that I the sd WILLIAM DUNN for a valuable consideration and in consideration of one thousand pounds of Tobb: and caske in hand paid by these presents sell unto RICHD. TAYLOR of the sd County Fifty acres of land lying in Rappa. County and bounded begining at a marked corner red Oake of WILLIAM LEAKs standing in the line of the aforesd RICHD. TAYLOR runing Southerly along the sd TAYLORs line to a marked corner red Oake and from thence Westerly by a line of marked trees to the head of a branch and from thence by the sd line to the head of another line branch to a corner Pine and from thence Northerly down the sd branch to line of the abovesd WILLIAM LEAKE and so Easterly alonge sd LEAKs line to the place it first began To have and to hold the sd land and premises to the sd RICHD. TAYLOR and his heirs forever with all woods and all other priviledges thereunto belonging without the lett of me the sd WM. DUNN my heirs, the sd TAYLER his heirs paying yearly unto our Sovereign Lord the King the rents when shall hereafter become due for the same, and do warrant sd land unto RICHD. TAYLER from the interest of any persons whatsoever As Witness my hand and seal this Eighteenth day of 7ber One thousand six hundred and ninety one

Signed sealed and delivered in the presents of us
JAMES BAUGHAN, WILLIAM DUNN
MARY BAUGHAN

Recognitr in Cur Comt Rappa 7 die 8ber 1691

pp. 267-268 THIS INDENTURE made this seventh day of October 1691 Between EDWIN THACKER of MIDDLESEX COUNTY in Virginia of one part and SYMO: COPNELL of Rappa County of other part Witnesseth that the sd EDWIN THACKER in consideracon of Eighteen hundred pounds of good sweet sented Tobb: already payed by sd SYMON COPNELL have granted unto sd SYMON COPNELL his heirs One hundred & fifty acres of land being in sd County of Rappa. being part of Fifteen hundred and sixty three acres granted unto sd EDWIN THACKER by Patent dated the 20th day of April 1687 Begining to be measured at a red Oake corner of Mr. HENRY AWBREYs lands and runing thence South West to a great white Oake on a brow by the HOLLY BRANCH, thence South East to a corner of JOHN GATEWOODs land to two corner trees, thence by his line South East to two Oakes, thence North by East to the land of sd Mr. HEN: AWBREY to two saplings thence by his line West by North to a corner of sd Mr. AWBREYs and lastly South by West to the begining place and also all profits belonging unto the sd One hundred and fifty acres of land with all rights which the sd EDWIN THACKER hath by force of the Patent or otherwise with all the priviledges unto the sd SYMON COPNELL his heirs and assigns from henceforth forever subject nevertheless to the quit rents which shall grow due unto their Majties. their heirs & Successors and further sd EDWIN THACKER doth grant that he the sd SYMON COPNELL his heirs shall at all times occupie the one hundred and fifty acres of land with the premises without the lett or the sd EDWIN THACKER his heirs or any other persons In Witness whereof the sd EDWIN THACKER hath hereunto sett his hand and seal

Signed sealed and delivered in the presents of us

HEN: BAUGHAN, EDWIN THACKER

LEONARD CHAMBERLANE

Recognitr in Cur Comt Rappa 7 die 1691

p. 168 THIS INDENTURE made the 9th day of 8ber 1691 Between EDWIN THACKER of MIDLESEX COUNTY in Virginia, Surveyor, of the one part & JOHN GATEWOOD of Rappa County, Plantr., of the other part Witnesseth

(This entry was not completed.)

324 pages A. S.

p. 269 State of Virginia

County of Essex, to Wit:

I HARRISON SOUTHWORTH, Clerk of the County Court for the County aforesaid in the State of Virginia do certify that I have verified the foregoing by a comparison of the same with the Original Record Book in my office and that it is a true copy thereof

Given under my hand this 24 day of March 1894

HARRISON SOUTHWORTH Clerk

(Note: In 1692, the County of (Old) Rappahannock was abolished and the Counties of ESSEX and RICHMOND were formed from it, the County of Essex lying to the South of the Rappahannock River; the County of Richmond lying to the North of the Rappahannock River.)

(Left Out - see page 115)

p. 248 KNOW ALL MEN by these presents that I the Subscriber do make over all my right and interest of this within menconed Deed of Sale for me my heirs and assigns unto DANLL. JACKSON him his heirs and assigns Witness my hand and seale this Sixth day of June in the yeare One thousand Six hundred and Ninety one

Teste DAVID BARWICK WM. his mark TONKIS

DAVID his mark JACKSON

Recognitr in Cur Com Rappa 1 die July 1691

www.ingramcontent.com/pod-product-compliance
Lightning Source LLC
LaVergne TN
LVHW061248100826
845148LV00008B/1060
9781680342253